# *Children's Books from Other Countries*

# Children's Books from Other Countries

**United States Board on Books for Young People**

## Carl M. Tomlinson
### Editor
*Northern Illinois University*

The Scarecrow Press, Inc.
Lanham, Md., & London
1998

# SCARECROW PRESS, INC.

Published in the United States of America
by Scarecrow Press, Inc.
4720 Boston Way
Lanham, Maryland 20706

4 Pleydell Gardens, Folkestone
Kent CT20 2DN, England

British Library Cataloguing in Publication Information Available

**Library of Congress Cataloging-in-Publication Data**

Children's books from other countries / Carl M. Tomlinson, editor.
    p.    cm.
    Includes bibliographical references and index.
    "United States Board on Books for Young People."
    ISBN 0-8108-3447-2 (pbk. : acid-free paper)
    1. Children—United States—Books and reading. 2. Children's
literature—Bibliography. I. Tomlinson, Carl M. II. United States
Board on Books for Young People.
    Z1037.C5428    1998
    028.5'5—dc21
                                           97-41768

ISBN 0-8108-3447-2 (paper : alk. paper)

# Contents

# *Foreword*

The United States Board on Books for Young People is proud to sponsor *Children's Books from Other Countries*. USBBY, as the United States national section of the International Board on Books for Young People, has as its mission the promotion of reading and international understanding through children's books. Sharing books first published in other countries with our children contributes to the achievement of this mission.

Identifying international books can be difficult for busy teachers, librarians, and parents. This book's primary purpose, therefore, is to help its readers identify quality international literature for children. Beyond this, the book offers suggestions in locating and sharing the books, once they have been identified. USBBY is grateful to the editor for writing the background and context sections of the book, for selecting the titles, and for editing the annotations. We also thank the many USBBY members who took an active interest in this project and contributed to it.

We hope that you will find the book useful and that it will be just the beginning of your experiences with international children's literature. Think of it as a travel guide, a listing of books, like places, that are worth seeing. You will plan your own trip, which books you will visit and in what order. And once you begin your journey, you will find yourself visiting new books that are not in the guide, recommending books to your friends and colleagues, and revisiting the books that you have loved. *Children's Books from Other Countries* is not only a guide, but also our postcard to you—"Having a great time. Wish you were here."

Joan I. Glazer
President, 1997
USBBY

# *Preface*

*Children's Books from Other Countries* is a brief and manageable reference to international children's literature. It was created in the belief that if librarians and teachers and others who work with children were more aware of the international books available to them, they would encourage children to read and enjoy them. Children in this way would be introduced to peers and cultures in other lands, thus helping to build bridges of understanding between the people of the world.

The concept of providing a bibliography of international books to interested professionals is not new. *Translated Children's Books*, compiled by Storybooks International in 1968, was an early publication of this sort. In 1972 the American Association of School Librarians division of the American Library Association, in commemoration of the International Book Year, published *Books from Other Countries, 1968-1971*, compiled by Elana Rabban. This publication was revised in 1978 by Anne McConnell (*Books from Other Countries, 1972-1976*). These commendable efforts were not continued, however, and for the last two decades we in the United States have been without a current reference devoted solely to international children's books.

*Children's Books from Other Countries* is, thus, long overdue. This bibliography of over seven hundred titles contains both translated books and books from English-speaking countries other than the United States. Selections include both in-print and out-of-print books from 1950-1996. The reason for including books from other English-speaking countries is that, though librarians and teachers often are aware of these titles, they are unaware that they are international. Including out-of-print titles is defensible in that they still are available through libraries and comprise a significant portion of the body of international books.

## Overview

### Part One: International Children's Literature

This section serves as a brief introduction to the field of international children's literature. First, definitions of terms and a rationale for the importance of this body of literature are offered. This is followed by milestones in the history of the field and current status of international children's literature globally and nationally. An explanation of how international books come to the United States, how they are identified as international, and how they are located sets the stage for Parts Two and Three.

## Part Two: International Literature and Children

This section addresses the many questions that librarians and teachers might have about how to share international books with children: How do I make the most of these books in my library or classroom? How do I encourage young people to read these books? How might these books be integrated into an existing plan or curriculum?

## Part Three: Annotated Bibliography

The bibliography is organized by genre. It includes poetry, picture books (realism, fantasy, informational), transitional books, realistic fiction, historical fiction, fantasy, informational books, biography, and short stories. Within each genre, entries are listed alphabetically by author's last name. Suggested age ranges and country of origin are included for each book. Annotations are also accessible through the author-title, subject, and country of origin indexes.

## *Acknowledgments*

This project could not have been completed without help from many people and institutions. I am particularly indebted to Advisory Committee members Lee Galda, Anne Lundin, Carol Lynch-Brown, Miriam Marecek, Maureen White, and Junko Yokota for their advice in the planning stages of this book, and to those who assisted me in book annotation for their cooperation, patience, and enormous contributions of time and effort. I am grateful to the Board of Directors of the United States Board on Books for Young People for giving me the opportunity to undertake this project and to USBBY past presidents Mary Lou White and Barbara Barstow for spearheading the project. To the Department of Curriculum and Instruction, Northern Illinois University, I owe thanks for general support during the years that this project was under way.

Thanks also are due to the following:

For help with initial planning: Susan Roman and Eileen Fitzsimons, Association of Library Service to Children, Chicago.

For help with copyediting: Hazel Rochman, assistant editor, *Booklist*, and USBBY Board member.

For help with Table 1: Olaf Winsløw, Danish Booksellers Association and Mai-Brit Nielsen, Dansk BiblioteksCenter, Copenhagen; Martha Baker, English Language Lector, International Youth Library, Munich; Bookseller Publications, London; Toin Duijx, IYL affiliate, The Netherlands; Judith Lechner, Department of Educational Foundations, Leadership, and Technology, Auburn University, Auburn, AL; Isabella Zeli, Cremona, Italy; and the Loyola University Library Staff, Chicago.

For help with locating books and information: Cooperative Children's Book Center Directors and Staff, University of Wisconsin, Madison; DeKalb Public Library Staff, DeKalb, IL; Marilyn Gardner, Association for Childhood Education International, Wheaton, MD; Charles Larry, children's librarian, Founders Library, Northern Illinois University, DeKalb; Judi McCallum, executive assistant, The Canadian Children's Book Centre, Toronto; Paula Quint, director, The Children's Book Council, New York; Rayma Turton, editor, *Magpies*, Sydney, Australia; and Margaret Coughlan, bibliographer, and John Kimball, Automation Section, Library of Congress.

For help with internet information: Mary Jo Aman, University of Wisconsin, Milwaukee.

For help with Details section: Alida von Krogh Cutts, Secretariat, USBBY, Newark, DE.

For computer assistance: Ilga Janouskovec, Computer Services, Northern Illinois University, DeKalb.

For photography: Dan Grych, Art/Photo, Northern Illinois University.

For general assistance: Tana Elias, Department of SLIS, University of Wisconsin, Madison; Heather Foreman, Department of C&I, Northern Illinois University; Cynthia Alby Johnston and Anita Peck, Department of Language Education, University of Georgia, Athens.

## *Advisory Committee*

Dr. Lee Galda
University of Georgia
Athens, GA

Dr. Miriam Marecek
Boston University
Boston, MA

Dr. Anne Lundin
University of Wisconsin
Madison, WI

Dr. Maureen White
University of Houston, Clear Lake
Houston, TX

Dr. Carol Lynch-Brown
Florida State University
Tallahassee, FL

Dr. Junko Yokota
National-Louis University
Evanston, IL

## Annotators

Mary Jo Aman
*University of Wisconsin, Milwaukee*
Martha Baker
*International Youth Library, Munich*
Denise Bowman
*Carpenter School, Deer Park, TX*
Edna Brabham
*Auburn University*
Caroline Brodie
*Kent State University*
Doris Dale
*Southern Illinois University (emerita)*
Barbara Elleman
*Marquette University, Milwaukee*
Lee Galda
*University of Georgia, Athens*
Doris Gebel
*Northport Public Library, NY*
Joan Glazer
*Rhode Island College, Providence*
Julie Kline
*University of Wisconsin, Milwaukee*
Judith Lechner
*Auburn University*

Susan Link
*Colony Bend School, Ft. Bend,TX*
Anne Lundin
*University of Wisconsin, Madison*
Carol Lynch-Brown
*Florida State University*
Barbara Nelson
*Auburn University*
Joan Nist
*Auburn University (emerita)*
Catherine Partridge
*Gregory Portland Sch., Portland, TX*
Hazel Rochman
*Booklist, ALA, Chicago*
Susan Stan
*White Owls, Minneapolis*
Barbara Tobin
*University of Pennsylvania*
Caroline Ward
*Nassau Library System, NY*
Maureen White
*University of Houston, Clear Lake*
Junko Yokota
*National-Louis University, Evanston*

## Illustrations Acknowledgments

**Cover art illustration**: © 1996 by Michael Foreman, from *The Secret Garden* card set. Reprinted by permission of Andersen Press, London. All rights reserved.

**Page 49.** Illustration from *All Join In*: © 1990 by Quentin Blake.

# PART ONE

*International Children's Literature*

It is through literature that we most intimately enter the hearts and minds and spirits of other people. And what we value in this is the *difference* as well as the human similarities of others: that way, as C. S. Lewis put it, we become a thousand different people and yet remain ourselves.
- Aidan Chambers

Many of us know a great deal more about international children's literature than we think we do. We have known and loved story characters such as Heidi, Pinocchio, Bambi, Peter Pan, Pippi Longstocking, Peter Rabbit, and Winnie-the-Pooh all our lives. As children, we listened again and again to the adventures of folktale characters such as Brer Rabbit, Cinderella, Baba Yaga, Red Ridinghood, Anansi the Spider, and the Three Billy Goats Gruff until we knew the stories by heart. Many of our classic children's stories and most memorable literary characters, including all of the abovementioned, are international. We claim these characters and their stories as part of our literary heritage.

## International Children's Literature and This Bibliography

Teachers and librarians are often surprised, but pleased, to find that a favorite children's book of theirs is international. It gives them yet another reason to share the book or another way to introduce or extend it. Others say that they would like to share more international books with the children and young people they serve, but do not know the titles or where to find the books.

*Children's Books from Other Countries* is an annotated bibliography of books written and first published outside the United States for reading and enjoyment by children aged 0-14. It is written for librarians and teachers and others who are interested in the education of children and who wish to learn more about the field of international children's literature.

*Definition. International children's literature*, for those who live in the United States, is that body of books originally published for children in a country other than the United States in a language of that country and later published in this country. It includes all types of literature—prose and poetry, fiction and nonfiction. These books can be subdivided into (1) books that were originally written in a language other than English and subsequently translated into English (e.g., *Heidi* by Johanna Spyri, originally published in Switzerland in German); (2) books that were originally written in English, but in a country other than the United States (e.g., *Peter Pan* by Sir James Barrie, originally published in England); and (3) books that were originally published in a country other than the United States in a language other than English and subsequently published in the United States in the original language (e.g., *Le Petit Prince* by Antoine de Saint Exupéry, originally published in France in French). *Children's Books from Other Countries* includes the first two types, that is, books published in the United States in English.

This bibliography does *not* include those children's books originally published in the United States for children of this country but whose characters or settings are foreign (e.g., *The Village of Round and Square Houses* by Ann Grifalconi). Likewise, books that treat some aspect of a microculture *within* the United States—often referred to as *multicultural literature*—are not considered international and are not included in this bibliography (e.g., *In the Year of the Boar and Jackie Robinson* by Bette Bao Lord).

*Rationale.* Is international literature necessary? With the thousands of children's books written and published in this country annually, do we also need children's books from other countries? For the following reasons, the answer to these questions is a resounding **YES**:

● Good stories from other countries bridge geographical and cultural gaps. Hearing stories enjoyed by children in other nations establishes in American children a foundation for international understanding. These stories connect us to the rest of the world.

● Some of the best works of children's literature are international. It would be a shame to miss such classics as Jules Verne's

*Twenty Thousand Leagues Under the Sea* (France), and the folktales of the Brothers Grimm (Germany), as illustrated by Lisbeth Zwerger (Austria), or such modern favorites as Christine Nöstlinger's *Konrad* (Austria), Anne Frank's *The Diary of a Young Girl* (The Netherlands), or Mitsumasa Anno's intriguing wordless picture book, *Anno's Journey* (Japan).

• International stories teach children about their peers in other lands, since they bring the people, history, and traditions of these countries to life and counteract stereotypes. The beauty of reading a good story from another country is that living, breathing *individuals* emerge, not a faceless mass of people, all with a common stamp. (Edman, 1969; Rochman, 1993)

• Both the emotional and the cognitive aspects of reading international literature make clear to young readers that they have much to gain from knowing about their peers in other lands. Adversely, having no exposure to books from other countries might give children the impression that there is little worth knowing outside the United States.

• By interpreting events in the everyday lives of their characters and by depicting long-term changes in the characters' lives, international authors of contemporary realistic fiction present truer and more understandable pictures of life in other countries than does the sensation-prone, narrow coverage of television and newspapers.

• Compelling stories build students' interest in the people and places they are reading about and pave the way to a deeper understanding and appreciation of the geographical and historical content encountered in textbooks.

• Literature written by natives of a country or region or those who have lived there and studied the country or region gives accuracy, authenticity, and an international perspective to classroom materials. Those who have taken the time to become thoroughly familiar with a culture write "from" the culture, based on their experience, rather than "about" the culture. (Italiano, 1995)

• International authors often confront issues that U.S. authors are reticent to discuss, but that children and young people benefit from knowing about. Examples include alienation, living with disabilities, human sexuality, interracial marriage, and poverty. Berlie Doherty's Carnegie Medal-winning young adult novel, *Dear Nobody*, an unwed teenager's account of her pregnancy, is

such a book. Babbis Friis-Baastad's *Don't Take Teddy*, concerning mental disabilities, is another.
● International picture book art is often fresh and distinctive.
● International literature reflects the cultural and language diversity found in our classrooms. By reading international books, students can learn to respect the heritage of others and to take pride in their own. Children who only read about characters just like themselves, on the other hand, limit their knowledge of others and, more importantly, of themselves.
● International and U.S. books work well together. Selecting a good mix of U.S. and international books for units of instruction, read-aloud, or independent reading is a daily reminder to students that similarities outweigh differences between cultures.

A corollary to the value of international books in translation is the value of having foreign language books in our libraries and classrooms. Frazier (1981) points out that lack of exposure to foreign-language books gives our students the false notion that all that is worth knowing is written in English. Regardless of whether students have facility in languages other than English, they benefit from seeing original versions of translated literature and seeing what other languages look like in print.

## An Overview of International Children's Literature

Some background knowledge of the field of international children's literature may add interest to your reading of these books or initiate further inquiry. The following summary presents only the highlights of the interesting history and features of this field.

*Early International Literature.* Surely, the first international stories were the traditional tales—myths, legends, and folktales—that originated long ago and followed humans as they populated the globe. Some anthropologists believe that this explains why many cultures share similar folktales. At any rate, such ancient stories as these and *Aesop's Fables* tend to be accepted as our own, since they were already present when the first books were published. (Meigs, Eaton, Nesbitt, and Viguers, 1953) Such early works from other lands laid the groundwork for the children's book field. Chief among these are the *Gesta Romanorum* of the Middle Ages, which provided many of the beginnings and basic situations for later stories and Comenius's Renaissance masterpiece, *Orbis Pictus*, or "The World Illustrated" (1657), thought to be the first picture book for children, which coupled for the first time the notions of books and joyful learning.

Formal international exchange of children's stories began several centuries ago. *Histoires du Temps Passés,* "Stories of Times Past," (1698), which we know as *Tales of Mother Goose,* written down by Charles Perrault in France at the end of the seventeenth century, and *Robinson Crusoe,* written by Daniel Defoe in England and published in 1719, are examples of early books enjoyed by children in many countries and in many different languages. Prior to this century the relative percentage of imported children's books to the total available was higher than today. The publishing industry was small compared to today's standards, and imported books helped to satisfy the demand.

*International Children's Literature Today.* Australia, Canada, the European nations, Great Britain, Japan, New Zealand, and the United States have well-developed bodies of children's literature. In 1995 in the United States alone there were over 100,000 books for children in print (Bowker, 1996). Most children's books originate in these countries.

Venezuela, Russia, China, South Africa, and India also actively publish children's books, though not in the variety or quality produced in the developed countries mentioned above. In some cases, social, political, and economic difficulties in these countries have spawned powerful works of protest literature that have attained international prominence, such as *The Streets Are Free* (Annick, 1995) by the Venezuelan, Kurusa, or *Journey to Jo'burg* and *Chain of Fire* (Lippincott, 1986, 1990) by the South African émigré, Beverley Naidoo. In China and India, while the numbers of children's books published are impressive, the quality and content of these books are less so. In these countries, where illiteracy is wide-spread, children's books are still primarily for the purpose of instruction, and so the lion's share of resources is devoted to textbook production. Legends, folktales, and myths are also widely published in order to convey cultural values. The few works of contemporary fiction that emerge are, with rare exceptions, didactic and obviously intended to teach moral values or to mold young readers' characters. (Khorana, 1993; Louie, 1996) We must remember that publishing in a country such as India, with its 17 languages and 1,652 dialects, presents challenges unimagined by publishers in the United States. Russia, still in a state of political flux, is making valiant efforts to establish a new, private publishing industry despite an unstable economy, huge inflation, and lack of booksellers. Independent Russian publishers, some devoted exclusively to children's books, have many problems, but relish the fact that, at long last, there is no censorship and no interference from government agencies. (Frenkel, 1994)

Many developing countries have yet to establish a children's book publishing industry, primarily due to economic constraints. In some countries of Africa, for instance, there are virtually no books for children. The notable exception is Zimbabwe and its capital, Harare, known as the "book capital of Africa," where the annual Zimbabwe International Book Fair is held. In most developing countries the publishing obstacles are formidable: numerous major language groups, requiring multiple translations and unprofitably small print runs of each title; few bookstores; no sales network; and few parents who can afford books for their children. The oral tradition prevails in these countries, with ancient stories, rich in history and culture, passed along by word of mouth from generation to generation. As young people abandon their villages for large cities, however, there is a danger that these oral histories will die out. Grassroots efforts to bring literacy to children in these countries are often inspiring. In Kenya, for example, women print letters, numbers, proverbs and pictorial messages on bright *kanga cloths*, the traditional all-purpose cloth used for clothing, curtains, tablecloths and other household purposes. These "primers" are economical, practical, versatile, and visible.

From time to time, authors who have visited or lived in developing countries have written stories set in these countries. Sometimes the author's intent is to help create a body of literature for the children of the country, and the books have been first published there. Worthy examples are Batchelder Award winners, *The Leopard,* a story by Cecil Bødker of Denmark, set in Ethiopia, and *Pulga*, a story by Siny R. van Iterson of Holland, set in Colombia.

*The International Children's Literature Movement.* The international children's literature movement was founded primarily through the efforts of Jella Lepman, a German Jew who fled the Nazi Holocaust of World War II but who returned to her devastated homeland immediately after the war. Determined to do something to prevent the recurrence of such destruction, Ms. Lepman convinced publishers from all over Europe to donate children's books for a traveling exhibit. These books, Ms. Lepman believed, would build bridges of understanding between the children who read them. For years this exhibit drew great crowds all over Europe, and in 1949 it became the foundation of the International Youth Library (IYL).

Today, the first of Ms. Lepman's great accomplishments, the International Youth Library (IYL), is housed in Schloss Blutenburg, a former castle, in Munich, Germany. It is the only institution in the world that systematically collects the world's literature for children. With more than 500,000 volumes in over 100 languages, the IYL is the world's largest collection of children's literature. Its publications include the quarterly *IJB Report,* the annual *IJB Bulletin,* and *The White Ravens,* an annual selection of recent international children's books recommended for translation.

Encouraged by the success of the international book exhibit and the fledgling IYL, Ms. Lepman and others founded in 1953 the International Board on Books for Young People, or IBBY. This nonprofit organization provides an international forum for those committed to bringing children and books together and is the centerpiece of the international children's literature movement. Its general mission is to promote international understanding and world peace through children's books. More specifically, IBBY also strives to:

* give children everywhere the opportunity to have access to books with high literary and artistic standards;
* encourage the publication and distribution of high quality children's books, especially in developing countries;
* provide support and training for those involved with children and children's books.
* stimulate research and scholarly works in the field of children's literature.

All countries are eligible to join IBBY. Currently, there are 62 member nations, each of which has a national organization affiliated with IBBY. The organization has its headquarters in Basel, Switzerland, and is supported through dues from the National Sections and donations. Individuals join the organization through their national section, if there is one. If not, individual membership in IBBY is possible. In the United States one joins the United States Board on Books for Young People (USBBY). IBBY's main activities are described below.

● The Hans Christian Andersen Medals. The best-known way in which IBBY and its member nations promote international children's literature is through its sponsorship of the Hans Christian Andersen Medal program. The Hans Christian Andersen Medal is the most prestigious children's book award in the world. Every two years each IBBY member nation is eligible to nominate a living children's author and illustrator from that country to compete for the medals. An international panel of jurists selects from the nominees an author and an illustrator whose complete works, in the jury's opinion, have made the most important international contributions to children's literature. Her Majesty Queen Margrethe II of Denmark is the patron of these awards, an appropriate link to Denmark's famous storyteller and award namesake, Hans Christian Andersen.

The Hans Christian Andersen award program was founded in 1956. Originally, only one medal was conferred every two years, but beginning in 1966 the committee gave separate medals for writing and for illustration. To date, four authors from the United States have won the medal: Meindert DeJong (1962); Scott O'Dell (1972); Paula Fox (1978); and Virginia Hamilton (1992). Maurice Sendak is the only U.S. winner for illustration (1970). See Appendix A for a complete listing of Hans Christian Andersen Award medalists.

• The IBBY Honour List. Every two years, IBBY produces a catalog of outstanding, recently published books, recommended by IBBY member nations as suitable for publication in other languages. Each National Section may submit three entries for excellence in writing, illustration, and translation. The catalog, available in English, French, German, and Spanish, is distributed throughout the world. Five traveling exhibitions of current Honour List books themselves are always on view, and past collections are kept permanently in some of the world's leading book institutions. The Honour List is credited with increasing the number of translations and foreign editions of excellent children's books. (Raecke and Maissen, 1994) For a copy of the Honour List, write to the Executive Director, IBBY Secretariat (See "Details" section below for address).

• *Bookbird.* Members of IBBY and its affiliate national organizations keep in touch through their journal, *Bookbird: World of Children's Books*, and their biennial world congresses. *Bookbird* was founded in 1966 and, since 1993, has been published in the United States. Each issue of this outstanding quarterly contains articles and shorter opinion pieces focused on a single theme, as well as letters from readers in response to earlier articles, a calendar of events, national book award listings, and important new trade and resource literature. A network of associate editors from IBBY member nations assists the editor, Dr. Meena Khorana of Morgan State University, Baltimore, MD, in producing the journal. The following is a sampling of *Bookbird* issue themes:

| | |
|---|---|
| *"Bad" Books, Good Reading* | *Children's Poetry* |
| *Southeast Asia* | *Sexuality in Books for Children* |
| *Violence in Children's Books* | *Philosophy for Children* |

Part of the task of producing this handsome international journal is providing translation services in many languages. This service encourages submissions from many nations, helping to ensure the global perspective that distinguishes *Bookbird* from most other children's literature journals.

- IBBY Biennial Congresses. IBBY holds an international conference every two years in a cultural and historic world center. The atmosphere at these gatherings is both exciting and inspiring. Language is not a problem for registrants from the United States, since many sessions are conducted in English and since translation services are provided. In 1990 the United States hosted the twentieth IBBY Congress in Williamsburg, Virginia.

- IBBY-UNESCO Workshops and Seminars for Developing Countries. The IBBY-UNESCO workshops focus on the writing, illustrating, production, publishing, promotion, and distribution of children's books in countries that publish few books. To date, workshops have been held in Costa Rica, Kenya, Argentina, Ghana, Mexico, Colombia, Mali, and Egypt. The most recent IBBY-UNESCO Workshop was held in 1996 in Bratislava, Slovak Republic, involving representatives from twenty Eastern European countries. One of the pioneers of the IBBY-UNESCO Workshop Project is Anne Pellowski, former director of the UNICEF Information Center on Children's Cultures and renowned teller of stories from around the world.

- The IBBY-Asahi Reading Promotion Award. This competitive award, co-sponsored and endowed by the Japanese newspaper company, Asihi Shimbun, is presented annually to a group or institution for making a lasting contribution to book promotion programs for children and young people. The 1996 winner of this award was The Little Library Project, Johannesburg, South Africa, in which ten picture books, an integrated language program, and teacher training materials were developed in six workshops, to serve ten million children in the area who have little or no access to good quality picture books. (Isaksson, 1996) For further information about the IBBY-Asahi Award, contact the IBBY Secretariat. (See "Details" section below for address)

- The IBBY Documentation Centre of Books for Disabled Young People. This center, with headquarters at the Norwegian Institute of Special Education in Oslo, Norway, promotes international exhibits, seminars, and bibliographic surveys of books for and about disabled young people. Some of its projects, co-sponsored by UNESCO, have been exhibited by IBBY worldwide.

• IBBY's International Children's Book Day. On or around Hans Christian Andersen's birthday, April 2, the International Children's Book Day is celebrated to call attention to children's books. Each National Section of IBBY is invited to sponsor ICBD for one year. Often the national sponsor commissions a poster to commemorate the day.

• Janusz Korczak Literary Prize. This international children's book prize commemorates the Polish humanitarian who established orphanages in Jewish ghettoes in Poland during World War II. It is sponsored by the Polish National Section of IBBY and is given biennially to living writers whose books are distinguished for their human and artistic values and for their promotion of understanding and friendship among children worldwide. Two awards are conferred: one for a book *for* children, and one for a book *about* children.

Those interested in a more personal account of the early days of IBBY should read Jella Lepman's *A Bridge of Children's Books* (1969) in which she tells the story of the establishment of an international children's book field. A current overview of the organization, *What Is IBBY?*, is available from the IBBY Secretariat (See "Details" section below for address.)

*International Literature in the United States*. Today in the United States relatively fewer children's books are imported than in the eighteenth and nineteenth centuries. This is due largely to the rapid growth in this century of U.S. children's book production. It is due also to the additional costs of translation and to the difficulty of selling many of these books in this country.

Reporting on the status of imported books in the United States is hampered by the fact that no U.S. agency officially tracks such information. We must rely on the estimates of children's book experts. Bamberger, in 1978, placed the number of children's book translations in the U.S., compared to total annual book production, at "no more than 1%." (p. 20) This estimate would seem to be borne out by more recent reports. White (1992) found 572 translated books out of 58,000 children's books listed in *Children's Books in Print 1989-1990*, or less than one percent. In 1993, the selection committee for the best translated children's book of the year (see discussion of the Batchelder Award below) decided not to confer an award, due to the weak field of submissions. Horning, Kruse, and Schleisman (1996), giving an overview of books received at the Cooperative Children's Book Center in Madison, Wisconsin, estimated that in 1995, at least 4,500 new books were published for children and young adults in the United States and that of these, fifty-four—1.2% of the total— were translations. Moreover, they noted that only eight of the 54 were translations of books of "substantial length." (p. 15) Even considering the titles missed in these estimations, the number of translated children's books brought to this country annually is a mere trickle.

A similar situation prevails in Great Britain where, during the recent past, only 3% of the sizeable number of children's books published annually are translations. (*Bookseller*, 1994) It might be tempting for consumers to conclude that they have no part in the decision to publish imported books, that publishers alone make these decisions, or that a large native book production precludes a need for imported books. The truth is that we, the reading public, *are* responsible, in part, for the degree to which our publishers look beyond our borders for the books they publish. Klaus Flugge, a British publisher of children's books, states that the reason for the paltry number of translations in his country is "...simply a lack of interest...in anything foreign." (Flugge, 1994) Could the same thing be said about us? Are we provincial? For purposes of comparison, Table 1 shows children's book production and percentages of imported books in several developed countries.[1]

Books originally written in English in other English-speaking countries and then published in the U.S. are more numerous than translations; but again, there are no exact figures for how many of these books are imported each year. Estimating these figures is further complicated by copublication arrangements (see discussion below), which sometimes make a book's country of origin difficult to determine. It is safe to say, however, that the great majority of imported English-language books comes from Great Britain, Canada, and Australia.

Children's magazines are an important reading resource. Notable in this field for its inclusion of international literature is *Cricket* magazine. Founder and editor Marianne Carus (1980) insists on having in *Cricket* "...translated stories from as many countries as possible and about as many different cultures as possible." (p. 174)

In 1966 the Children's Services Division (now Association of

---

[1] Australia tracks publishing information by total sales rather than by title. In 1994, of 21,300,000 children's hardbacks sold, 17,800,000 or 83%, were imported. Of 9,900,000 paperbacks sold, 3,400,000, or 34%, were imported. *Source: Australian Bureau of Statistics, Department of Communications and the Arts.*

| Translated Children's Books Imported Annually in Selected Developed Countries Total Production (% of Total Translated)* | | | | | |
|---|---|---|---|---|---|
| Country | 1991 | 1992 | 1993 | 1994 | 1995 |
| Denmark | 1226 (54%) | 1296 (57%) | 1255 (56%) | 1147 (54%) | 1237 (51%) |
| Germany | 4415 (28%) | 4780 (31%) | 4594 (29%) | 4777 (28%) | 5168 (28%) |
| Italy | 1278 (51%) | 1374 (50%) | 1498 (45%) | 1594 (46%) | 1590 (56%) |
| Japan | unavailable | unavailable | 2857 (16%) | 3167 (16%) | 2988 (19%) |
| The Netherlands† | 2136 (41%) | 1954 (42%) | 1907 (44%) | unavailable | unavailable |
| Sweden †† | 972 (67%) | 1016 (64%) | 841 (67%) | 962 (61%) | 1016 (66%) |
| United Kingdom | 4582 (2.7%) | 5090 (3.7%) | 5259 (3.5%) | 5393 (3.7%) | 5865 (4%) |
| United States | 4000+(<1%)** | 4500+(<1%)** | 4500+(1.7%)** | 4500+(1.7%)** | 4500+(1.2%)** |

Table 1

* These figures are for children's and young adult trade literature exclusive of comics, except where otherwise noted. ** Rough estimates. † Figures for The Netherlands include comic books. †† Figures for Sweden are for fiction only. Breakdown of nonfiction publications by origin was unavailable. Numbers of Swedish nonfiction children's titles published are approximately 20-25% of totals given.

Sources: Denmark-The Danish Booksellers Association and the Dansk BiblioteksCenter, Copenhagen; Germany-*Buch und Buchhandel in Zahlen* (1991-1996). Börschenverein des Deutschen Buchhandels e.v.; Italy-*Liber Data Base*, 1997, Biblioteca Gianni Rodari, Campi Bisenzio, Firenze, Italy; Japan-Center for Children's Books, Tokyo; The Netherlands-Toin Duijx, International Youth Library affiliate, The Netherlands; Sweden-Center for Children's Books, Stockholm; United Kingdom-*The Bookseller*, London; United States-Cooperative Children's Book Center.

Library Services to Children), a division of the American Library Association, founded the **Mildred L. Batchelder Book Award Program** to encourage international exchange of high quality children's books. This annual award is made to an American publisher for a book considered to be the most outstanding of those books originally published in a foreign language in a foreign country and subsequently translated into English and published in the United States during the previous calendar year. The award program recognizes publishers of such books in translation in the United States and honors its namesake, Mildred Batchelder, who devoted her entire career to children's librarianship and who was outspoken on the need for greater exchange of children's books around the world. In a 1966 publication Ms. Batchelder wrote, "To know the classic stories of a country creates a climate, an attitude for understanding the people for whom that literature is a heritage. When children know they are reading in translation the same stories that children in another country are reading, a sense of nearness grows and expands. Interchange of children's books between countries, through translation, influences communication between the peoples of these countries, and if the books chosen for traveling from language to language are worthy books, the resulting communication may be deeper, richer, more sympathetic, more enduring. I accept and believe in these assumptions." (Wheeler, 1967, p. 180) The children's literature community is indebted to those who proposed this award program and to Mildred Batchelder, whose work inspired it, for giving international children's literature an enduring presence in this country.

Winners of the Batchelder Award are selected by a five-person committee (four members and a chair) appointed each year by the president-elect of the Association of Library Services for Children. The winner is announced each year at the Mid-Winter Conference of the American Library Association. Since 1990 the committee has been authorized to name an honor book or books in addition to the winner. Among other selection criteria are the provisions that the book retain enough of its original flavor that the reader can sense that it came from another country, that folk literature is ineligible, and that the original illustrations are retained.

Some well-known titles that first came to the attention of librarians and teachers as a result of winning the Batchelder Award include *Konrad* by Christine Nöstlinger from Austria, *Hiroshima No Pika* by Toshi Maruki from Japan, and *The Island on Bird Street* by Uri Orlev from Israel. If you want to become familiar with the best translated international children's books available in this country, the Mildred L. Batchelder Award list is a good place to begin. A complete listing of the Batchelder winners is included in the appendix; these titles are also annotated in Part Three.

The **United States Board on Books for Young People (USBBY)** is the United States National Section of IBBY. USBBY's purposes are to explore and promote excellent children's reading materials that have been created throughout the world; to cooperate with IBBY and with other groups whose goals are comparable to those of USBBY; to facilitate exchange of information about books of international interest; and to promote access to and reading of these books by children and young adults in the United States and elsewhere. It provides support for, and disseminates information to, those involved with children and children's literature, and it stimulates research and scholarship in the field of children's literature. In addition, USBBY has several important projects which are described below.

● IBBY Regional Conferences. Not everyone can make it to the far-flung IBBY congresses, and so the U.S. regional IBBY conferences are a welcome addition to USBBY's activities. The first IBBY Regional Conference was held at Callaway Gardens, Georgia, in 1995, and the second was held in Albuquerque, New Mexico, in 1997. Both conferences were highly rated by all who attended. Future conferences are planned for Madison, Wisconsin (1999), and Seattle, Washington (2001).

● The Bridge to Understanding Award promotes, through reading, sensitivity to our global environment. It was established in 1994 in memory of devoted internationalist, Arlene Pillar. Schools, libraries, scout troops, clubs, and bookstores are eligible for this award for one-time events or ongoing programs that serve children in grades K-10. The award carries a $500 prize and a certificate.

● Discovery Project. The goal of this project is to promote writing for children among those groups of people who have little or no support for such endeavors. Two writing workshops, one in New York and one in California, were funded in 1996. USBBY oversees the Discovery Project and, in conjunction with it, has developed the brochure, *10 Tips for Becoming a Children's Writer*.

● USBBY Newsletter. Members of USBBY receive the *USBBY Newsletter* semiannually. This informative bulletin contains news reports, brief articles, a calendar of events, and book reviews related to national and international children's literature.

- USBBY Home Page. The USBBY Homepage contains information about IBBY and USBBY, excerpts from the *USBBY Newsletter*, and reviews of outstanding international books and international book award news. One can join USBBY through the Homepage. Eventual links to other IBBY National Sections and appropriate listservs are planned. Homepage Address: www\usbby.uwm.edu

- USBBY Liaisons to IBBY Activities. USBBY oversees U.S. participation in the Hans Christian Andersen Medal competition, the IBBY Honour List Project, the IBBY-Asahi Award competition, the Janusz Korczak Literary Prize competition, the Outstanding Books for Young People with Disabilities Project, and selection of the U.S. associate editor of *Bookbird*.

USBBY holds board of directors and general membership meetings and presents literature-related programs at the annual conferences of the American Library Association, the International Reading Association, and the National Council of Teachers of English. These organizations and the Children's Book Council are patrons of USBBY. Those interested in attending general membership meetings and programs should consult the respective conference program for details. See "Details" section below for specifics about subscribing to *Bookbird* and joining USBBY.

## How International Books Come to the United States

*International Book Fairs.* For most international books the journey to American book shelves is long and challenging. It usually begins at the annual international bookfairs in Frankfurt, Germany, and Bologna, Italy, and, to a lesser extent, Harare, Zimbabwe, where publishers, editors, and literary agents from all over the world meet to negotiate publishing and licensing rights for foreign publication.

The Frankfurt Bookfair exhibits books for all ages, but the Bologna Fair is devoted to children's books exclusively. At these vast fairs, publishers arrange extensive displays of their wares to encourage reading and browsing in hopes of selling the right to publish their books in other countries. Negotiations are begun, deals are struck, and in some instances where limited text is involved (e.g., concept books, nearly wordless books), on-the-spot translations are made. International children's book publishing is now a serious consideration for publishers. (Beneduce, 1991)

Another international event that attracts the attention of children's book publishers is the Biennale of Illustrations Bratislava, or BIB. This juried competition for excellence in picture book illustration has been held in Bratislava, the capital of the Slovak Republic, every two years since 1967. A Grand Prix winner and up to five recipients of Golden Apple awards are selected by an international jury, whose selection criteria emphasize artistic creativity. In 1995 there were 290 entrants from 45 countries.

*Selection.* Many considerations precede the decision to publish an international book in the United States. Publishers must first ask themselves, "Will this book appeal to American children?" Fully aware of this, foreign authors and editors who hope to sell their books in the United States are often influenced by their perceptions of what will and will not be accepted here. There is much truth in New Zealander Margaret Mooney's statement (1987), "A good book is a good book anywhere," but literary tastes can differ from culture to culture and from country to country. Clear evidence of this fact is the absence of works of many Hans Christian Andersen Medal and BIB Grand Prix winners in the United States. For example, are you familiar with the works of Bohumil Riha (Czechoslovakia), Tormod Haugen (Norway), or Michio Mado (Japan), Hans Christian Andersen medal winners in 1980, 1990, and 1994, or John Rowe, winner of the BIB Grand Prix in 1995?

There is also the issue of whether aspects of foreign books must be changed or "Americanized" to make them more marketable in this country. (Whitehead, 1996a, 1996b) Some editors believe that all children want to read about their peers in other lands, however different. Others believe that children in this country only want to read about people who are just like themselves. Ideally, in the process of editing a foreign book for the United States audience, a balance is achieved between the book's integrity and its marketability so that the flavor of the book's origins is apparent, and yet the story is easily understood by the new audience. Luckily, many foreign stories over the years have transcended national borders with ease. Their themes are universal, and their content is relevant to the needs and interests of all children. These are the stories sought after by publishers today.

Tastes in illustration also vary from culture to culture. Publishers have found that the stylistically sophisticated and symbol-rich picture books of some European artists such as Dušan Kalláy's *December's Travels* (Czechoslovakia) and Jörg Müller's *The Animals' Rebellion* (Switzerland), have not proven successful with young American audiences. It is to be hoped that the trend toward increased use of picture books for older readers in U.S. middle and high school grades will change this situation, since many of these works are artistically inspiring and thought-provoking.

Publishers must sometimes consider potential for censorship of international children's books in this country. Foreign authors and illustrators of children's books are often more straightforward than their U.S. counterparts in discussing topics like sexuality and religion, and in depicting nudity. Thankfully, some publishers have not been hampered by this concern, and so we can enjoy such culturally authentic books as Nomura's delightful picture storybook from Japan, *Grandpa's Town* (1991), and Newth's sobering young adult novel set in seventeenth-century Greenland and Norway, *The Abduction* (1989).

Publishers must consider the extra expense of publishing an international book. First, there is the cost of buying publication rights. Then, there is the cost of translation, which varies by length of the book and difficulty of the project, but in the case of a novel could cost several thousand dollars. In order to recoup these extra expenses, the publisher must either charge more for the book or generate extra sales. This is problematic, since international books traditionally have a limited audience in the United States. (Batchelder, 1988) This situation helps to explain why publishers market more international picture books than novels (they are cheaper to translate), and more international classics and folk literature than contemporary works (older works are in the public domain; classics have a surer market).

*Translation.* Many of the children's books imported to this country come from other countries where English is a major language—Australia, Canada, New Zealand, South Africa, and Great Britain. United States publishers or editors can base their decisions to buy the rights to these books on personal readings, since the books are written in English. If a book is written in a language unknown to the publisher or editor, however, he or she must then rely on secondhand information—a synopsis or book review or the opinion of a literary agent or professional reader—a risky basis for what could be an expensive publishing venture.

When rights to a foreign-language book have been purchased, the publisher must then arrange for the book to be translated. A good translation is critical to a book's success. Some people think of translation as a mechanical, word-by-word process of exchange that can be accomplished by anyone with the requisite bilingualism. Not so. Word-for-word translations are, at best, awkward, and at worst, unintelligible. To translate successfully is

•to rewrite the original text while remaining true to the original story and to the author's tone, voice, and emotion;

•to make the book appealing to children of one culture while retaining the flavor of another;

•to know to what extent foreign terms and place names will intrigue child readers without confusing them;

•to know the idioms of both languages, both contemporary and

historical, so that appropriate idiomatic substitutes retain the original linguistic verve and cultural authenticity;
•to understand the complementary nature of text and illustrations and to consider the illustrations when translating.

Translators must be skillful writers as well as skillful linguists, and they must be attuned to authors' and readers' sensibilities. Stephen Croall (1990), translator of the Swedish picture book, *The Cat Hat* (Kane/Miller, 1989), suggests that translators also consult the author, if possible, take time for multiple drafts, and read the final draft to children.

*Copublication.* In order to reduce costs, publishers sometimes enter into copublication agreements. The nature of these agreements varies, but copublishing a book generally means that two or more publishers share initial production costs. In this way, publishers can afford to publish more books or to issue larger print runs than they could manage independently, and they can procure publishing rights to foreign books less expensively or avoid them altogether. Sometimes publishers in different countries agree to publish a number of one another's books in translation every year, as is the case with the American publisher, Farrar, Straus and Giroux, and the Swedish publisher, Rabén and Sjögren. On occasion, many publishers participate in a project, as is the case in The Creative Company's copublication of Hoffmann's *Nutcracker*, illustrated by Roberto Innocenti, with eleven foreign publishers. One of the most outstanding examples of copublication is UNESCO's Asian-Pacific Copublication Program, which, since its inception in 1973, has published 20 children's titles, involving 30 Asian countries and 40 languages (including English), and has disseminated 4.5 million copies of these books. (Tajima, 1995) Also noteworthy in this regard are bilingual picture books which are naturally suitable for copublication in countries that do not share a language, since one printing can be marketed in both countries.

Copublication agreements allow publishers to bring together far-flung authors, illustrators, and editors. In this way a child in Kansas can read a book written by an author from Austria, illustrated by an artist from Indonesia, and first published by a small company in Switzerland, as is the case with *Andrew's Angry Words* (1995) by Dorothea Lachner and illustrated by Thé Tjong-Khing (born in Indonesia, now living in Holland) and copublished by North-South Books. Of concern to some observers (Jobe, 1996) is that, to make books acceptable to several cultures for the purposes of copublication, their creators will omit most culture-specific features, producing books that will neither offend, nor excite, anyone. Many cooperative publishing ventures have been enormously successful. Such international best-sellers as Pfister's *The Rainbow Fish* (Switzerland), Wild's *The Very Best of Friends* (Australia), and Browne's *Gorilla* (England) have gained publishers' attention. Cooperative publishing is a definite wave of the future.

## Identifying and Locating International Children's Books

Knowing how to identify a children's book as international and where to find information about these books is a necessary first step in establishing an international children's literature information network. There is no single, surefire way to ascertain that a book at hand is international, particularly since copublishing agreements sometimes mask a book's country of origin. Nonetheless, one or more of the following clues may provide the answer.

•Check for the listing of a translator on the title page.

•Note foreign award medallions on the cover.

•Check the catalog page on the reverse side of the title page (in some recent picture books, this information is found on the last page), where the book's cataloging in publication (CIP) information is given. There, the listing of an original publisher, original date of publication, and original title would be another indication that the book is international. In the case of the French picture book, *Star of Fear, Star of Hope* by Jo Hoestlandt with illustrations by Johanna Kang, the catalog page includes the following lines—

Copyright © 1993 by Editions Syros
Originally published in Paris in 1993 as *La grande peur sous les étoiles*

—both of which indicate that the book is international. Older international books sometimes do not include all of this information, but most include the translator's name and original country and year of publication.

If you think that a title may be international, and original publication information is not provided, numerous indices may be consulted for more complete bibliographic information. *Children's Books in Print* and electronic databases such as the "Marvel" link to the Library of Congress or OCLC are good references to begin with.

For obtaining copies of international titles that your local library does not own, the interlibrary loan system is a godsend. Even the remotest libraries are linked electronically to larger systems so that locating almost any title is possible. Ideally, the search continues in ever-widening circles until the desired title is located. Usually, the books themselves can be procured in about a week.

The following sources of information about international children's books are worth investigating.

• Recommended international titles can be found in the appropriate section of survey-type children's literature textbooks. *Canadian Connections* (Jobe & Hart, 1991), co-authored by a former IBBY president, Ronald Jobe, lists key Canadian children's books.

• Complete lists of winners of major book awards in other English-language countries can be found in the Children's Book Council's *Children's Books: Awards & Prizes* (CBC, 1996).

• *The International Companion Encyclopedia of Children's Literature* (Hunt & Bannister, Eds., 1996) contains over 30 essays on the literature of individual countries and regions.

• Short Story International, a quarterly featuring stories from around the globe, is available on three levels, *Seedling Series* (Grades 4-7), *Student Series* (Grades 8-12), and *Short Story International* (adult). (See "Details" Section for address)

• Booklists developed in the past by the Selection of Children's Books and Materials from Various Cultures Committee (recently disbanded) of ALA's Association for Library Service to Children. For information about these lists, published in *Booklist*, contact ALSC.

• "News from Down Under" and "News from the North" columns in *The Horn Book Magazine* feature notable books from Australia and Canada, respectively. The "Hunt Breakfast" column lists winners of the major book awards in the English-speaking countries.

• The International Reading Association's IRA Children's Book Awards in three categories (younger readers, older readers, informational book) for an author's first or second published book often recognizes international works.

• Annual notable book lists and bibliographies often flag international books. Notable among these are:
•ALA's "Notable Children's Books" and "Best Books for Young Adults." These lists are published annually in the March issue of *School Library Journal* and the March 15th issue of *Booklist*. *Booklist* features its "Editor's Choice" list in January. (See

"Details" Section for addresses)
•"100 Best Books," a selection of the best current children's paperbacks, is published annually in Great Britain by Book Trust and is available for £1.50 plus postage. (See "Details" Section for address)
•"CCBC Choices." This booklist is published by and for the members of the Friends of the CCBC, Inc. (Cooperative Children's Book Center, Madison, Wisconsin). Trends and outstanding titles on the international scene are a feature in this annual publication. (See "Details" Section for address)
•"New York Times Best Illustrated Children's Books of the Year." This list, which appears in the literary supplement of the *New York Times*, often includes international titles.
•"Notable Children's Books in the Language Arts (K-8)." This list is published in the October issue of *Language Arts*.
•"Notable Children's Trade Books in the Field of Social Studies." This list appears in the April/May issue of *Social Education* and is available through the Children's Book Council (See "Details" Section for address)
•"Notable Science Trade Books for Children." This list appears in the March issue of *Science and Children* and is available through the Children's Book Council (See "Details" Section for address)
• Publishers' catalogs are another excellent source of both recent and backlisted international titles. In most catalogs, imports are well marked or can be determined by noting translation and publishing histories. Determined internationalists soon learn which publishers specialize in international books, and make sure that they receive these catalogs. Publishers known for their support of international children's literature include:
•African Imprint Library Services, 236 Main Street, Falmouth, MA 02540. This company will send lists of recent English-language children's books available in the U.S. from all African nations. Caribbean Imprint Library Services, same address, provides the same service for recent Caribbean children's books. 508-540-5378; Fax 508-548-6801.
•Candlewick Press, 2067 Massachusetts Avenue, Cambridge, MA 02140, is the American branch of Walker Publishers of London, one of the few publishers devoted exclusively to children's books. Candlewick is responsible for bringing the works of some of the best British authors and illustrators to this country. 617-661-3330;

Fax 617-661-0565.
•The Creative Company, 123 S. Broad Street, P.O. Box 227, Mankato, MN 56002 regularly publishes a number of high quality international picture books, primarily from France and Germany. 507-388-6273; Fax 507-388-2746.
•Dorling Kindersley Publishing, Inc. 95 Madison Avenue, New York, NY 10016. DK specializes in beautifully photographed informational books in a variety of formats for all ages. Many recent DK books are available in CD-ROM and video. Many DK titles are imported from England. 212-213-4800; Fax 212-213-5240.
•Farrar, Straus & Giroux, 19 Union Square West, New York, NY 10003. As a result of a translation and distribution agreement with the largest Swedish publisher of children's books, Rabén and Sjögren, this company publishes a number of translated Swedish picture books every year. In addition, the company publishes translated fiction for young adults. 212-741-6900.
•Front Street Publishers, P.O. Box 280, Arden, North Carolina 28704, a recently established small press, publishes a number of books in translation from the Dutch publisher, Lemniscaat. 704-681-0811; Fax: 704-681-0508.
•Henry Holt and Company, 115 West 18th Street, New York, NY 10114-0378. Holt's imprint, Edge Books, features international young adult fiction.
•Kane/Miller Book Publishers, P.O. Box 529, Brooklyn, NY 11231-0005. This small press specializes in translated children's picture books from around the world under the Cranky Nell imprint. 718-624-5120; Fax: 718-858-5452.
•Lerner Publications Company/Carolrhoda Books, Inc., 241 First Avenue North, Minneapolis, MN 55401. This company publishes international fiction and nonfiction for children in series.
•North-South Books, 1133 Broadway, Suite 1016, New York, NY 10010. North-South Books is the English language imprint of Nord-Süd Verlag, the Swiss children's book publisher. The company emphasizes high quality multinational copublications featuring lesser-known authors and illustrators, and regularly reissues older international titles. North-South also publishes the English-language editions of Michael Neugebauer Books (formerly Picture Book Studio), another Swiss publisher.
•Simon & Schuster/Margaret K. McElderry Books, Macmillan

Publishing Company, 866 Third Avenue, New York, NY 10022. This company publishes picture books and chapter books from other English-speaking countries and translated children's chapter books. Margaret K. McElderry, children's book publisher and editor, is recognized for her leadership in bringing more international children's books to the United States.

•Tundra Books of Northern New York, Box 1030, Plattsburgh, NY 12901 is a subsidiary of the Canadian publisher McClelland & Stewart. This company specializes in Canadian, Native American, and French/English bilingual books for children and exceptional picture book art. 416-598-4786; Fax: 416-598-4002.

•Turton and Chambers Ltd., Station Road, Woodchester Stroud, Glos GL5 5EQ, England. This firm specializes in translating into English and publishing foreign children's books for distribution in England and Australia. Books can be ordered by catalog from England.

•Wellington Publishing Company, P.O. Box 14877, Chicago, IL 60614. This small press specializes in translated children's books by Czechoslovakian authors and illustrators, but also has books from Israel, France, and Belgium. 312-472-4820; Fax: 312-472-4924.

• Some professional library and education journals regularly include annotated lists of recent children's books around themes or topics, and occasionally this will include international books. *Bookbird: World of Children's Books* and *USBBY Newsletter* list global literature of note in every issue, and *Book Links*, *The Horn Book Magazine*, *The Journal of Children's Literature*, *Language Arts*, *The New Advocate*, and *The Reading Teacher* all feature reviews of international books from time to time.

For a more direct line to current news about children's books in other English-speaking countries and a different perspective on the international book scene, the following foreign journals are invaluable. They are easily subscribed to, and their cost is nominal, relative to their worth.

•*Bookchat*. P.O. Box 541, Grabouw, 7160 South Africa. Tel: 27-24-59-30-81; Fax: 27-24-59-40-00. This quarterly magazine gives an overview of children's literature in the Republic of South Africa through news items, book reviews, and articles, and also serves as the voice of IBBY in that country.

•*Children's Book News*. Canadian Children's Book Centre, 35

Spadina Road, Toronto, Ontario M5R 2S9. Tel: 416-975-0010; Fax: 416-975-1839. Published quarterly as an instrument of the Canadian Children's Book Centre, this informative magazine gives an overview of Canadian children's literature through news items, Canadian children's book award programs and winners, national and regional book promotion programs, author and illustrator profiles, a Canadian view of international literature, publishing news, and reviews of recently published books.

•*Our Choice.* Canadian Children's Book Centre (See above). Published annually in September, this bibliography of approximately two hundred titles includes the best Canadian children's titles published in the preceding year.

•*Magpies: Talking about Books for Children.* P.O. Box 563, Hamilton, Queensland 4007, Australia. Tel: 61-7-3256-0064; Fax: 61-7-3256-0922. Published bimonthly, this journal provides a current overview of children's literature in Australia through numerous book reviews, award listings, author and illustrator profiles, an Australian view of international literature, and articles.

•*Young Book Trust News.* Book House, 45 East Hill, Wandsworth, London SW18 2QZ, England. Tel: 44-181-870-9055; Fax: 44-181-874-4790. Published quarterly, this journal provides an overview of British children's literature through articles, author-illustrator profiles, award and promotional programs and winner updates, publisher news and trends, and reviews of recent notable children's books.

• The internet promises access to information about children's literature and direct links to others interested in these materials on a scale never before imagined. World Wide Web Sites, Children's Literature Review Journals, Listservs (Electronic Discussion Groups), and Commercial Sites currently available on the internet do not include a specifically international option. The notion of "world wide web" seems tailored for bringing together those interested in learning about books from other countries.

Electronic Discussion Groups (Listservs) seem the likeliest of the current internet sites in which to find discussion of international children's books. The following listservs may well include opinions about international books:

**Child_lit**
*majordomo@email.rutgers.edu*

This list is devoted to discussion and critical analysis of children's literature.

**CCBC-Net**

*listserv@ccbc.soemadison.wisc.edu*

This is a forum for the discussion of contemporary children's and young adult literature.

**Kidlit-L**

*listserv@bingvmb.cc.binghamton.edu*

Discussion about children's literature involves teachers, librarians, students, and others interested in the field.

**Booktalk**

*listserv@nervm.nerdc.ufl.edu*

Discussion about using children's literature in the classroom.

**LM_NET**

*listserv@listserv.syr.edu*

Discussion about school library services and related activities.

**PUBYAC**

*listserver@nysernet.org.*

Discussion for children's and young adult librarians in public libraries.

**ALSC-L**

*listserv@uicvm.uic.edu*

Discussion group sponsored by the Association for Library Services to Children.

**BR_Cafe**

*listproc@micronet.wcu.edu*

Discussion among children about what they are reading. Discussions can be between individuals or general forum. For children only.

The electronic media raise many questions about the future of literature, reading, publishing, and information services, as noted by Ellis (1997). Ellis's article features one of the first children's novels to be published on (and *only* on) the internet, *The End of the Rainbow* (Dutton, 1996), by the Dane, Bjarne Reuter. The Batchelder Committee's decision to disqualify this story from competition, since it did not appear in book form, suggests the many issues that will inevitably arise as more and more information becomes available over the internet.

# PART TWO

*International
Literature
and Children*

## Sharing International Books with Children

The same good practices work well with domestic and international books alike. The main point is that these books be shared regularly and often with children in pleasant, nonthreatening contexts, and that children be given opportunities to respond in a variety of ways to these stories. The following ideas, suggestions, and advice for sharing international books with children come from experienced librarians and teachers.

• Understand that children, like their adult caregivers, must sometimes be led or helped into an acceptance of anything new or different. In the case of books from other countries, your enthusiastic interest in and promotion of these stories is often enough to convince children to try them. Rochman (1993) notes, furthermore, that sharing good international books need not be confined to the "gifted." See Tomlinson and Lynch-Brown (1989) for one classroom example that supports this notion.

• Read international books aloud. No other adult-led activity works as well as often with children as the read-aloud. Research studies (e.g., Durkin, 1966; Butler, 1975; Carlsen & Sherrill, 1988) show that all age groups benefit. These benefits are doubled, if the read-aloud selection is one that students would be unlikely to choose for independent reading, but will love, once brought into the story, as is often the case with international books.

• Booktalk international books regularly. Finding and noting similarities between international books, authors, and illustrators and well-known and well-liked American books, authors, and illustrators is an effective way to bridge from the known to the unknown. After one or two examples, children can begin to look for these author or illustrator pairs themselves. Table 2 demonstrates some likely U.S.-international pairings.

### U.S.-International Author/Illustrator Pairs and Comparisons

| International Author/ Illustrator | United States Author/Illustrator | Points of Comparison |
| --- | --- | --- |
| Anthony Browne (U.K.) *Hansel and Gretel* | Nancy E. Burkert *Snow-White and the Seven Dwarfs* | Use visual symbols; create multilayered visual narratives; pay great attention to details |
| Robin Klein (Australia) *Hating Allison Ashley* | Judy Blume *Are You There, God? It's Me, Margaret* | Mostly female characters; address contemporary issues; popular reading |
| John Marsden (Australia) *So Much to Tell You* | Chris Crutcher *Staying Fat for Sarah Byrnes* | Teen-aged characters; often difficult adolescent issues |
| Jörg Müller (Switzerland) *The Bear Who Wanted to Be a Bear* | Chris Van Allsburg *The Wretched Stone* | Surrealist artistic style; visual symbols; picture books for older readers |
| Uri Orlev (Israel) *The Island on Bird Street* | Gary Paulsen *Hatchet* | Themes of maturing by overcoming adversity; survival stories; mostly male characters |

Table 2

• Display international books. At regular intervals, call children's and adults' attention to these books by displaying them on a

special "Good Books" shelf in your library or classroom.
   • Use lists or maps as story aids. Simple, handwritten lists of character and place names written on posterboard and kept in view as the story is read can make all the difference in stories with numerous characters or characters and places with unusual names. Figure 1 illustrates what such a list might look like for Cecil Bødker's Ethiopian mystery, *The Leopard,* the 1978 Batchelder Award winner.

---

Characters and Terms in **THE LEOPARD**

| | |
|---|---|
| Tibeso | A shepherd, about 10 |
| The Great Man | A community leader |
| The Blacksmith | |
| Belaynesh | Owner of the marketplace cafe |
| Magersa | |
| Darasso | } Three traders |
| Bonko | |
| Sokineh | Saffay's granddaughter, about 10 |
| Saffay | Elderly woman |
| Baritte | Sokineh's mother |
| Abdallah | Tibeso's made-up name |
| Hadji Jarra | Man who helps Tibeso |
| Fatuma | Little, old woman who lives with Hadji Jarra |
| Hassan | Older boy disguised as a girl |
| Befekadu | A beggar |
| *torosho* | fried cornbread |
| *gaby* | cotton shawl |
| *koda* | milk basket |
| *merka* | porridge |
| *tella* | homemade beer |
| *tej* | honey wine |
| *tej-bet* | a bar where honey wine is sold |
| *teff* | straw |

Figure 1

---

   • Do not be intimidated by foreign words. Before reading an international book aloud, look for and practice any foreign terms or unusual names. (A private reading prior to a read-aloud session is a good rule to follow regardless of the book's origin.) Authentic pronunciation of foreign terms, though desirable, is not a necessity. As long as the reader is consistent, any agreed-upon pronunciation of foreign names and unusual words will suffice for listeners. If the story is good enough, unfamiliar words will not bother the child.

● Integrate international and American books with instructional or thematic units. International books coordinate particularly well with social studies and history units, since they give authentic, "I was there," vicariousness to classroom experiences. Well-integrated text sets such as the following not only address curricular needs but also serve to transcend the boundaries of culture:

**Theme: Friendship** (Grades K-2)
*Best Friends for Frances* by Russell Hoban (United States)
*Crusher Is Coming* by Bob Graham (Australia)
*Ernest and Celestine* by Gabrielle Vincent (Belgium)
*Frog and Toad* by Arnold Lobel (United States)
*May I Bring a Friend?* by Beatrice S. de Regniers (United States)
*Mimi Gets a Grandpa* by Viveca Sundvall (Sweden)
*Stevie* by John Steptoe (United States)
*The Very Best of Friends* by Wild and Vivas (Australia)
*Willy and Hugh* by Anthony Browne (Great Britain)

**Theme: World War II** (Grades 4-7)
*The Island on Bird Street* by Uri Orlev (Israel, set in Poland)
*Journey to Topaz* by Yoshiko Uchida (United States)
*Rose Blanche* by Christophe Gallaz and Roberto Innocenti (Switzerland, set in Germany)
*Summer of My German Soldier* by Bette Greene (United States)
*Upon the Head of the Goat* by Aranka Siegal (United States, set in Hungary)
*The Winter When Time Was Frozen* by Els Pelgrom (Netherlands)

**Theme: Growth and Maturity** (Grades 5-7)
*The Friends* by Kazumi Yumoto (Japan)
*A Gathering of Days* by Joan Blos (United States, set in 1830s)

*The Great Gilly Hopkins* by Katherine Paterson (United States)
*Hatchet* by Gary Paulsen (United States, set in Canada)
*Paper Bird* by Maretha Maartens (Republic of South Africa)
*Playing Beatie Bow* by Ruth Park (Australia, set in 1980s & 1880s)

**Theme: Meeting the Challenges of New Frontiers** (Grades 6-9)
*Ajeemah and His Son* by James Berry (Great Britain, set in 1800s Jamaica)
*Beyond the Divide* by Kathryn Laskey (United States, set in 1800s)
*Chain of Fire* by Beverly Naidoo (Great Britain, set in 1980s Republic of South Africa)
*Eva* by Peter Dickinson (Great Britain, set in the future)
*Invitation to the Game* by Monica Hughes (Canada, set in the future)
*An Old Tale Carved Out of Stone* by Aleksandr Linevski (Russia, set in Stone-Age Siberia)

● Introduce an international story by locating the country of origin on a world map and relating its location to that of the United States. Call to mind what the students already know about this place, people, and culture. A brief search may provide background information or a native of the country living within your community to give a context for understanding and appreciating these books.

● Encourage children to search for information about the country that a favorite international book or current read-aloud originated in or the culture that the story describes. As information, visuals, and artifacts are collected, make a display. Likely resources are the magazines *Calliope: World History for Young People* and *Faces: A Magazine About People*, both published by Cobblestone Publishing. (See "Details" Section for address)

● Emphasize the similarities as well as the differences in book characters' lives and the lives of the children you are reading to. Help children to understand that the similarities (being human, having families, needing love, food, and shelter, etc.) are more fundamental and more important than the differences, and the differences are interesting. Chart or web and discuss these similarities and differences. Let children look for similarities and differences in illustrations in picture books.

Primary-graders, for example, might be helped to chart similarities and differences between their lives and that of Amoko in the Ghanaian picture book, *Amoko and Efua Bear* (Macmillan, 1988), as in the following example.

| SIMILARITIES | DIFFERENCES |
|---|---|
| We live in houses | |
| We live with our families | |
| We like to play with our friends | |
| We bathe | Amoko bathes out of doors |
| We have toys that we love | |
| I hold Teddy or he rides in a carriage. | Amoko carries Efua in a cloth. |
| When we lose our toys, we are sad | |
| We have mothers and fathers | |
| Our parents take care of us | |
| We go grocery shopping | Amoko's grocery store is outdoors |
| etc. | |

• Post titles of other books by the author or illustrator of a current favorite international book; or post titles of good books by other authors or illustrators from the same country.

• Call students' attention to children's book award programs in other countries, particularly those in Canada, England, Australia, and New Zealand, to generate interest in reading books on these lists.

## Activities to Promote International Understanding

• Develop an international book shelf in your library or classroom.

• Introduce an international pen pal program in your library or school. For names and addresses of children in other lands contact the

U.S. Committee for UNICEF Office in your region:

    East - 212-824-6275     Midwest - 312-670-2379

    West - 310-277-7608     Southeast - 404-584-5955

Or write to:

    U.S. Committee for UNICEF

    Public Information

    333 East 38th Street

    New York, NY 10016

UNICEF also endorses a penpal club organized by Dorling Kindersley Publishers. See information in the DK publication, *Children Just Like Me*, or write to:

    Children Just Like Me Penpal Club

    DK Publishing, Inc.

    95 Madison Avenue

    New York, NY 10016

• Develop a card file of community resource people who might contribute to your international program. Likely possibilities include exchange students, recent immigrants, Peace Corps veterans, and parents or other adults who have lived abroad.

• Involve your library or classroom in international holidays or special observances such as International Children's Book Day (April 2), United Nations Day (October 24), Human Rights Day (December 10), UNICEF "Trick or Treat."

• Become familiar with the work and publications of the Association for Childhood Education International. Of particular interest: Annual international focus issue of the journal, *Childhood Education: Infancy through Early Adolescence* and collected readings from that journal, *International Perspectives*. (See "Details" Section for address)

• Write to the information office in Washington, DC, of the embassy of the country in which you are interested, requesting information.

• Show children original language versions of international children's books. Read aloud or have a qualified person read aloud or tape some passages in the original language.

• Make sure that children understand that many excellent, well-loved stories were first written in a language other than English. The classics and many popular folktales offer this opportunity.

## Conclusion

Preparing this bibliography has revealed several key points about the past, present, and future of international children's literature. Primary among these is that books from other countries have always been an important part of our literary estate and continue to be so today. Some of our most loved and enduring books come from other countries. In addition:

• The presence of international literature is not assured. It must be promoted and supported. Featuring international books through booktalks, read-aloud, author studies, and integration into instructional units are effective ways of doing this.

• Integrating international literature with native literature whenever possible emphasizes the important messages that cultural differences are interesting and that people of the world are fundamentally more alike than different.

• The forces that bring translated books to our shores are weak. The best books from many countries are not to be found in translation in this country. One way to bring more good translated books to this country is to support the ones on the market today.

• Contemporary realistic fiction that honestly and accurately portrays young readers' peers in other lands is particularly lacking in today's book market. Folktales are valuable and plentiful, but they alone cannot give an accurate portrayal of today's world.

• Copublication is an important and promising publishing trend. Care must be taken, however, to preserve the flavor of the culture or country of each story's origin. Librarians and teachers influence publishers in this by selecting culturally specific books over blandly homogeneous books.

• Currently, no system exists for tracking international literature in the United States. Thus, we can only estimate the status of international literature in our country. A central tracking system would be a valuable asset to the publishing industry and to others interested in international literature.

• Publishing data are often incomplete in international books. Publishers should be encouraged to include in every book complete cataloging in publication (CIP) data, including original title, language, publisher, date, and translator's name, and to clearly indicate copublications.

- Electronic media hold much promise for international literature, from electronic publishing to forums for discussion and dissemina-
tion of issues and information about notable international titles.

- We all share a responsibility for determining the books made
available to us. Our selection, reading, use, and promotion of books help
determine the publishing trends of the future. When exploring the world
of books, we must make sure that it is the *whole* world.

## Details (Names, Addresses, Membership Procedures)

For information about materials from and membership in the Association of Childhood Education International:

Association of Childhood Education International
11501 Georgia Avenue, Suite 315
Wheaton, MD 20902-2443
Tel: 800-423-3563

For information about *Booklist*, *Book Links*, and *The Journal of Youth Services in Libraries*:

Association for Library Service to Children
% American Library Association
50 East Huron Street
Chicago, IL 60611
Tel: 800-545-2433

For information about *Calliope* or *Faces* magazines:

Cobblestone Publishing
7 School Street
Peterborough, NH 03458

For information about *CCBC Choices*:

% Friends of the CCBC, Inc.
P.O. Box 5288
Madison, WI 53705

For information and materials from the Children's Book Council:

The Children's Book Council
568 Broadway, Suite 404
New York, NY 10012
Tel: 212-966-1990

For information about the British *100 Best Books* publication:

Young Book Trust
Book House - 45 East Hill
London SW18 2QZ
Tel: 011-44-181-870-9055; Fax: 011-44-181-874-4790

For information about *The Horn Book Magazine*:

The Horn Book Magazine
11 Beacon Street, Suite 1000
Boston, MA 02108

For information about IBBY or its projects:

    Executive Director

    IBBY Secretariat

    Nonnenweg 12, Postfach

    CH-4003 Basel, Switzerland.

For information about *Outstanding Books for Young People with Disabilities*:

    IBBY Documentation Centre of Books for

        Disabled Young People

    P. O. Box 1140

    N-0317 Oslo, Norway

    FAX +47-22 85 80 02

For information about *School Library Journal*:

    School Library Journal

    P.O. Box 1978

    Marion, OH 43305-1978

For information about *Short Story International*:

    Mr. Sam Tankel, publisher

    Short Story International

    6 Sheffield Road

    Great Neck, NY 11021

    Tel: 516-466-4166

For information about USBBY:

    Secretariat

    USBBY

    P.O. Box 8139

    Newark, DE 19714-8139

    Tel: 302-731-1057, ext. 274 or 229; Fax: 302-731-1057

    or consult USBBY's Homepage at www\usbby.org

# References

Appiah, Sonia. (1988). *Amoko and Efua Bear.* New York: Macmillan.

Association of Library Service to Children. (1995). *Mildred L. Batchelder Award Selection Committee Manual.* Chicago: ALA.

Bamberger, R. (1978). The influence of translation on the development of national children's literature. In Klingberg, G., Ørvig, M., & Amor, S. (Eds.). *Children's books in translation: the situation and the problems.* Stockholm: Almqvist & Wiksell International.

Batchelder, M. (1988). Children's books in translation. *The Five Owls,* *2*(5), 65-67.

Beneduce, A. (1991). Children's publishing in a shrinking world. *Publishers Weekly,* November 8 issue, 30-34.

Butler, D. (1975). *Cushla and her books.* Boston: Horn Book.

Carlsen, G. R. & Sherrill, S. (1988). *Voices of readers: How we come to love books.* Urbana, IL: National Council of Teachers of English.

Carus, M. (1980). Translation and internationalism in children's literature. *Children's Literature in Education, 11*(4), 171-179.

Children's Book Council (Compiler, Ed.). (1996). *Children's Books: Awards & Prizes.* New York: the Children's Book Council, Inc.

Croall, Stephen. (1990, June). *Infallible guide to a successful translation.* Paper presented at the World Congress on Reading, Stockholm, Sweden.

Durkin, D. (1966). *Children who read early.* New York: Columbia Teachers College Press.

Edman, M. (1969). Be sure to mind your P's and P's. In *Children and International Education.* (unpaginated). Washington, DC: Association for Childhood Education International.

Ellis, S. (1997). Buster on the screen. *The Horn Book Magazine, 73*(3), 289-293.

Flugge, K. (1994, April 8). Crossing the divide. *The Bookseller,* pp. 18-19.

Frazier, J. H. (1981). "Internationalism" and the children's literature community in the United States: A second look. *Library Quarterly, 51*(1), 54-67.

Frenkel, P. (1994). Russia, an equation with many, many unknowns. *Bookbird, World of Children's Books, 32*(1), 11-15.

Hearne, B. (1991). Coming to the states: Reviewing books from abroad.

*The Horn Book Magazine, 67,* 562-568.

Horning, K., Kruse, G. & Schleisman, M. (1996). *CCBC choices 1995.* Madison, WI: University Publications, University of Wisconsin - Madison.

Hunt, P. & Ray, S. (Eds.). (1996). *International companion encyclopedia of children's literature.* New York: Routledge.

Isaksson, B. (1996). The IBBY-Asahi reading promotion award 1996. *Bookbird, World of Children's Books, 34*(1), 32-34.

Italiano, G. (1995, October). *Can cultural authenticity be identified?* Paper presented at the IBBY Regional Conference, Callaway Gardens, GA.

Jobe, R. & Hart, P. (1991). *Canadian connections.* Markham, ON: Pembroke Publishers Limited.

Jobe, R. (1996). Translation. In P. Hunt & S. Ray (Eds.). *International companion encyclopedia of children's literature* (pp. 519-529). New York: Routledge.

Khorana, M. (1993). *The Indian subcontinent in literature for children and young adults.* New York: Greenwood Press.

Klingberg, G., Ørvig, M., & Amor, S. (Eds.). (1978). *Children's books in translation: The situation and the problems.* Stockholm: Almqvist & Wiksell International.

Lepman, J. (1969). *A bridge of children's books.* Chicago: American Library Association.

Louie, B. Y. (1996). Children's literature in the People's Republic of China. *The Reading Teacher, 49*(6), 494-496.

Meigs, C., Eaton, A., Nesbitt, E., & Viguers, R. (1953). *A critical history of children's literature.* New York: Macmillan.

Mooney, M. (1987, December). A good book is a good book anywhere. *Teachers Networking,* unpaginated.

Raecke, R. and Maissen, L. (1994). *What is IBBY?* Basel, Switzerland: International Board on Books for Young People.

Reuter, Bjarne. (1996). *The end of the rainbow.* Translated by Anthea Bell. New York: Dutton. http://www.penguin.com/usa/buster/index. html

Rochman, H. (1993). *Against borders.* Chicago: ALA Books/Booklist Publications.

*Subject Guide to Children's Books in Print.* (1996). New Providence, NJ: R. R. Bowker.

Tajima, S. (1995). Hope in numbers: Cooperative book development in

Asia. *Bookbird, 33*(2), 28-33.

Tomlinson, C. M. and Lynch-Brown, C. (1989). Adventuring with international literature: One teacher's experience. *The New Advocate, 2*(3), 169-178.

Wheeler, S. H. The Mildred L. Batchelder award. *Top of the News, 23*(2), 180-181.

White, M. (1992). Children's books from other languages: A study of successful translations. *Journal of Youth Services in Libraries, 5*(3), 261-275.

Whitehead, J. (1996a). "This is NOT what I wrote!": The americanization of british children's books—part I. *The Horn Book Magazine, 72*(6), 687-693.

Whitehead, J. (1996b). "This is NOT what I wrote!": The americanization of british children's books—part II. *The Horn Book Magazine, 73*(1), 27-34.

# PART THREE

*Annotated Bibliography*

# Using This Bibliography

The 724 titles in this bibliography are organized by the following genres or sections: poetry, realistic picture books, fantasy picture books, informational picture books, transitional books, realistic novels, historical fiction novels, fantasy novels, informational novels, biography, and anthologies and short stories. Entries within each section are listed in alphabetical order by author's last name.

Each entry is identified by a number, such as **1.234**. The numeral to the left of the decimal indicates the genre or section. The numerals to the right of the decimal indicate the individual entry. These ID numbers are used as referents in the indexes. Following the ID number are the bibliographic data. These include:

1. Author
2. Book title in boldface
3. Translator
4. Illustrator
5. Publisher
6. Year of publication
7. Original title in italics

8. Original publisher
9. Original publishing date
10. Paperback publishing data
11. ISBN or LCCN
12. Number of pages
13. Age range of target audience
14. Country of origin in boldface

Any omission of these data indicates that the data either were not applicable or were unavailable. Annotations follow the bibliographic data. Awards and annotator's initials follow the annotation in italics.

Well-known international classics, as well as a few modern favorites such as the works of Roald Dahl, were not included in this bibliography in the belief that they need no further introduction. Although traditional fantasy (folktales, myths, and fables) is the genre most imported to the United States for the children's book market, many of these stories do not appear in this bibliography, having been retold by American authors, illustrated by American artists, and, in many cases, first published in this country (previously existing only in oral form). Although, as the title indicates, the focus of this bibliography is books for children, some particularly outstanding young adult and crossover titles are included for the benefit of those who work with more mature young readers.

Selection criteria included the following:
• high literary and artistic quality

• worthy and up-to-date treatment of people and their cultures outside the United States (dates of inclusion are 1950-1996, but the great majority of selections were published during the last decade)

• interesting presentation of information specific to a country other than the United States or presentation of information about the United States from a foreign perspective

• appropriate for readers aged 0-14, with the exception noted above

Key to annotators: Mary Jo Aman *(mja)*; Martha Baker *(mb)*; Denise Bowman *(db)*; Edna Brabham *(eb)*; Caroline Brodie *(cb)*; Doris Dale *(dd)*; Barbara Elleman *(be)*; Lee Galda *(lg)*; Doris Gebel *(djg)*; Joan Glazer *(jg)*; Julie Kline *(jk)*; Judith Lechner *(jvl)*; Susan Link *(sl)*; Anne Lundin *(al)*; Carol Lynch-Brown *(clb)*; Barbara Nelson *(bkn)*; Joan Nist *(jsn)*; Catherine Partridge *(cp)*; Hazel Rochman *(hr);* Susan Stan *(ss)*; Barbara Tobin *(bt)*; Carl Tomlinson *(cmt)*; Caroline Ward *(cw)*; Maureen White *(mew)*; Junko Yokota *(jy)*.

# POETRY

**1.1** Agard, John (compiler). **Life Doesn't Frighten Me at All.** Holt, 1990. Originally published by William Heinemann Limited in 1989. ISBN 0-8050-1237-0. 96 p. (12-14). Poetry. **Great Britain.**
The eighty-five poems in this collection represent the work of both known and unknown poets from many ethnic and cultural backgrounds. They were collected by John Agard, a Guyanese poet living in England. The poems focus on themes of growing up, family, love, and justice. The various sounds of spoken English are captured in the diverse dialects represented. *jg*

**1.2** Akaza, Norihisa. **Smell of the Rain, Voices of the Stars.** Translated by Eiji Sekine. Illustrated by Yoshiharu Suzuki. Harcourt, 1994. Originally published as *Ame No Nioi Hoshi No Koe* by Komine Shoten in 1987. ISBN 0-15-302204-3. 32 p. (7-9). Poetry. **Japan.**
After seventeen years as a teacher in a school for blind children, the author wanted sighted people to realize the richness of the lives of his students. This book is a collection of the author's reflections on his teaching experiences and poems written by his students. *jy*

**1.3** Baumann, Kurt. **The Hungry One.** Translated and adapted by

Naomi Lewis. Illustrated by Stasys Eidrigevičius. North-South, 1993. Originally published as *Der Sterngrauch Nimmersatt* by Nord-Süd Verlag in 1993. ISBN 1-55858-121-9. 27 p. (10-12). Picture book. **Switzerland**.

Rum Tum Tum was born with an insatiable appetite. He ate everything around him. Then he met the miller's daughter and knew that her love alone would fill the emptiness inside him. The miller, however, fearful of losing everything, sent Rum Tum away. Seven years later he returned, and this time he ate miller, daughter, and the mill as well. Prison? He ate that, too. Photographs of humans behind abstract masks result in surrealism, and hint at the "monster" human devouring the world. *cmt*

**1.4** Berry, James. **Celebration Song**. Illustrated by Louise Brierley. Simon & Schuster, 1994. Originally published by Hamish Hamilton Ltd. in 1994. ISBN 0-671-89446-3. 24 p. (7-9). Picture book. **Great Britain**.

It is Jesus's first birthday and Mary tells him about his birth in this poem giving the Nativity a Caribbean setting. The poem reflects the rhythms of the West Indian dialect. *jg*

**1.5** Berry, James. **When I Dance**. Illustrated by Karen Barbour. Harcourt, 1991. Originally published by Hamish Hamilton, 1988. ISBN 0-15-295568-2. 120 p. (12-14). Poetry. **Great Britain**.

These poems reflect life in Britain's inner cities as well as life in the Caribbean. They focus on the hopes, dreams, joys and sorrows of young black youth. Subjects include stories of football games, hurricanes, Caribbean proverbs, and being alone. *Signal Poetry Award. mja*

**1.6** Blake, Quentin. **All Join In**. Illustrated by the author. Little, Brown, 1991. Originally published by Jonathan Cape in 1990. ISBN 0-316-09934-1. 32 p. (3-6). Picture book. **Great Britain**.

Seven rollicking verses invite children to join in the merrymaking. Entire verses can be memorized or just the repeated phrases. Excellent for choral reading. Wonderfully exaggerated illustrations are convincing proof that joining in can be fun. *Kurt Machler Award. cmt*

**1.7** Booth, David. **'Til All the Stars Have Fallen**. Illustrated by Kady MacDonald Denton. Viking, 1990 (paperback: Puffin, 1994). Originally published by Kids Can Press, 1989. ISBN 0-670-83272-3. 93p. (7-12). Poetry. **Canada**.

A wonderful collection of poetry arranged within broad themes, this book is further graced by interpretive illustrations that add to the poetic vision. The poems speak of children's wishes and dreams, joys and fears, as well as of the physical and spiritual heritage of Canada. *Amelia Frances Howard-Gibbon Award. lg*

**1.8** Cousins, Lucy (collector). **The Little Dog Laughed and Other Nursery Rhymes.** Illustrated by the collector. Dutton, 1990. Originally published by Macmillan Children's Books in 1989. ISBN 0-525-44573-0. 64 p. (1-3). Poetry anthology. **Great Britain.**
Brilliantly colored and boldly designed art will hold the attention of young listeners as these fifty nursery rhymes are recited. Adults will be glad to know that old favorites like "Humpty Dumpty," "Baa, Baa, Black Sheep," "Three Blind Mice," and "Little Miss Muffet" are included. A table of contents provides easy access to the rhymes. *bb*

**1.9** Ho, Minfong (compiler). **Maples in the Mist: Children's Poems from the Tang Dynasty.** Translated by Minfong Ho. Illustrated by Jean and Mou-sien Tseng. Lothrop, 1996. Originally published in China in A.D. 618-907. ISBN 0-688-12044-X. 32 p. (7-12). Picture book. **China.**
This outstanding collection of poems written more than a thousand years ago in China deals primarily with the beauty of nature. These brief, simple poems were traditionally taught to children in China and, in this translation, are unrhymed. Large, serene watercolor illustrations complement each poem. Chinese script in the borders provides the author, title and text of each selection. A translator's note and biographical sketches of the poets are included. *cmt*

**1.10** Hughes, Shirley. **The Big Alfie and Annie Rose Story Book.** Illustrated by the author. Lothrop, 1989. Originally published by The Bodley Head in 1988. ISBN 0-688-07672. Unpaginated. (4-8). Illustrated anthology. **Great Britain.**
Delightful vignettes about toddler Annie Rose and her big brother Alfie alternate with poems about their family and events of their day. *djg. See also Anthologies and Short Stories.*

**1.11** Hughes, Shirley. **Out and About.** Illustrated by the author. Lothrop, 1988. Originally published by Walker. ISBN 0-688-07690-4. 48 p. (4-6). Picture book. **Great Britain.**

Elements of nature (wind, rain, mud, hills) and the changing seasons are the inspiration for these rhymes. A spirited little girl and her baby brother take great joy in the world around them, and are the cohesive element in this collection. Winsome illustrations convey the children's curiosity and pleasure. *ALA Notable Books for Children; CCBC Choices.* *jl*

**1.12** Hughes, Shirley. **Rhymes for Annie Rose**. Illustrated by the author. Lothrop, 1995. Originally published by The Bodley Head in 1995. ISBN 0-688-14220-6. 32 p. (1-3). Poetry. **Great Britain**.
The illustrator's expressive paintbrush and her innate ability to grasp the details of childhood bring warmth and credibility to the twenty-plus rhymes in this lively collection. *be*

**1.13** Mado, Michio. **The Animals**. Translated by The Empress Michiko of Japan. Illustrated by Mitsumasa Anno. McElderry Books, 1992. Poems originally published in three volumes in Japanese. ISBN 0-689-50574-4. 45 p. (4-14). Poetry anthology. **Japan**.
Gleaming, crystal clear poems offer fresh insights into the natural world of insects, birds, and animals. Wonderfully condensed, these brief poems speak volumes about the beauty of nature and the great rewards paid to those who will see it. Afterword explains the provenance of this collection and the part the Japanese branch of IBBY played in its creation. *Mado and Anno, Hans Christian Andersen Medalists for Writing and Illustration, respectively. cmt*

**1.14** Mahy, Margaret. **Nonstop Nonsense**. Illustrated by Quentin Blake. McElderry, 1989. Originally published by Dent in 1977. ISBN 0-689-50483-7. 120 p. (10-12). Short stories and poetry. **New Zealand**.
Hilarious vignettes and anecdotes about the ridiculous Delmonico family are interspersed throughout this collection of humorous poetry. *djg. See also Anthologies & Short Stories.*

**1.15** Marshak, Samuel. **The Pup Grew Up!** Translated by Richard Pevear. Illustrated by Vladimir Radunsky. Holt, 1989. Originally published in 1926. ISBN 0-8050-0952-3. 28 p. (4-12). Poetry/Picture book. **Russia**.
A woman checked her tiny Pekingese at the train station with her other luggage, but when she arrived at her destination, the dog delivered to her

was a Great Dane! The response to her frustrated queries: "Maybe during the trip your little pup grew up!" Illustrations provide a late 1920s setting for this humorous poem ridiculing bureaucratic ineptitude. *cmt*

**1.16** Morgenstern, Christian (Lisbeth Zwerger, selector). **Lullabies, Lyrics and Gallows Songs.** Translated by Anthea Bell. Illustrated by Lisbeth Zwerger. North-South Books, 1995. Originally published as *Kindergedichte & Galgenlieder* by Michael Neugebauer Verlag AG in 1992. ISBN 1-55858-364-5. 41 p. (5-9). **Switzerland.**
Morgenstern's nonsense verse has been compared to that of Edward Lear and Lewis Carroll, and his lyric poems about seasons and nature to those of Robert Louis Stevenson. One of the first to write concrete poems (cf. "Fish's Night Song"), Morgenstern is primarily noted for his nonsense verse published posthumously in 1917. "Lullabies and Lyrics" are gentle and humorous; "Gallows Songs" include poems of a darker nature. Translator's Notes provide insight into the challenge of translating poetry. *Parenting's Reading Magic Award. mew*

**1.17** Service, Robert W. **The Cremation of Sam McGee.** Illustrated by Ted Harrison. Introduction by Pierre Berton. Greenwillow Books, 1986. Originally published in 1986 by Kids Can Press. ISBN 0-688-06903-7. 24 p. (10-12). Poetry. **Canada.**
In this tongue-in-cheek narrative poem, a frozen miner appears in a northern Canadian outpost, is thought dead, and is cremated. As the fire thaws him out, the miner, quite alive after all, announces that he is finally comfortable. Service originally wrote this poem of the Yukon in 1907. The illustrator's distinctive abstract paintings bring new life to this well-known work. The illustrator, himself an émigré to the Yukon from England, adds his own notes about the paintings. *dd*

**1.18** Volavková, Hana (ed.). **...I never saw another butterfly...: Children's Drawings and Poems from Theresienstadt Concentration Camp 1942-1944.** Translated by Jeanne Němková. Illustrated with drawings by children. McGraw Hill, 1962. Originally published by Nakladatelstvi Orbis in 1962. LCCN 64-1557367570. 80 p. (10-14). **Czechoslovakia.**
This collection of poems and drawings of children kept at Theresienstadt reveals the amazing power of the imagination to transcend oppression,

as well as the despair of children who knew that they would soon die. Includes explanatory notes and catalogue of drawings with notes on child artists. *cmt*

# PICTURE BOOKS

## Realistic Picture Books

**2.1** Adams, Jeanie. **Pigs and Honey**. Omnibus/Penguin (paperback), 1989. ISBN 1-86291-050-2. 32p. (6-10). Picture book. **Australia**.
A family from the Aurukun Aboriginal community on Cape York Peninsula, in Far North Queensland, goes camping one weekend. Everyone, including Grandad, Aunty, babies, and cousins, pile into the family truck and head out into the Bush, where they set up camp. While the women track down wild honey, the men hunt and kill a wild pig for roasting by the campfire. Told through the eyes of a young boy, the story is written by a white woman, and is endorsed by the Aboriginal community as a means of showing others how they enjoy their way of life on their own land. *Australian Children's Book of the Year for Younger Readers Award. bt*

**2.2** Ahlberg, Allan. **Starting School**. Illustrated by Janet Ahlberg. Viking, 1988. (paperback: Puffin, 1990). Originally published by Penguin Books, London, in 1988. ISBN 0-670-82175-6. 32 p. (3-6). Picture book. **Great Britain**.
From the first day of school through the final day before the Christmas break, readers follow in detail the activities of kindergartners Gavin,

Errol, Sophie, Sushma, and their classmates in the classroom, on the playground, and in the gym. Vignettes of the children engaged in activities—several to a page—expand the text and enable readers to follow each child's participation. The Ahlbergs' inviting introduction to school speaks to preschoolers' concerns everywhere. *ss*

**2.3** Allen, Judy. **Eagle.** Illustrated by Tudor Humphries. Candlewick Press, 1994. Originally published by Walker in 1994. ISBN 1-56402-143-2. 26 p. (7-9). Picture book. **Great Britain.**

Information about the endangered Philippine eagle and its diminishing habitat is delivered in a fictional narrative told from the perspective of Miguel, youngest of the schoolboys who are trekking through the jungle with their teacher. At first, Miguel is frightened by the eagle, but when it swoops down to seize a nearby cobra, the boy's fears evaporate, replaced by awe and delight. Humphries's illustrations convey the misty quality of the dense jungle habitat, alive with indigenous creatures and, in places, laid waste by logging crews. Includes information about the status of the Philippine eagle and efforts under way to preserve the species. *ss*

**2.4** Andrews, Jan. **Very Last First Time**. Illustrated by Ian Wallace. McElderry, 1986. Originally published by Groundwood Books in 1985. ISBN 0-689-50388-1. 29 p. (7-9). Picture book. **Canada.**

Eva Padlyat, an Inuit living in northern Canada, is old enough to go alone under the ice at low tide to search for mussels. During her first solo trip she is overenthusiastic, wanders far from her ice hole, and nearly panics when her candle goes out. She remembers her spare candle, however, and finds her way back to the ice hole and her mother. It has been a satisfying experience. Richly colored impressionistic illustrations provide details of modern Inuit life as well as a glimpse of the wondrous world under the ice. *cmt*

**2.5** Anno, Mitsumasa. **All in a Day**. Illustrated by ten international artists. Philomel, 1986. Originally published as *Marui chikyu no marui ichinichi* by Dowaya in 1986. ISBN 0-399-21311-2. 22 p. (4-7). Picture book. **Japan.**

On New Year's Day the narrator calls out to children all around the world to see how they are spending their day. Each double-page spread has eight illustrations representing eight countries around the world.

Each time the page is turned, three hours has passed. The time zones, seasons, and activities all differ, but somewhere in the book, each child sleeps, eats, celebrates, and plays. Anno, in the preface, remarks that despite the differences in how we live, the faces of children laughing and crying throughout the world are the same. *jy*

**2.6** Anno, Mitsumasa. **Anno's Journey**. Illustrated by the author. Philomel, 1992 (Originally published in U.S., 1978). Originally published as *My Journey* by Fukuinkan Shoten in 1977. ISBN 0-529-05418-3. 47 p. (7-12). Picture book. **Japan**.
A man travels through northern Europe gathering impressions of the landscapes, the people, and their cultures. Though a record of the author/illustrator's own recent travels through Europe, the Brueghel-esque, double-page illustrations in this wordless picture book are set in an earlier time. Visual references are made to notable works of art, games, fairy tales, and literary works. Endnotes explain the author's purpose in creating this book. *cmt*

**2.7** Appiah, Sonia. **Amoko and Efua Bear**. Illustrated by Carol Easmon. Macmillan, 1989. Originally published by André Deutsch Ltd. in 1988. ISBN 0-02-705591-4. 27 p. (4-6). Picture book. **Ghana**.
Amoko's favorite toy is her bear, Efua. Like many five-year-olds, she carries her bear everywhere. When she gets a new toy, Amoko forgets Efua and leaves him in the yard overnight. In the morning he is gone and Amoko is inconsolable. Father soon finds a tattered Efua, repairs are made, and Amoko is happy again. Many details of life in Ghana are shown in large, bright illustrations. *cmt*

**2.8** Ardizzone, Edward. **Tim All Alone**. Illustrated by the author. Oxford, 1956. Originally published by Oxford, 1956. (paperback: Oxford University Press, 1990). ISBN 0-19-279125-9 (paperback). Unpaginated. (6-8). Picture book. **Great Britain**.
When young Tim returns from a holiday, he finds his mother and father gone and their house boarded up. Tim signs on as a ship's cabin boy in order to search for his missing parents. Expressive watercolors and pen and ink drawings portray Tim's many adventures along the way. *Kate Greenaway Medal. al*

**2.9** Baillie, Allan. **Rebel**. Illustrated by Di Wu. Ticknor & Fields, 1994.

Originally published by Ashton Scholastic in 1994. ISBN 0-395-69250-4. 32 p. (4-8). Picture book. **Australia.**

The general of a new regime rolls into a Burmese village with his tanks, gathers all the villagers in front of the school, and wantonly crushes playground equipment to proclaim his power. A single sandal comes flying out of the window and hits the general. Enraged, he orders all the children out of the school to reveal the guilty party. But the children emerge barefoot, leaving a pile of sandals indoors. The author deliberately uses the name, Burma, noting that the people prefer it over the name imposed by the military government—Myanmar. Based on a true incident. *ss*

**2.10** Baker, Jeannie. **Where the Forest Meets the Sea.** Illustrated by the author. Greenwillow, 1987. Originally published by Julia MacRae Books in 1987. ISBN 0-688-06363-2. 28 p. (4-9). Picture book. **Australia.**

On a day trip with his father to the Daintree Wilderness in North Queensland, Australia, a boy explores the spectacular tropical rainforest. He imagines the earth as it was in ancient times, but fears that human expansion may soon destroy this living history. Using intricate collage and photographic overlay, the artist projects views of the past and the future. *cmt*

**2.11** Baker, Jeannie. **Window.** Illustrated by the author. Greenwillow, 1991. Originally published by Julia MacRae, 1991. ISBN 0-688-08917-8. Unpaginated. (7-12). Picture book. **Australia.**

In a series of intricate collages framed by a window, changes to the landscape outside a boy's home are chronicled across two decades. Rapid ecological destruction and its degrading effects on the quality of human life are made clear in this wordless book. *Australia's Picture Book of the Year Award. cmt*

**2.12** Baum, Louis. **One More Time.** Illustrated by Paddy Bouma. Morrow, 1986. Originally published as *Are We Nearly There?* by The Bodley Head in 1986. ISBN 0-688-06586-4. 26p. (4-6). Picture book. **Great Britain.**

Simon and Dad enjoy a trip to the park where Simon sails his toy boat. When Dad announces that it is time to go, Simon says, "One more time." During the train ride home, Dad quietly assures Simon that it is not far.

This warm contemporary story ends with Dad bringing Simon home to his mother, giving him a hug, and saying good-bye as he leaves. *jg*

**2.13** Björk, Christina and Anderson, Lena. **Linnea's Almanac.** Translated by Joan Sandin. Illustrated by Lena Anderson. Farrar, 1989. Originally published as *Linneas årsbok* by Rabén & Sjögren in 1982. ISBN 91-29-59176-7. 59 p. (7-9). Picture book. **Sweden.**

Linnea receives an almanac for Christmas, which inspires her to record events throughout the year—feeding birds, tending plants, making kites, making flower garlands, and creating Swedish heart baskets for the Christmas tree. Linnea's activities show children how to remain close to nature while living in the middle of a large city. Sunny, informative, well-formatted illustrations provide much information in this and all of the "Linnea" books. *clb*

**2.14** Björk, Christina and Anderson, Lena. **Linnea in Monet's Garden.** Translated by Joan Sandin. Illustrated by Lena Anderson. Farrar, 1987. Originally published as *Linnea i målarens trädgård* by Rabén & Sjögren in 1985. ISBN 91-29-58314-4. 53 p. (7-9). Picture book. **Sweden.**

Linnea and her friend, Mr. Bloom, a retired gardener, go on a trip to France where they explore Claude Monet's garden in Giverny. In museums in Paris Linnea discovers more about Monet and his art. This carefully researched book is filled with interesting details on impressionism, Monet's life and works, and the flowers in his garden. An excellent resource for developing skill in research and writing. *clb*

**2.15** Björk, Christina and Anderson, Lena. **Linnea's Windowsill Garden.** Translated by Joan Sandin. Illustrated by Lena Anderson. Farrar, 1988. Originally published as *Linnea Planterar; Kärnor, Frön och Annet* by Rabén & Sjögren in 1978. ISBN 91-29-59064-7. 59 p. (7-9). Picture book. **Sweden.**

Linnea gives a tour of her indoor garden. With illustrations and diagrams she tells how to grow and care for orange trees, watercress, and avocados. Linnea's plant newspaper, "The Green Gazette," serves a model for a class project. *clb*

**2.16** Bogart, JoEllen. **Gifts.** Illustrated by Barbara Reid. Scholastic, 1994. Originally published by North Winds in 1994. ISBN 0-590-24177-X. 32 p. (7-9). Picture book. **Canada.**

Rhythmic verse and unusual plasticine illustrations capture the spirit of adventure and unabashed delight of a globetrotting grandmother. As grandma travels, she and her granddaughter age, so by the end, it is the granddaughter and her child who are off on an adventure of their own. *Amelia Frances Howard-Gibbon Award. lg*

**2.17** Bour, Danièle. **The House from Morning to Night.** Illustrated by the author. Kane/Miller, 1985. Originally published as *La Maison du Matin au Soir* by Editions du Centurion in 1978. ISBN 9-916291-01-4. 14 p. (4-9). Picture book. **France.**
The daily lives of residents in a French apartment house are followed through large, colorful, double-page cutaway illustrations. As the day progresses from 6:00 a.m. to 11:00 p.m., routines of several families can be followed, showing both similarities to and differences from U.S. culture. *cmt*

**2.18** Bradman, Tony and Browne, Eileen. **Through My Window.** Illustrated by Eileen Browne. Silver Burdett, 1986. Originally published by Methuen in 1986. ISBN 0-382-09258-9. 26p. (7-9) Picture book. **Great Britain.**
Jo stays home sick, cared for by her father while her mother goes off to work. All day she awaits her mother's return and the surprise she has been promised, rushing to the window each time she hears someone. The predictable pattern is broken when her mother returns, bringing something that Jo has always wanted—a stethoscope. *jg*

**2.19** Bradman, Tony. **Wait and See.** Illustrated by Eileen Browne. Oxford, 1988. Originally published by Metheun in 1987. ISBN 0-195-20644-4. 26p. (1-3). Picture book. **Great Britain.**
Jo and her mother are going to the post office. On the way, they meet the greengrocer, the baker, and the fishmonger. At each place, Jo wonders if she should spend the money that she has saved, but decides to "wait and see." This is lucky, since she must use her money to pay the postage for her card and her mother's package to Granny, as her mother has forgotten her wallet. *mja*

**2.20** Breeze, Lynn. **This Little Baby's Bedtime.** Illustrated by the author. Little, 1993. Originally published by Orchard in 1990. ISBN 0-316 -58419-3. 8 p. (1-3). Picture book. **Great Britain.**

This extensive series of board books depict wide-eyed, happy toddlers, their friends and toddler siblings, going about the daily business of growing and learning. Couplets on each page will encourage repeated readings. Other titles in the series: *Baby's Playtime; Baby's Morning; Baby Goes Out; Baby Goes to the Farm. mb*

**2.21** Brott, Ardyth. **Jeremy's Decision**. Illustrated by Michael Martchenko. Kane/Miller, 1990. Originally published by Oxford in 1990. ISBN 0-916291-31-6. 29 p. (7-9). Picture book. **Canada**.
Jeremy's father is a symphony conductor. Jeremy loves music, but he does not like people asking him if he will be a conductor, too. Finally, a journalist notices Jeremy's interest in dinosaurs and asks about this instead. During his enthusiastic response, Jeremy decides that what he wants to be is a paleontologist. To his surprise, everyone is delighted. In a time-forward ending, Jeremy's sister, Allegra, provides an unexpected, but satisfying, conclusion. *cmt*

**2.22** Browne, Anthony. **Zoo**. Illustrated by the author. Alfred A. Knopf, 1993. Originally published by Julia MacRae in 1992. ISBN 0-679-83946-1. 32p. (8-10). Picture book. **Great Britain**.
A young boy and his family take a less than idyllic trip to the zoo. Contrasted with realistic illustrations of the majestic zoo animals, slightly surreal depictions of the family, behaving more primitively than the animals they are viewing, leave readers to ponder who really belongs in a cage. One child in the family is later bothered by the concept of imprisonment, a visual theme of the story. *Kate Greenaway Medal. al*

**2.23** Burningham, John. **Granpa**. Illustrated by the author. Crown, 1985. Originally published by Jonathan Cape in 1984. ISBN 0-224-02279-2. 32 p. (4-6). Picture book. **Great Britain**.
A little girl and her grandfather are best friends. They understand one another, and sharing their days makes everything they do more enjoyable. Pencil sketches and highly narrative, large, spare illustrations develop the relationship and show the passing of time. One day, Granpa's chair is empty. *Kurt Maschler Award. cmt*

**2.24** Carrier, Roch. **The Boxing Champion**. Translated by Sheila Fischman. Illustrated by Sheldon Cohen. Tundra Books of Northern New York, 1991. Originally published as *Un champion* by Tundra in 1991.

(paperback: Tundra, 1991). ISBN 0-88776-249-2 (paperback 0-88776-257-3). 24 p. (7-12). Picture book. **Canada**.

Reminiscing about his childhood in Quebec in the 1940s, the author tells about his decision, at ten, to order a muscle-building kit so as to better compete with his sturdy neighbors, the Côtés, in the annual springtime boxing matches. Despite his training and self-motivation, he was still knocked out, but the prettiest girl in class threw him flowers. Expressive illustrations add humor and interest through odd perspectives and numerous details. *cmt*

**2.25** Carrier, Roch. **The Longest Home Run**. Translated by Sheila Fischman. Illustrated by Sheldon Cohen. Tundra Books of Northern New York, 1993. Originally published as *Le Plus Long Circuit* by Tundra in 1993. (paperback: Tundra, 1993). ISBN 0-88776-300-6 (paperback: 0-88776-312-X). 24 p. (7-12). Picture book. **Canada**.

In 1947 in his village of Ste. Justine, Quebec, the author and his friends were surprised one day by a girl, Adeline, who walked up and immediately hit their baseball farther than anyone...ever...all the way through cranky Sgt. Bouton's window! "I'm a magician," Adeline explained, and that evening after her sideshow performance, she and her father left town. Sgt. Bouton is all smiles the next day and returns the ball willingly to the author, thinking that he made the amazing hit and is a future world champion. Illustrations provide many details of village life in 1940s Canada. *cmt*

**2.26** Chekhov, Anton. **Kashtanka**. Translated by Ronald Meyer. Illustrated by Gennady Spirin. Harcourt, 1995. Originally published by Verlag J. F. Schreiber in 1994. ISBN 0-15-200539-0. 24 p. (7-10). Picture book. **Russia**.

Kashtanka the dog loses its master and is taken in by a man who has a trained animal act in a circus. Kashtanka learns to perform tricks and, when one of the animals dies, is integrated into the circus act. On the night of his first performance, Kashtanka sees his former master in the audience, rejoins him, and leaves the strange life of the circus forever. Sensitive illustrations capture the animals' emotions. *New York Times Best Illustrated Books. mew*

**2.27** Collington, Peter. **The Coming of the Surfman**. Illustrated by the author. Knopf, 1994. Originally published by Jonathan Cape Ltd. in

1993. ISBN 0-679-84721-9. 32 p. (8-14). Picture book for older readers. **Great Britain.**
In a blighted urban neighborhood plagued by warring gangs, a man, unbelievably, opens a surfing store, although the nearest water is two hours away. The gangs watch with increasing interest (and less animosity) as the Surfman converts an abandoned factory into a wave machine. For awhile everyone surfs; no one fights. But the wave machine is shut down for repairs, and one gang, piqued at losing its turn, destroys the machine. The Surfman leaves; the neighborhood blight resumes. Opportunity lost. Clinically stark, monotone illustrations echo the boring emptiness of these young people's lives, the Surfman's bright red toolbox on the narrator's desk being the sole sign of hope. *ss, cmt*

**2.28** Cooke, Trish. **So Much.** Illustrated by Helen Oxenbury. Candlewick, 1994. Originally published by Walker in 1994. ISBN 1-564-02344-3. Unpaginated. (1-6). Picture book. **Great Britain.**
As relatives arrive for a family birthday party, they each give in to their desire to hold, squeeze, kiss, and play with the baby, who is delighted by "so much" attention and "so much" love. Rhythmic dialect, repetitive language, and a cumulative structure are positive features. Illustrations show that this is an African-British family. *British Book Design and Production Award; Kurt Maschler Award; Smarties Prize for 5 & Under. cmt*

**2.29** Cowcher, Helen. **Tigress.** Illustrated by the author. Farrar, 1991. (paperback: Sunburst/FSG, 1993). Originally published by Picture Corgi in 1991. ISBN 0-374-37567-4. 40 p. (7-9). Picture book. **Great Britain.**
The conflict between environmentalists and farmers is played out in this story set on the Indian subcontinent where herdsmen graze their flocks on land next to an animal sanctuary. When a tigress ventures out of the sanctuary to kill a bullock and then a camel, the herdsmen talk of poisoning the meat before the tigress returns to feed. The sanctuary's ranger devises a better solution, setting off firecrackers that frighten the tigress and her cubs back to safety. Captivating illustrations alternate head-on views of the animals with panoramic visions of the plains at various times of day and night. *ss*

**2.30** Cowley, Joy. **The Duck in the Gun.** Illustrated by Robyn Belton. Shorthand, 1992 (Dist. in U.S by Rigby). Originally published by

Doubleday in 1969. Unpaginated. (4-6). Picture book. **New Zealand.** Having laid siege to a town, the General was ready to fight. He could not fire his cannon, however, because a duck had nested there and would not come out. While waiting for the eggs to hatch, the General and his soldiers made friends with the townspeople. When the eggs hatched and they could fight again, they chose not to. Instead, the General married the Prime Minister's daughter. Previous edition (Doubleday, 1969) illustrated by Edward Sorel. *Russell Clark Award for Illustration, 1985.* cmt

**2.31** Crew, Gary. **First Light.** Illustrated by Peter Gouldthorpe. Gareth Stevens, 1996. Originally published by Lothian in 1993. (paperback, Lothian, 1995, distributed in the U.S. by Seven Hills). ISBN 0-83681-664-1. 32p. (8-12). Picture book. **Australia.**
Davey would rather work on his model plane, but his gruff father insists he accompany him fishing before first light. Somber, foreboding illustrations portray menacing images, like flashing knife blades and partially submerged shots of animals' bulging eyes, tentacles, and claws. Reluctant to throw in his line, Davey waits in the eerie darkness. As light creeps over the water, his father hooks something big that takes his bait, and then lifts the dinghy momentarily from the water. The two sit shaken, staring at the bloodied remains of the bait fish, as the day's first light finally reveals the father's face. The ominous tone now lifts and the two row home, seemingly bonded by the strange power of the sea. *Australian Children's Picture Book of the Year Award.* bt

**2.32** Daly, Niki. **Not So Fast Songololo.** Illustrated by the author. McElderry, 1985. Originally published by Human & Rousseau in 1985. ISBN 0-689-50367-9. 32 p. (4-9). Picture book. **Republic of South Africa.**
Malusi, about seven, goes with Gogo, his grandmother, to the city to help her with her shopping. In one shop window he admires a pair of bright red tennis shoes. Gogo notices that Malusi's shoes are worn out, and so on the way home, she takes her grandson into the store and buys the shoes for him. This makes them both very happy. Illustrations show the similarity of life in the Republic of South Africa and the United States. *Katrine Harries Award for Illustrations, (South Africa) 1987.* cmt

**2.33** Davidge, Bud. **The Mummer's Song.** Illustrated by Ian Wallace.

Orchard, 1994. Originally published by Groundwood Books in 1993. ISBN 0-531-06825-0. 32 p. (5-8). Picture book. **Canada**.

The Mummer's Song memorializes a centuries-old Newfoundland Christmas tradition, in which neighbors don outlandish costumes and go from house to house. Residents guess who is under each costume, and, if correct, are rewarded by removal of the mask. Pencil illustrations show the absurdity and variety of costumes. All are taken in stride by Granny, who says it just wouldn't be Christmas without the mummers. A musical score is included. *ss*

**2.34** Denton, Kay MacDonald. **Dorothy's Dream**. Illustrated by the author. McElderry, 1989. Originally published by Walker in 1989. ISBN 0-689-50482-9. Unpaginated. (4-6) Picture book. **Great Britain**.

Because there is so much going on in her house at bedtime, Dorothy does not want to go to sleep at night, for fear of missing something. She looks at books, sings, dances, and draws pictures instead of sleeping. The problem is solved when Dorothy decides to go to sleep early so that she won't miss any dreams. Pale, watercolor illustrations provide the backdrop for this fanciful story which may be useful for bedtime conversation. *cb*

**2.35** Dupasquier, Philippe. **I Can't Sleep**. Illustrated by the author. Orchard, 1990. Originally published by Walker Books in 1988. ISBN 0-531-05874- 3. 32 p. (4-6). Picture book. **Great Britain.**

Father cannot sleep. He is joined first by his daughter, then his son, then his wife. All four have a snack, go outside to view the night sky, and finally settle down to sleep, only to oversleep the next morning. A wordless picture book with a contemporary setting. *jg*

**2.36** Edwards, Dorothy. **Emmie and the Purple Paint**. Illustrated by Priscilla Lamont. Oxford, 1987. Originally published by Methuen in 1984. ISBN 0-195-20599-5. Unpaginated. (3-6). Picture book. **Great Britain**.

Emmie does not like her play group, but she does like the play group activity of playing in paint. This is fun, until it gets out of hand. (FirstSearch) *cmt*

**2.37** Egger, Bettina. **Marianne's Grandmother**. Illustrated by Sita Jucker. Dutton, 1987. Originally published by Bohem Press in 1986.

ISBN 0-525-44335-5. 24 p. (4-6). Picture book. **Switzerland**.
Marianne remembers her grandmother's death and funeral, but she also remembers the times she and her grandmother spent together, taking walks, playing games, and baking at Christmastime. The swirling watercolor illustrations of grays and blues express both the sadness of loss and the joy of remembrance. *CCBC Choices. jl*

**2.38** Escudié, René. **Paul and Sebastian**. Translated by Roderick Townley. Illustrated by Ulises Wensell. Kane/Miller, 1988. Originally published as *Poulou et Sebastien* by Éditions du Centurion/Les Belles Histoires de Pomme d'Api in 1987. ISBN 0-916291-19-7. 29 p. (4-9). Picture book. **France**.
Paul and Sebastian are neighbors and good friends, although Paul lives in a trailer and Sebastian lives in an apartment. Their mothers, however, forbid them to play together, saying, "They are not our kind of people." On a school outing, the boys take refuge from a storm in a cabin, and fall asleep. Their mothers find them and, in the dark, mistakenly take each other's child home and lovingly put him to bed. In the morning they discover their mistake and realize the folly of their prejudice. Now, they are all friends. *cmt*

**2.39** Foreman, Michael. **War Game**. Illustrated by the author. Arcade, 1994. Originally published by Pavilion in 1993. ISBN 1-55970-242-7. 72 p. (7-10). Picture book for older readers. **Great Britain**.
Four young soldiers are transported from the sunny fields of Suffolk to the cold, muddy trenches of France to fight against the Germans in World War I. They soon realize that war is not a glorious game. They find temporary relief from the brutal and seemingly endless struggle in the trenches when, on an extraordinary Christmas Day, they celebrate the holiday with their German enemies with a soccer match. Profusely illustrated with watercolor and pen and ink drawings and facsimiles of war posters. Based upon a true story of the author's four uncles who were killed in World War I. *American Library Association Notable Books for Children; IBBY Honour List; Smarties Grand Prize. mja*

**2.40** Fox, Mem. **Shoes from Grandpa**. Illustrated by Patricia Mullins. Orchard, 1990. Originally published by Ashton Scholastic in 1989. (paperback: Orchard, 1992). ISBN 0-531-05848-4. (paperback: 0-531-08448-5). 32 p. (4–7). Picture book. **Australia**.

Grandpa gives Jessie shoes; her dad adds socks; her mom, a skirt; her cousin, a blouse; her sister, a sweater; her grandma, a coat; her aunt, a scarf; her brother, a hat; and her uncle, mittens. But Jessie, though thankful, just wants jeans. This rhythmic cumulative tale of family and clothes is alliterative and rhyming. Illustrations are colorful torn-paper collage, featuring a tousled redheaded Jessie. *jsn*

**2.41** Fox, Mem. **Tough Boris.** Illustrated by Kathryn Brown. Harcourt, 1994. ISBN 0-15-289612-0. 30 p. (4-6). Picture book. **Australia.**

A tough, greedy captain of a pirate ship finds treasure. A stowaway boy steals a violin from the treasure trove and plays it for the crew. Then the pirate's parrot dies and the stowaway sees the captain cry, so he helps him bury the parrot at sea in the violin case. Spare, predictable text with many visual clues promote independent reading. *bkn*

**2.42** Fox, Mem. **Wilfrid Gordon McDonald Partridge.** Illustrated by Julie Vivas. Kane/Miller, 1985. (paperback: Kane/Miller, 1989). Originally published in Australia by Omnibus Books in 1984. ISBN 0-916291-04-9. (paperback: 0-916291-26-X). 30 p. (4-6). Picture book. **Australia.**

A small boy becomes concerned when his parents tell him that ninety-five-year-old Miss Nancy, whom he loves, has lost her memory. He asks the other residents of the old people's home what a memory is. From the collective response that memory is warm, is from long ago, makes one cry, makes one laugh, and is precious as gold, he brings Miss Nancy things that trigger her memory. Humorous illustrations show Wilfrid's concern for his friend. *bkn*

**2.43** Gajadin, Chitra (reteller). **Amal and the Letter from the King.** Adapted from the play *The Post Office* by Rabindranath Tagore. Illustrated by Helen Ong. Boyds Mills, 1992. Originally published by Lemniscaat in 1992. ISBN 1-56397-120-8. 36 p. (7-9). Picture book. **Netherlands.**

Amal, who is ill, is not allowed outdoors, and so he sits by his window and interrogates the passersby about the places in his native India that he can imagine but has never seen. The mayor jokingly assures him that he will receive a letter from the king. When Amal's friend, the holy man, reiterates this, he means that Amal will soon receive a summons to Heaven. All who knew him will remember Amal's bright spirit. An allegory about life and death, the story also gives insight into village life in India. *cmt*

**2.44** Gallaz, Christophe and Innocenti, Roberto. **Rose Blanche.** Translated from the French by Martha Coventry and Richard Graglia. Illustrated by Roberto Innocenti. Creative Education, 1985. Originally published by Éditions 24 Heures, Lausanne, in 1985. ISBN 0-87191-944-x. 32 p. (10-12). Picture book. **Switzerland.**
Rose follows an army truck into the woods surrounding her German village. There she comes upon starving children held behind barbed wire fences—a Nazi concentration camp. From that day on, the compassionate Rose gives her meager food ration to the imprisoned children, putting her own life in peril. One day she finds the camp destroyed and surrounded by soldiers who, in the turmoil, mistake her for an enemy. Rose is never seen again. Detailed illustrations provide an uneasy mood, a sombre setting, and appallingly realistic glimpses of the death camp. A picture book for older readers. *Mildred Batchelder Award. cmt*

**2.45** Garland, Sarah. **Billy and Belle.** Illustrated by the author. Reinhardt Books, 1992. Originally published by Reinhardt Books in association with Viking in 1992. ISBN 0-670-84396-2. 29 p. (4-9) Picture book. **Great Britain.**
A biracial couple with two children named Billy and Belle, believe that their third child will be born today. Billy is taken to school and preschooler Belle goes along for the day while Mom and Dad go to the hospital. It's Pet Day, and Billy has taken his hamster to show. During art time Belle accidently lets all of the pets loose on the playground. After all the pets are safely recovered, Billy and Belle go home with their father and learn that they have a new baby brother named Adam. Vivid watercolor illustrations bring to life this one special day in the life of a loving family which just happens to be biracial. *cb*

**2.46** Garland, Sarah. **Polly's Puffin.** Illustrated by the author. Greenwillow, 1989. Originally published by The Bodley Head, London, in 1988. ISBN 0-688-08748-5. 24 p. (4-6). Picture book. **Great Britain.**
Polly finds it a nuisance to go shopping with her toddler-aged brother. She lets him play with her stuffed toy puffin, but, unbeknownst to Polly, he throws it, and it lands in the jacket hood of a passing stranger. Through serendipity—or is it magic—Polly and her puffin are reunited.

A melody woven through the story helps to show how we are more connected to one another than we think. *mb*

**2.47** Geraghty, Paul. **The Hunter**. Illustrated by the author. Crown, 1994. Originally published by Hutchinsons Children's Books in 1994. ISBN 0-517-59692-8. 32 p. (4-6). Picture book. **Great Britain**.
As young Jamina and her grandfather set out across the African plain, she tells him that she wants to hunt elephants. But after she rescues a baby elephant whose mother has been killed by hunters, and huddles in the darkness with it to evade poachers, she changes her mind about becoming a hunter. Detailed illustrations of native plants and animals used as frames highlight the African setting, and silhouettes in night scenes add drama. A strong statement about the dangers posed by hunters and poachers to African wildlife. *jg*

**2.48** Gleeson, Libby. **The Great Big Scary Dog**. Illustrated by Armin Greder. Tambourine, 1994. Originally published as *Big Dog* by Ashton Scholastic in 1991. ISBN 0-688-11293-5. 32 p. (4-6). Picture book. **Australia**.
A neighborhood dog seems fearsome to the children who must pass it. None of the advice they are given helps. When they decide to turn the tables on the dog by donning a Chinese dragon costume to scare it, they find that the dog is not fearsome at all, but friendly. The loose pencil and watercolor illustrations humorously convey both motion and emotion and support the author's suggestion that the unfamiliar should be approached rather than avoided. *ss*

**2.49** Gomi, Taro. **Summer Is Here**. Illustrated by the author. Chronicle, 1989. Originally published by Libroport in 1989. (paperback: Chronicle, 1995). ISBN 0-87701-626-7. 32 p. (4-6). Picture book. **Japan**.
Spring arrives and a calf is born. Readers journey through the seasons, as illustrations are imaginatively displayed on the body of the calf. *Graphic Prize, Bologna Children's Book Fair. Other titles by Gomi: The Big Book of Boxes; Bus Stops; The Crocodile and the Dentist; Everyone Poops; Guess What?; Guess Who?; Hide & Seek; Santa Through the Window; My Friends; Where's the Fish; Who Ate It?; Who Hid It?* *jy*

**2.50** Graham, Bob. **The Adventures of Charlotte and Henry**. Illustrated by the author. Viking, 1987. ISBN 0-670-81660-4. 45 p. (4-8).

Picture book. **Australia.**

Five stories in comic book format present daring Charlotte and cautious Henry, two true friends who complement each other. When, despite Henry's warnings, Charlotte rolls down a hill in a tire, Henry is there to efficiently bandage her scraped knees, without recriminations. When Henry's favorite stuffed dog loses its stuffing, Charlotte patches him so he looks better than ever. The light watercolors and bolder outlines help further define Charlotte and Henry's personalities. *Commended: Australian Picture Book of the Year. jvl*

**2.51** Graham, Bob. **Crusher Is Coming**. Illustrated by the author. Viking Kestrel, 1988. Originally published by Lothian Publishing Company in 1987. ISBN 0-670-82081-4. Unpaginated. (4-9). Picture book. **Australia.**

Peter has taken care to give his room a "manly" image in preparation for tough Crusher's after-school visit. His mother is not to kiss him and his little sister Claire is to stay out of his room while Crusher is around. But Crusher, huge and tough-looking as he is, falls for Claire and happily plays her little girl games all afternoon. Peter finds new respect for both Crusher and Claire. Amusing cartoon-style illustrations detail Claire and Crusher's bonding. *Australia's Picture Book of the Year Award. cmt*

**2.52** Graham, Bob. **Greetings from Sandy Beach**. Illustrated by the author. Kane/Miller, 1992. Originally published by Lothian Publishing Company in 1990. ISBN 0-916291-40-5. Unpaginated. (4-9). Picture book. **Australia.**

Much can happen on a two-day family camping trip to the beach. Despite the best efforts of this mother and father, nothing goes according to plan. Hope for solitude and quiet is dashed by a busload of children on a school outing, and relaxation is threatened when a motorcycle gang pitches camp nearby. But the school children make good playmates, and the illustrations reveal a growing friendship between the family and the motorcycle gang. *Australia's Picture Book of the Year Award. cmt*

**2.53** Graham, Bob. **Rose Meets Mr. Wintergarten**. Illustrated by the author. Candlewick Press, 1992. Originally published by Walker Books in 1992. (paperback: Candlewick, 1994). ISBN 1-56402-039-8 (paperback: 1-56402-395-8). Unpaginated. (4-9). Picture book. **Australia.**

After moving into her new home, Rose hears dreadful rumors about her next-door neighbor, Mr. Wintergarten. It is even suspected that he eats people! But when her ball goes over Mr. Wintergarten's fence, Rose goes to see him, taking cookies and flowers. She discovers a lonely old man who, because of Rose's kindness, soon opens his heart and yard to the neighborhood children. *Australia's Picture Book of the Year Award.* cmt

**2.54** Gray, Nigel. **A Country Far Away**. Illustrated by Philippe Dupasquier. Orchard, 1989. Originally published by Andersen Press Ltd. in 1988. (paperback: Orchard, 1991). ISBN 0-531-05792-5 (paperback: 0-531-07024-7). 26 p. (7-9) Picture book. **Great Britain**.
In a split-page format, the day-to-day activities of two boys, one from Great Britain and one from a tropical African country, are compared. Homelife, chores, school, games, shopping, siblings, and celebrations are featured, mainly in the information-rich illustrations. Basic similarities and interesting differences of the two cultures are emphasized. *Best Books of the Year,* Parents Magazine; *Notable Children's Trade Book in the Field of Social Studies.* cmt

**2.55** Gray, Nigel. **I'll Take You to Mrs. Cole**. Illustrated by Michael Foreman. Kane/Miller, 1992. Originally published by Andersen Press Ltd. in 1985. ISBN 0-916291-39-1. 30 p. **Great Britain**.
A little boy's mother often threatened to take him to Mrs. Cole's house down the street when he didn't do his chores. Because of this, the boy thought that Mrs. Cole must have terrible punishments for children. Curious, he went to Mrs. Cole's house one day and found her to be the jolliest, most child-friendly person imaginable. Now he does his chores so that he *can* visit his friend, Mrs. Cole. Humorous illustrations show Mrs. Cole to be a very relaxed housekeeper. cmt

**2.56** Guy, Rosa. **Billy the Great**. Illustrated by Caroline Binch. Dell, 1994. Originally published by Gollancz in 1991. ISBN 0-440-40920-9. 30 p. (4-6). Picture book. **Great Britain**.
Billy's parents try to plan his life for him, including his choice of friends, but he has ideas of his own. Illustrations show that Billy is a child of African descent. (FirstSearch). cmt. *Editor's note: The author is American, the illustrator is British.*

**2.57** Harrison, Joanna. **Dear Bear**. Illustrated by the author. Carolrhoda,

1994. (paperback: First Avenue Editions, 1994). Originally published by HarperCollins, London, in 1994. ISBN 1-87614-839-9. 32 p. (4-6). Picture book. **Great Britain.**
Young Katie imagines a ferocious bear under the stairs, and fear begins to haunt her. Her mother suggests she write a letter to the bear telling him to go away. The bear writes back, and soon they are engaged in regular correspondence. When Katie is invited under the stairs for tea, she arrives to find not only tea and a large stuffed bear, but also a note from the bear asking if he can come live with her. Minimal text is supplemented with reproductions of the correspondence and illustrated panels that convey Katie's changing emotional responses to a common childhood situation. *ss*

**2.58** Harrison, Ted. **A Northern Alphabet.** Illustrated by the author. Tundra, 1982. (paperback: Tundra, 1989). ISBN 088-776-233-6. (paperback: 088-776-233-6). 30 p. (4-9). Picture book. **Canada.**
Each letter of the alphabet, shown in capital and lower case, is featured in a sentence describing a scene typical of northern, rural Canada. The illustrations' appealing abstract style and bold blues, pinks, and oranges capture the vastness and cold crispness of the Far North. Borders provide place names beginning with the featured letter and occasionally challenge the reader to think of more places that begin with the letter. *IBBY Honour Book for Illustration; Amelia Frances Howard-Gibbon Illustrator Honor Book. jvl*

**2.59** Harrison, Ted. **O Canada.** Illustrated by the author. Kids Can, 1992. ISBN 1-55074-087-3. 30 p. (7-9). Picture book. **Canada.**
The author shows his love for his adopted country by giving his personal impressions of each of the provinces and the Northwest Territories through words and fluorescent colored images. The words of the Canadian National Anthem also run through the book, in larger type, and the music for the anthem is provided at the end. *jvl*

**2.60** Harvey, Amanda. **The Iron Needle.** Illustrated by the author. Lothrop, 1994. Originally published by Pan Macmillan Children's Books in 1994. ISBN 0-688-13192-1. 32 p. (4-6). Picture book. **Great Britain**.
When Elizabeth loses her needle, neither her mother nor the village shop has another, so she goes to the iron foundry at the foot of the hill to make one. With the help of the men at the foundry and the female

blacksmith, she makes a needle in time to complete a birthday sampler for her mother. Watercolor illustrations show the workings of the foundry and blacksmith shop in nineteenth-century England. *jg*

**2.61** Hathorn, Libby. **Way Home**. Illustrated by Gregory Rogers. Crown, 1994. Originally published by Random House Australia in 1994. ISBN 0-517-59909-0. Unpaginated. 7-9. Picture book. **Australia**.
Shane finds a stray kitten in an alley of the city where he lives, befriends it, and decides to take it home. Through the nighttime city they dodge threatening gangs and rushing traffic, greet friendly street people, and escape snarling dogs. Shane's warm references to home belie the fact that he lives alone in a box at the end of an alley. Shadowy brown and grey tones and vertical lines underscore the somber, severe, unfeeling urban setting. Well-lit showroom windows provide stark contrast with Shane's grimy life. Remarkably, Shane appears both resilient and tenuously hopeful. *Kate Greenaway Award. al, cmt*

**2.62** Hayashi, Akiko. **Aki and the Fox**. Illustrated by the author. Doubleday, 1991. Originally published as *Kon and Aki* by Fukuinkan Shoten in 1989. ISBN 0-385-41948-1. Unpaginated. (2-6). Picture book. **Japan**.
The toy fox, Kon, has been Aki's beloved companion from the day she was born, but as Aki grows up, Kon becomes worn. Aki and Kon travel by train to Grandmother's seaside town so Kon can be mended. The softly-framed watercolor and pen illustrations provide an accurate look at many cultural details of modern Japan. *cw*

**2.63** Hayes, Sarah. **Happy Christmas Gemma**. Illustrated by Jan Ormerod. Lothrop, 1986. Originally published by Walker in 1986. (paperback: Morrow, 1992). ISBN 0-688-06508-2. (paperback: 0-688-11702-3). 28 p. (1-3). Picture book. **Great Britain**.
Baby Gemma's first Christmas is full of excitement as she and her big brother decorate the tree, help make the Christmas pudding, and share the day with Mom, Dad, and Grandma. Realistic, well-defined watercolor figures on white backgrounds clearly show the fun and love this black family share. Pages of durable stock make this book appropriate for hands that are ready to move beyond board books. *bb*

**2.64** Heine, Helme. **Merry-Go-Round**. Translated by Chatto &Windus

Ltd. Illustrated by the author. Barron's Educational Series, 1980. Originally published by Gertraud Middelhauve Verlag in 1979. ISBN 0-8120-5393-1. 25 p. (4-6). Picture book. **Germany**.

Katie was spending her summer vacation with her Aunt Dumpling who cooked, her Uncle Plod who guarded the house, and Mr. Brainy who read books all day. Katie had no one to play with until she convinced the adults, one by one, to change their jobs so that she would have a companion. Eventually, the three adults took turns at everything, and everyone was happier. Illustrations use exaggeration to lend humor. *cmt*

**2.65** Henderson, Kathy. **The Little Boat**. Illustrated by Patrick Benson. Candlewick, 1995. Originally published by Walker in 1995. ISBN 1-564-02420-2. Unpaginated. (4-6). **Great Britain**.

A little boy playing at the seashore makes a toy sailboat that is swept out to sea. After surviving storms, hungry fish, and bigger boats, the sailboat is finally found by a little girl at the opposite shore. (FirstSearch). *Kurt Maschler Award. cmt*

**2.66** Heymans, Annemie and Heymans, Margriet. **The Princess in the Kitchen Garden**. Translated from the Dutch by Johanna H. Prins and Johanna W. Prins. Illustrated by the authors. Farrar, 1993. Originally published as *De prinses van de moestuin* by Em. Querido's Uitgeverij B.V. in 1991. ISBN 0-374-36122-3. 44 p. (8-11). Picture book. **Netherlands.**

Hannah, eleven, and her younger brother Matthew have slowly accepted their mother's death, but their father remains absorbed in his grief and neglects his children. In reaction, Hannah hides in her mother's kitchen garden shed to contemplate the problem. When a windstorm (Hannah believes the wind to be her mother) forces Matthew and Father to join Hannah in the shed, Father realizes his children's need for his love and attention and his need for theirs. Loose, ethereal pencil and chalk drawings reflect Hannah's sense of insecurity as well as her belief in her mother's presence. *Honor Book: Mildred Batchelder Award; ALA Notable Book. mew, cmt*

**2.67** Hidaka, Masako. **Girl From the Snow Country**. Translated by Amanda Mayer Stinchecum. Illustrated by the author. Kane/Miller, 1986. Originally published as *Yukinko* by Fukutake Publishing in 1984. ISBN 0-916291-06-5. 32 p. (4-7). Picture book. **Japan**.

Mi-chan, a little girl, enjoys her rural, winter world by building snow bunnies in the garden. She gives them ears of camillia leaves. She accompanies her mother to the open-air market and on the way brushes snow from the statue of Jizo, protector of children. A kind flower vendor gives Mi-chan some berries for her snow bunnies' eyes. Large, snowy illustrations are filled with cultural information about contemporary rural Japanese life. *cmt*

**2.68** Hoestlandt, Jo. **Star of Fear, Star of Hope.** Translated from the French by Mark Polizzotti. Illustrated by Johanna Kang. Walker, 1995. Originally published as *La grande peur sous les étoiles* by Éditions Syros in 1993. ISBN 0-8027-8374-0. 28 p. (7-12). Picture book. **France.**
Helen, now over 60, recalls the evening of her ninth birthday in 1942 in northern France. Her best friend Lydia was spending the night. Frightened by Jews seeking refuge in the apartment, Lydia, also Jewish, asked to be taken home, and Helen's birthday was spoiled. Angry, Helen shouted, "You're not my friend anymore!" The next day, Lydia disappeared, and Helen was never able to recant her words. After years of anger over the Jewish holocaust, Helen now only hopes that her friend survived. The sickness and hatred of the Nazi regime and the evil behind the yellow stars that Jews had to wear are reflected in flat, sinister, mustard-yellow illustrations. *Honor Book: Mildred Batchelder Award; ALA Notable Book. mew, cmt*

**2.69** Hoffman, Mary. **Amazing Grace.** Illustrated by Caroline Binch. Dial Books, 1991. Originally published by Frances Lincoln, 1991. ISBN 0-8037-1040-2. Unpaginated. (4-9). Picture book. **Great Britain**
Grace loves stories and acts out the parts of characters such as Joan of Arc, Anansi, and Mowgli. When her classmates tell her that she cannot be Peter Pan in the class play because she is a girl and black, her grandmother, Nana, takes her to the theater to see Rosalie, the daughter of a friend from Trinidad, in the role of Juliet. Grace realizes that it is hard work and talent that will get her what she wants. She gets the role of Peter Pan. In a sequel, *Boundless Grace*, Nana helps Grace understand that families are what one makes them. *Winner of more than 15 awards and prizes. djg*

**2.70** Hoffman, Mary. **Nancy No-Size.** Illustrated by Jennifer Northway. Oxford University, 1987. Originally published by Methuen in 1987.

ISBN 0-19-520596-0. 24 p. (4-6). Beginning reader. **Great Britain**.
Nancy is no size at all—too big for some things, too small for others, too
tall for last year's tights, but too short to reach the top bunk. Nancy
wants to be SOMETHING special, and when it turns out to be her fifth
birthday, she finds out that she is just right for her age after all. *CCBC
Choices. jl*

**2.71** Honda, Tetsuya. **Wild Horse Winter**. Translated by Susan Matsui.
Illustrated by Tetsuya Honda. Chronicle, 1992. (paperback: Chronicle,
1995). Originally published as *Dosanko-Uma No Fuyu* by Fukutake
Shoten in 1991. ISBN 0-8118-0251-5. 40 p. (4-6). Picture book. **Japan**.
When winter comes to Japan's Hokkaido island, the hardy band of
native horses migrate to the coastal feeding grounds. This story traces
one such journey, when a fierce blizzard buries the horses en route until
the only sign of them is the puff of steam from their breath. The next
morning, they manage to dig themselves out of the high drifts and
complete their journey. Full-page illustrations show the landscape of the
island, foregrounding the horses in their recurring battle against nature.
An editor's note provides information about the history of the diminishing breed of Dosanko horses. *ss*

**2.72** Hughes, Shirley. **Angel Mae: A Tale of Trotter Street**. Illustrated
by the author. Lothrop, 1989. (paperback: Puffin). Originally published
by Walker Books in 1989. ISBN 0-688-08538-5. Unpaginated. (4-6).
Picture book. **Great Britain**.
Mae Morgan lives with her mum and dad and her brother Frankie in the
flats on the corner of Trotter Street, but there is a new baby on the way.
Mae feels left out until she gets a special part in the Christmas play.
Things do not go according to plan, but all ends well in this pleasant
story which will appeal to all members of the family. *djg*

**2.73** Hughes, Shirley. **The Big Concrete Lorry**. Illustrated by the
author. Lothrop, 1989. Originally published by Walker Books in 1989.
0-688-08534-2. Unpaginated. (4-6). Picture book. **Great Britain**.
The Patterson family lives at number 26 Trotter Street and though the
rooms in their small home are full to bursting, the Pattersons wouldn't
dream of moving away. They decide to build an extension and everyone
helps. Events proceed in an orderly manner until the concrete lorry
brings an unexpected delivery! Quick action and the help of all the

Trotter Street neighbors save the day. *djg*

**2.74** Hughes, Shirley. **Bouncing**. Illustrated by the author. Candlewick, 1993. First published by Walker in 1993. ISBN 1-564-02128-9. Unpaginated. (1-3). Concept book. **Great Britain**.
First in a series of concept books featuring toddlers at play and work. Each story explains the action indicated by the title. In *Giving*, a little girl and her baby brother discover the joy of giving, whether it be a gift, a smile, or a kiss. In *Chatting*, a little girl likes to chat to her cat and with friends in the park and at the supermarket. Others in the series: *Giving* (1993, ISBN 1-564-02129-7); *Chatting* (1994, ISBN 1-564-02340-0); *Hiding* (1994, ISBN 1-564-02342-7). *djg*

**2.75** Hughes, Shirley. **An Evening at Alfie's**. Illustrated by the author. Lothrop, Lee and Shepard, 1984. Originally published by The Bodley Head in 1984. ISBN 0-688-04122-1. Unpaginated. (4-6) Picture book. **Great Britain**.
Alfie loves it when Maureen baby-sits, because she always reads him a story. Tonight she reads "Noah's Ark." After he is tucked into bed, Alfie begins to hear water running and then discovers water raining down in his house! It is a broken water pipe, and Maureen, with the help of her mum and dad, find and close the water main. All is well by the time Alfie's parents return from their evening out. Alfie cannot wash up the next morning, but he does not mind, because, after all, he had more than enough water the night before. *djg*

**2.76** Hughes, Shirley. **Lucy & Tom's 1.2.3**. Illustrated by the author. Viking Kestrel, 1987. Originally published by Gollancz in 1987. (paperback: Dutton). ISBN 0-670-81763-5 (paperback: 0-14-050782-5). 32 p. (4-6). Concept book. **Great Britain**.
From the moment Lucy and Tom wake up, their day is full of math as they count the kittens, notice the numbers on houses and how they progress, weigh foods, fill a bowl with water, and play on a see-saw. The simple story allows the various math concepts to be discussed or overlooked, according to the disposition of the reader or listener. Illustrations show ruddy-cheeked and very real children as they play, visit Grandma, or shop in a comfortable, cozy British neighborhood. *bb*

**2.77** Hughes, Shirley. **The Snow Lady: A Tale of Trotter Street**.

Illustrated by the author. Lothrop, 1990. Originally published by Walker in 1990. ISBN 0-688-09875-4. Unpaginated. (4-6). Picture book. **Great Britain**.

Sam and Barney build a snow lady that resembles their elderly neighbor, "mean" Mrs. Dean. The children learn a hard lesson when Mrs. Dean returns home from holiday early and their prank is nearly discovered. *cmt*

**2.78** Hughes, Shirley. **Wheels: A Tale of Trotter Street**. Illustrated by the author. Lothrop, 1991. Originally published by Walker in 1991. ISBN 0-688-09881-9. Unpaginated. (4-6). Picture book. **Great Britain**.

Carlos desperately wants a new bike just like his friend Billy's for his birthday, but his mum can't afford one. When, at last, his birthday arrives, he gets, not a new bike, but a go-cart! He happily joins all the children at the park with his new wheels. Set in a multi-ethnic working class neighborhood, this warm and appealing story exhibits Hughes' sure touch for the familiar details of family life. *cw, djg*

**2.79** Hutchins, Pat. **The Doorbell Rang**. Illustrated by the author. Greenwillow Press, 1986. Originally published by The Bodley Head in 1986. (paperback: Mulberry, 1987). ISBN 3-44-58298-0. Unpaginated. (4-6). Picture book. **Great Britain**.

Victoria and Sam's mouths water in anticipation as Ma takes a dozen cookies out of the oven. Six cookies each (even if they are not as good as Grandma's). But the doorbell rings and keeps ringing and more and more friends arrive. With each arrival, the children see their allotment of cookies grow smaller. Each child has just one cookie when the doorbell rings and it is...Grandma with an enormous tray of cookies! Illustrations help keep tabs on the number of children who will have to divide the cookies. *djg*

**2.80** Hutchins, Pat. **My Best Friend**. Illustrated by the author. Greenwillow, 1993. Originally published by ? in 1988. ISBN 0-688-11485-7. 32 p. (4-6). Picture book. **Great Britain**.

Sometimes a best friend can do everything well: run faster, climb higher, jump farther, and read better than anyone else. But sometimes even a best friend can get scared and need to be comforted. That's what friends are for. *CCBC Choices. jl*

**2.81** Hutchins, Pat. **The Wind Blew**. Illustrated by the author. Macmillan, 1974. Originally published by The Bodley Head in 1974. (paperback: Aladdin, 1990). ISBN 0-027459101 (paperback: 0-689-71744-X). 32p. (3-6). Picture book. **Great Britain**.

When the wind sweeps through a town, it steals first an umbrella, then a balloon, then many other possessions from the townspeople, all of whom are compelled to chase after their belongings *en masse*. Simple text and vibrant tempera paintings create an engaging cumulative story. *Kate Greenaway Medal. al*

**2.82** Impey, Rose. **Joe's Cafe**. Illustrated by Sue Porter. Little Brown, 1990. Originally published by Orchard, London, 1990. ISBN 0-316-41777-7. Unpaginated. (4-6). Picture book. **Great Britain**.

Joe loves his sister, but she is just too little to play. One day, when he is supposed to be minding her, his sister hides, but Joe doesn't seek. Instead, he plays his favorite game—mud pies. A neighbor comes by and buys some "mud cakes," and when she leaves, Joe forgets to close the gate. Little sister toddles out of the gate and down the road, and it is quite some time before Joe misses her. His worried search ends when his neighbor appears with his sister by the hand, safe and sound. *National Book League's Children's Books of the Year List. djg*

**2.83** Itoh, Mamoru. **I Want to Tell You About My Feelings**. Translated by Leslie M. Nielsen. Illustrated by Hiromi Isogawa. Morrow, 1996. Originally published as *Kono kimochi tsutaetai* by Discover 21, Inc. in 1992. ISBN 0-688-14630-9. 76 p. (7-14). Picture book. **Japan**.

Comparing communication to a game of catch, the author tells what promotes and hinders this act. The basic assertion is that we need to tell each other our feelings (throwing the ball) and hear what others are saying to us (catching the balls that are thrown to us) to communicate. Text and illustrations are uncomplicated, underlying the message that communication is simple, if we will do it. *cmt*

**2.84** Izawa, Yohji and Funakoshi, Canna. **One Morning**. Translated by the publishers. Illustrated by the authors. Picture Book Studio, 1986. Originally published as *Asa* by Suemori Chieko Books, G. C. Press, in 1985. ISBN 0-88708-033-2. 30 p. (1-3). Picture book. **Japan**.

A pet cat greets the sights, sounds, and smells of a new day as her master gets ready for work. Spare text and simple collage illustrations effectively invite readers to supply the details. *First Prize for Graphics, Bologna International Children's Book Fair. cmt*

**2.85** Jam, Teddy. **Night Cars.** Illustrated by the author. Orchard Books, 1989. Originally published by Groundwater Books in 1988. (paperback: Orchard Books, 1991). ISBN 0-531-08393-4. (paperback: 0-530-08393-4). 30 p. (1-3). Picture book. **Canada.**
A baby is lulled to sleep as he watches the street life through his window at night. He sees cars, a fire truck, people, and dogs passing on the street below. For most of the book the observant baby is outside the illustrations, looking into the scenes, but in the morning he enters into the pictures when his daddy takes him down onto the street and into one of the stores that he has been watching. *Elizabeth Mrazik-Cleaver Canadian Picture Book Award. bkn*

**2.86** Kaldhol, Marit. **Good-bye Rune.** Translated by Michael Crosby-Jones. Illustrated by Wenche Øyen. Kane/Miller, 1987. Originally published as *Farvel, Rune* by Det Norske Samlaget in 1986. ISBN 0-916291-11-1. 24 p. (4-9). Picture book. **Norway.**
For all of their five years, Sara and Rune have been best friends. Tragically, Rune drowns, and Sara, over the next year, must learn to live with her grief. Softly glowing, full-page watercolor illustrations depict real scenes during this time, while small black and white vignettes depict Sara's memories of her friend. A fittingly quiet, thoughtful book. *cmt*

**2.87** Karvoskaia, Natacha (story told by Zidrou). **Dounia.** Illustrated by the author. Kane/Miller, 1995. Originally published by Rainbow Graphics International in 1995. ISBN 0-916291-58-8. 26 p. (4-7). Picture book. **Belgium.**
Dounia, an orphan, has been adopted. She is black and her new parents are white, and she has had to move to a new country. On her first day in her new home, she is too shy to express her delight, but she knows that she will be happy. The warm hues and loose style of the illustrations underscore the easy feeling that Dounia, three or four years old, has about her new situation. *cmt*

**2.88** Khalsa, Dayal Kaur. **My Family Vacation.** Illustrated by the author. Clarkson N. Potter, 1988. 0-517-56697-4. 22 p. (4-9). Picture book. **Canada.**

May and her family take a trip by car to Florida from the snowy north. They enjoy sightseeing and swimming before making the long drive back. *dd*

**2.89** Khalsa, Dayal Kaur. **Sleepers**. Illustrated by the author. Clarkson N. Potter, 1988. ISBN 0-517-56917-5. 22 p. (1-3) Picture book. **Canada.**
A young child, insisting that she never sleeps, tells how her family and her pets, as well as flamingoes, camels, a cowboy and a clown sleep. In the end, as she goes to sleep herself, she says, "Well...I *hardly* ever sleep." Minimal text is accompanied by colorful, childlike illustrations. *bkn*

**2.90** Khalsa, Dayal Kaur. **Tales of a Gambling Grandma**. Clarkson N. Potter, 1986. (paperback: Potter, 1986). ISBN 0-517-56137-9. (paperback: 0-517-88262-0). 32 p. (7–9). Picture book. **Canada.**
A girl tells of her Grandma, who came from Russia to Brooklyn as a child and later married a plumber. To earn extra money, she gambled. After her husband's death, the grandmother lived with her working daughter and son-in-law and cared for her granddaughter, telling her stories and playing cards with her. Most of the colorful illustrations focus on Grandma and girl together, enjoying Coney Island and a Chinese restaurant, penny-polishing, and playing poker. *New York Times Notable. jsn*

**2.91** Kurelek, William. **A Prairie Boy's Winter**. Illustrated by the author. Houghton Mifflin, 1973. Published simultaneously by Tundra Books of Montreal. ISBN 0-395-17708-1. Unpaginated. (8-10). Picture book. **Canada.**
In realistic and detailed paintings and lively reminiscences, the author portrays farm life in the 1930s in Manitoba, Canada. The games, chores, social life, and weather associated with the five months of winter in this rural area are featured. Although the conditions were harsh, the author saw beauty and humor everywhere. *New York Times Best Illustrated Books of the Year*. See also: *A Prairie Boy's Summer* (Houghton Mifflin, 1975; ISBN 0-395-20280-9). *cmt*

**2.92** Kurusa. **The Streets Are Free**. Illustrated by Monika Doppert. Translated by Karen Englander. Annick Press, 1995(1985). Originally published as *La Calle es Libre* by Ediciones Ekaré/Banco del Libro, Caracas, Venezuela, in 1981. ISBN 1-55037-370-6. Unpaginated. (7-9). Picture book. **Venezuela.**

As the slums or *barrios* build up around a large city in Venezuela, the children are left with no place to play except the streets. They organize themselves, make a plan for a playground, and appeal to the mayor for help. He makes promises but does nothing. Finally, the children convince their parents to build the playground themselves, and this time it works. Illustrations depict the raw poverty of the *barrios*. *cmt*

**2.93** Landström, Olof and Lena. **Will Goes to the Post Office.** Translated by Elisabeth Dyssegaard. Illustrated by Olof Landström. R&S Books, 1994. Originally published as *Nisse Går til Posten* by Rabén & Sjögren in 1993. ISBN 91-29-62950-0. 24 p. (2-5). Picture book. **Sweden.**

Will goes to the post office and returns home bearing a large, clumsy box. The importance with which Will views this commonplace errand and the pleasure he takes in carrying it out are evidenced in his small grin and the way he continually examines the notice he carries with him to the post office. The engaging pictures tell the whole story, while the economical text provides the dialogue. Other titles in this series: *Will's New Cap* (1992); *Will Gets a Haircut* (1993); and *Will Goes to the Beach* (1995). *ss*

**2.94** Landström, Lena. **Will Goes to the Beach.** Translated by Carla Wiberg. Illustrated by Olof Landström. R&S Books/Farrar, 1995. Originally published as *Nisse Går til Stranden* by R&S Books in 1994. ISBN 912-96291-44. Unpaginated. (3-6). Picture book. **Sweden.**

Young Will and his mother prepare a picnic lunch and ride their bikes to the beach so that Will can practice swimming. A sudden shower sends the crowds away, but prompts Will and his mother to enjoy the warmth of the water. Before long, Will discovers that he is actually swimming. Cartoon-style illustrations add much humor to this story. Other titles in this series: *Will's New Cap* (1992); *Will Gets a Haircut* (1993); *Will Goes to the Post Office* (1994). *cp*

**2.95** Lester, Alison. **Rosie Sips Spiders.** Illustrated by the author. Houghton Mifflin, 1989. Originally published by Oxford University, Melbourne, in 1988. ISBN 0-395-51526-2. 32 p. (4-9). Picture book.

**Australia.**

The hobbies and habits of seven very different boys and girls are presented as cameo portraits side by side on double-page spreads. The work, home, favorite food, play, gardens, pets, bath routine, and sleep habits are shown and described. Illustrative ingenuity and sophisticated vocabulary add interest. *Australian Book Publishers Association Book Design Award. mb*

**2.96** Lewin, Hugh. **Jafta: The Homecoming**. Illustrated by Lisa Kopper. Knopf, 1994. Originally published by Hamish Hamilton in 1992. ISBN 0-679-84722-7. Unpaginated. (4-8). Picture book. **Great Britain.**

Told from the point of view of a small child, Jafta, this simple, moving story tells what a father's return means to a family separated by apartheid. Other titles in the *Jafta Family* series (Carolrhoda): *Jafta*; *Jafta's Mother*; *Jafta's Father*; *Jafta and the Wedding*; *Jafta: The Journey*; *Jafta: The Town. hr*

**2.97** Lewis, Kim. **The Shepherd Boy**. Illustrated by the author. Four Winds, 1990. Originally published by Walker in 1990. ISBN 0-02-758581-1. 32 p. (4-6). Picture book. **Great Britain.**

As young James waits to be "old enough" to be a shepherd like his father, he and his stuffed lamb imitate the work of his parents as they tend the sheep. On Christmas day James is rewarded with a special gift. Soft, textured illustrations enhance the Scottish farm setting and the boy's antics with his toy companion. *be*

**2.98** Lindgren, Astrid. **I Want a Brother or Sister**. Translated by Eric Bibb. Illustrated by Ilon Wikland. Farrar, 1988. Originally published as *Jag Vil Också Ha ett Syskon* by Rabén & Sjögren in 1977. ISBN 9-129-58778-6. 32 p. (4-6). Picture book. **Sweden.**

Peter, having asked for and gotten a new baby sister, Lena, soon wishes that he had asked for a tricycle instead! He finds ways to get even with this new rival for his parents' attention until his mother takes him on her lap and enlists his help in caring for Lena. Swedish homes, small-town surroundings, and supportive adults are portrayed in a warm, sympathetic style, offering a feeling of community and belonging. *clb*

**2.99** Lindström, Eva. **The Cat Hat**. Translated by Stephen Croall. Illustrated by the author. Kane/Miller, 1989. Originally published as

*Kattmössan* by Alfabeta Bokförlag in 1988. ISBN 0-916291-23-5. 32 p. (4-8). Picture book. **Sweden.**

This humorous tale of false accusation begins when Lena's cat, Bruno, goes missing. In her distress she becomes convinced that her neighbor, Roland, has killed Bruno and made a winter hat of his fur! No sooner has she confiscated Roland's hat and given it a proper burial than she sees dozens of identical "Bruno" hats in the village hat shop. She exhumes the buried hat. Taking the "coffin" to her cellar to burn, Lena discovers Bruno, returned at last. Troubled that she has wronged Roland, she returns the hat to him only to find that he hates it and wants her to have it after all. *cmt*

**2.100** Lobe, Mira. **Christoph Wants a Party**. Retold by Marcia Lane. Illustrated by Winfried Opgenoorth. Kane/Miller, 1995, Originally published as *Christoph Will Ein Fest* by Verlag Jungbrunnen in 1984. ISBN 0-916291-59-6. 20 p. (4-6). Engineered picture book. **Austria.**

Christoph, soon to be five, wants to invite his five best friends to his birthday party, but cannot, since his apartment is too small. At a pastry shop on his birthday, Christoph imagines the dessert tray into a fantastic, multitiered birthday playground enjoyed by all of his friends. The next day, he and his parents construct a miniplayground in his bedroom where it is easy to have imaginary adventures. Riotously illustrated, six-panel foldout details Christoph's imaginary party. *cmt*

**2.101** Loh, Morag. **Tucking Mommy In**. Illustrated by Donna Rawlins. Orchard, 1988. Originally published by Ashton Scholastic in 1987. (paperback: Orchard, 1991). ISBN 0-531-05740-2. (paperback: 0-53107025-5). 32 p. (3–6). Picture book. **Australia.**

Mommy is very tired, so daughter Sue tells a bedtime story about their cat Mitzi while Mommy falls asleep on Jenny's bed. The girls rouse Mommy, help her into her pajamas, tuck her in, and tell Daddy about it when he comes home from work and tucks them in. Watercolor and colored pencil illustrations combine with text to create a reassuring bedtime story. *ALA Notable Book. jsn*

**2.102** Mahy, Margaret. **The Great White Man-Eating Shark.** Illustrated by Jonathan Allen. Dial, 1990. (paperback: Puffin Pied Piper, 1996). Originally published by Dent in 1989. ISBN 0-8037-0749-5. 32 p. (4-6). Picture book. **Great Britain.**

Sick of sharing the beach with other swimmers, Norvin, who looks a bit like a shark already, straps on a dorsal fin and scares the other swimmers out of the water. Each time they venture back in, he repeats his little game, but the day he finds a female shark swimming alongside him, it is Norvin himself who decides to remain on land for the rest of the summer. Allen's cartoon illustrations, which succeed in communicating both broad movements and minute expressions, are catalysts for the humor found in Mahy's spirited text. *ss*

**2.103** Mahy, Margaret. **Jam : A True Story.** Illustrated by Helen Craig. Atlantic Monthly Press, 1985. Originally published by J. M. Dent in 1985. (paperback: Little, Brown, 1986). ISBN 0-87113-048-3. 26 p. (4-6). Picture book. **New Zealand.**
When Mrs. Castle takes an important job, Mr. Castle becomes a very efficient househusband. When he discovers that their plums are ripe, he harvests them and fills every container in the house with plum jam. After eating it every conceivable way, and even using it to stop leaks and stick down tiles, they finally consume the last of it—just as the new crop of plums ripen. Humorous, cartoon-style illustrations show Mr. Castle's enthusiasm and the family's growing disenchantment with the ever-present jam. *bkn*

**2.104** Mahy, Margaret. **The Man Whose Mother Was a Pirate.** Illustrated by Margaret Chamberlain. Viking Kestrel, 1986. Originally published by J. M. Dent in 1985. (paperback: Viking, 1987). ISBN 0-670-81070-3. (paperback: 0-140-50624-1). 26 p. (5–8). Picture book. **New Zealand.**
A little man in a respectable brown suit and shoes takes his mother, an old pirate, away from the city to the sea. On the way, a farmer and a philosopher try to dissuade them, but when pirate mother and little man reach the shore, they are delighted. She becomes bo'sun to a sea captain, and her son, now Sailor Sam, is cabin boy. Themes of self-fulfillment and freedom are reflected in the humorous, loosely drawn illustrations. The lively dialog and the narrative become poetically alliterative at the climactic sea-scene. *jsn*

**2.105** Mandelbaum, Pili. **You Be Me, I'll Be You.** Translated by the publisher. Illustrated by the author. Kane/Miller, 1990. Originally published as *Noire Comme le Café, Blanc Comme la Lune* by Pastel,

L'Ecole des Loisirs, Paris, in 1989. ISBN 0-916291-27-8. 32 p. (4-9). Picture book. **Belgium**.

Anna, a biracial child, does not like the way she looks. She wants to look like her white father, until they paint their faces and dress up as one another. Father points out to Anna how people often try to change their appearance. Anna decides that she is fine the way she is. Textured collage illustrations add realism. *cmt*

**2.106** Maruki, Toshi. **Hiroshima no Pika**. Translated from the Japanese through Kurita-Bando Literary Agency. Illustrated by the author. Lothrop, 1982. Originally published by Komine Shoten Co., Ltd. in 1980. ISBN 0-688-01297-3. 48 p. (10-12). Picture book. **Japan**.

Mii and her parents were eating breakfast in their Hiroshima home on the morning of August 6, 1945, when American armed forces dropped the atomic bomb that destroyed the city and killed over 100,000 inhabitants. Desperate to get her badly burned husband to water, Mii's mother carried him through terrifying carnage to the river. The author's powerful expressionist illustrations graphically depict the hell of war. Intended as an antiwar statement, the book serves to remind us that "It can't happen again, if no one drops the bomb." A picture book for older readers. *Mildred Batchelder Award, 1983; ALA Notable Book; Boston Globe Horn Book Award Honor Book for Nonfiction, 1983; Jane Addams Peace Award, 1983. cmt*

**2.107** McFarlane, Sheryl. **Waiting for the Whales**. Illustrated by Ron Lightburn. Orca, 1991. ISBN 0-920501-66-4. Unpaged. (7-9). Picture book. **Canada**.

A lonely old man lives on a bluff overlooking the Pacific where he grows a huge garden, walks in the woods, and watches for the orcas. His daughter and granddaughter appear one spring day and as his granddaughter grows, the old man shares his knowledge with her. When he dies, the child is sad, but with the return of the orcas, who bring with them a new calf, she is comforted. *Amelia Frances Howard-Gibbon Award.*

**2.108** McMullan, Kate. **Good Night Stella**. Illustrated by Emma Chichester Clark. Candlewick, 1994. Originally published by Walker in 1994. ISBN 1-56402-065-7. Unpaginated. (4-6). Picture book. **Great Britain**.

Stella's father tucks her into bed and says, "Good night, sleep tight, sweet dreams," but her hamster gallops on his squeaky wheel, and she can't sleep. Father comforts her through scary shadows, drinks of water, and other nighttime troubles as they wait up for Mother. First, Father sleeps while Stella waits up, then Stella sleeps and Father keeps the vigil. Watercolor illustrations portray Stella as the text indicates—"charming and lively and naughty." *djg*

**2.109** Mennen, Ingrid. **One Round Moon and a Star for Me.** Illustrated by Niki Daly. Orchard, 1994. Originally published by The Bodley Head in 1994. ISBN 0-531-06804-8. Unpaginated. (4-7). Picture book. **Republic of South Africa.**
A young boy of rural Lesotho needs reassurance that his father is still his father, too, when a new baby is born into the family. (FirstSearch) *cmt*

**2.110** Mennen, Ingrid, and Daly, Niki. **Somewhere in Africa.** Illustrated by Nicolaas Maritz. Dutton, 1992. Originally published as *Ashraf of Africa* by Songololo Books in 1990. (paperback: Red Fox, 1992). ISBN 0-525-44848-9 (paperback: 0-09-989890-X). 32 p. (5-9). Picture book. **Republic of South Africa.**
In a delightful overthrow of stereotypes, a young Malay boy in Cape Town, South Africa, reads about wild, untamed Africa in a book borrowed from the big city library. Vibrant illustrations show similarities and differences between Cape Town and all big cities of the world. *cmt*

**2.111** Morimoto, Junko. **My Hiroshima.** Illustrated by the author. Viking, 1990. Originally published by William Collins Pty. in 1987. ISBN 0-670-83181-6. 34 p. (9-12). Picture book for older readers. **Australia.**
The author, a survivor of the atomic blast that destroyed the city of Hiroshima on August 6, 1945, recalls life before, during, and after the bomb. Frightening images of slaughtered masses interspersed with archival photographs of the ruined city hint at the horror of this time. Includes facts about Hiroshima and a letter to parents and teachers. *cmt*

**2.112** Müller, Jörg. **The Changing Countryside.** Illustrated by the author. Atheneum, 1977. Originally published as *Alle Jahre wieder saust der Presslufthammer nieder* by Sauerländer in 1973. ISBN 0-689-50085-8. (7-14). Wordless portfolio. **Switzerland.**

A series of eight oversized murals dated at three-year intervals depicts the transformation of a pleasant bucolic area into suburban sprawl. Richly detailed and realistic illustrations suggest economic and political forces behind change and its social impact on the lives of those who must live with it. Excellent for older readers. *Müller: Hans Christian Andersen Medal for Illustration. cmt*

**2.113** Müller, Jörg. **The Changing City**. Illustrated by the author. Atheneum, 1977. Originally published as *Hier faullt ein Haus, dort steht ein Kran und ewig droht der Baggerzahn, oder Die Veränderung der Stadt* by Sauerländer in 1977. ISBN 0-689-50084-X. (7-14). Wordless portfolio. **Switzerland**.
Companion volume to *The Changing Countryside* (see annotation above), these eight murals chronicle the destruction over two decades of a charming urban neighborhood through the inroads of "progress": big business, big highways, and big buildings. Excellent for older readers. *cmt*

**2.114** Mullins, Patricia. **V for Vanishing**. Illustrated by the author. Harper-Collins, 1994. Originally published by Margaret Hamilton Books in 1993. (paperback: HarperTrophy, 1997). ISBN 0-06-023556-X. 32 p. (3-7). Picture book. **Australia**.
The concept underlying this alphabet book is vanishing species. For each letter, an endangered creature is presented in collage, using tissue paper, paint, and crayon. Accompanying the illustration are the creature's common name, its Latin name, and its native country. In a foreword, Mullins explains the role of humans in this process of extinction and suggests ways that we can change this trend. *ss*

**2.115** Murphy, Jill. **A Quiet Night In**. Illustrated by the author. Candlewick, 1994. Originally published by Walker in 1993. (paperback: Candlewick, 1996). ISBN 1-56402-248-X. 28 p. (3-5). Picture book. **Great Britain**.
Jill Murphy's books about the Large family capture the essence of family life and add a memorable elephant family to the world of children's literature. In the fourth story about the Larges, Mrs. Large hustles the children into their pajamas before dinner in hopes of securing a quiet evening in which to celebrate Mr. Large's birthday. As it turns out, Mr. and Mrs. Large's night in is very quiet indeed, as they end up falling

asleep on the couch before dinner and are tucked in by their four children. Other books in this series: *Five Minutes' Peace* (1986); *All in One Piece* (1987); and *A Piece of Cake* (1987). *ss*

**2.116** Nakawatari, Harutaka. **The Sea and I**. Translated by Susan Matsui. Illustrated by the author. Farrar, 1992. Originally published as *Umi-to Boku* by Fukutake Publishing in 1990. ISBN 0-374-36428-1. Unpaginated. (4-7). Picture book. **Japan**.
A fisherman's son living on the coast of Japan watches his father's boat leave, as he does every day. Today, the waves, the gulls, and the wind warn him of an approaching storm. He fears for his father's safety out on the water, but evening brings calm weather, and his father returns to give his son a big sea hug and to tell him stories of his many voyages. Beautifully rendered panoramas of the shore at different times of the day capture the beauty and magnitude of the ocean and emphasize the importance of nature to the characters' lives. *cmt*

**2.117** Nichol, Barbara. **Beethoven Lives Upstairs**. Illustrated by Scott Cameron. Orchard, 1994. Originally published by Lester Publishing in 1993. ISBN 0-531-06828-5. 48 p. (8-12). Picture book for older readers. **Canada**.
In 1822 in Vienna, Christoph, ten, writes to his Uncle Karl in Salzburg to complain about the noisy new tenant upstairs, the composer Beethoven. Letters written during the ensuing three-year correspondence show that Christoph gradually comes to befriend the troubled genius, to sympathize with his anguish caused by deafness, and finally to revere him for his splendid music. Oil paintings evoke the early nineteenth-century setting by their careful attention to details of attire and furnishings. *cmt*

**2.118** Nomura, Takaaki. **Grandpa's Town**. Translated by Amanda Mayer Stinchecum. Illustrated by the author. Kane/Miller, 1991. Originally published as *Ojiichan no Machi* by Kodansha in 1989. ISBN 0-916291-36-7. 32 p. (4-7). Picture book. **Japan**.
Little Yuuta is concerned that his recently widowed grandfather is lonely living alone. But after spending an eventful day with him walking through the town and bathing at the public bath, Yuuta understands why Grandpa is happy here among all his friends. Japanese customs, clothing, and architecture are presented in strong wood-cut illustrations.

Some nudity in section set in public bath. Text is presented in both English and Japanese. *cmt*

**2.119** Onyefulu, Ifeoma. **Emeka's Gift: An African Counting Story**. Photographs by the author. Cobblehill Books, 1995. Originally published by Frances Lincoln Limited in 1995. ISBN 0-525-65205-1. Unpaginated. (7-9). Concept book. **Great Britain**.
Emeka, a little boy, sets off to visit his grandmother. But what can he bring Granny for a present? His journey takes him through the market and he counts out handmade objects, some for everyday use and some for special occasions. The author was born and raised in eastern Nigeria as a member of the Igbo tribe. Beautiful, full-color photographs illustrate this informative picture book. *djg*

**2.120** Ormerod, Jan. **Messy Baby**. Illustrated by the author. Lothrop, 1985. 18 p. (1-3). Picture book. **Australia**.
Each book in the **Baby Books** series shows a toddler and his/her father interacting. In **Messy Baby**, Dad tidies up Baby's room, telling all the while where each item goes, while Baby follows him around, undoing his work. It all ends, however, with a big, reassuring hug for Messy Baby. The realistically drawn people and objects and Baby's and Dad's expressive faces help convey the affectionate mood of the story. Other books in **Jan Ormerod's Baby Books** series: **Dad's Back**, ISBN 0-688-04126-4; **Reading**, ISBN 0-688-04127-0; **Sleeping**, ISBN 0-688-04129-9. *jvl*

**2.121** Ormerod, Jan. **Our Ollie**. Illustrated by the author. Lothrop, 1986. Originally published by Walker in 1986. ISBN 0-688-04208-2. 20 p. (1–3). Concept book. **Australia**.
In the **Little Ones** series, simple words and colorful illustrations on a white background show young children learning basic concepts. **Our Ollie** is compared with a cat, hippo, cock, hedgehog, parrot, frog, and bear. In **Silly Goose** a child compares her actions to those of a gibbon, flea, kangaroo, duck, bat, peacock, ostrich—and a silly goose. As **Young Joe** counts up to ten on his fingers, he thinks of animals—one fish, two frogs...and ends with one puppy. In **Just Like Me** a toddler compares her brother to an egg, a rabbit, a toad, a puppy, and a piglet, but concludes that he will grow up to be just like her. Other books in **Jan Ormerod's Little Ones** series: **Silly Goose**, ISBN 0-688-04209-0;

**Young Joe,** ISBN 0-688-04210-4; **Just Like Me,** ISBN 0-688-04211-2. *jsn*

**2.122** Ormerod, Jan. **The Saucepan Game**. Illustrated by the author. Lothrop, 1989. Originally published by Walker in 1989. ISBN 0-688-08519-9. 17 p. (1-3). Picture book. **Great Britain.**
A baby and a black and white cat play with a saucepan. They look inside and feel inside. Then they take turns sitting on it. The baby tries to hide in it and finally crawls away as the cat disappears into it. Minimal text and uncomplicated, but intriguing, illustrations invite reader-listener dialog. *bkn*

**2.123** Ormerod, Jan. **Sunshine**. Illustrated by the author. Puffin, 1981. Originally published by Kestrel in 1981. ISBN 0-140-50362-5. Unpaginated. (4-6). Picture book. **Australia.**
A little girl and her parents go through their morning ritual before setting off for work. The illustrations in this wordless book show that it is the child who keeps her parents on schedule. *Australia's Picture Book of the Year Award. cmt*

**2.124** Oxenbury, Helen. **All Fall Down**. Macmillan, 1987. Originally published by Walker in 1987. ISBN 0-027-69040-7. Unpaginated. (1-3). Board book. **Great Britain**
Part of a set, this large board book presents three toddlers joyfully singing, running round and round, bouncing on the bed, and all falling down. Participation activities, delightful illustrations of happy, multi-ethnic toddlers, and sturdy construction are features sure to appeal to the very young. Other books in this series: *Tickle, Tickle*; *Clap Hands*; and *Say Goodnight. djg*

**2.125** Pfanner, Louise. **Louise Builds a House**. Illustrated by the author. Orchard, 1989. Originally published by John Ferguson Pty Ltd. in 1987. ISBN 0-531-05796-8. 29 p. (4-6). Picture book. **Australia.**
In her imagination, the author builds her dreamhouse. Each addition is accompanied by her reason for having it. Large illustrations show each stage of the house and Louise putting it to use. Good concept book about dwellings.

**2.126** Picó, Fernando. **The Red Comb**. Translated and adapted by

Argentina Palacios. Illustrated by María Antonia Ordóñez. Bridgewater, 1994. Originally published as *La peineta colorada* by Huracán, Río Piedras, and Ekaré-Banco del Libro in 1991. (paperback: Bridgewater, 1994). ISBN 0-8167-3539-5. 48 p. (7-9). Picture book. **Puerto Rico, Venezuela.**

Vitita and her old neighbor, siña Rosa, help to hide a runaway slave from a slavecatcher in nineteenth-century Cuba. The female protagonists show great wit and spirit in the process. This story, based upon an actual event, originated in response to a contest encouraging the writing of historical fiction in Puerto Rico. *CCBC Choices; Américas Award Commended Title. jl*

**2.127** Poulin, Stéphane. **Could you stop Josephine?** Illustrated by the author. Tundra Books of Northern New York, 1988. Originally published by Tundra Books in 1988. ISBN 0-88776-216-6. 23 p. (4-6). Picture book. **Canada.**

Daniel's family celebrates his birthday with a visit to their country relatives. It's Josephine the Cat's birthday, too, and she sneaks a ride to the country in the trunk. Daniel's whole day is spent chasing Josephine all over the farm, a chase that includes Cleo, the dog, Cousin Norman, and Norman's cat, Rupert. Daniel gets back in time to enjoy his party, and later, Josephine enjoys it, too. Strong, expressive illustrations capture scenes of Canadian farmlife. *IBBY Honour List, Canada.* See also: *Have you seen Josephine?*; *Can you catch Josephine?. cmt*

**2.128** Rodda, Emily. **Power and Glory.** Illustrated by Geoff Kelly. Greenwillow, 1996. Originally published by Allen & Unwin Pty Ltd. in 1994. ISBN 0-688-14214-1. 32 p. (5-7). Picture book. **Australia.**

A child tries to finish his new video game, "Power and Glory," but is interrupted time and again by family members. At last he wins the game...the first level, that is. Large, expressive illustrations suggesting a resemblance between video characters and family members add humor. Repetitive, patterned text and large print make this a good book for beginning readers. *cmt, djg*

**2.129** Romanova, Natalia. **Once There Was a Tree.** Translated by Anne Schwartz. Illustrated by Gennady Spirin. Dial, 1985. Originally published as *Chei eto pen?* by Detskaya Literatura in 1983. ISBN 0-8037-0235-3. 27 p. (7-14). Picture book. **Russia.**

Between the time that an old tree dies and a new one grows in its place, a succession of animals and insects lay claim to the old tree's stump as it serves them in various ways. Who really owns the tree stump? Perhaps it belongs to all for whom earth is home. Beautifully detailed illustrations and vignettes elevate this lesson in ecology to a celebration of nature. *cmt*

**2.130** Ross, Christine. **Lily and the Present**. Illustrated by the author. Houghton Mifflin, 1992. Originally published by Methuen in 1992. ISBN 0-395-61127-X. 24 p. (4-7). Picture book. **New Zealand**.
Lily sets off in search of a big, bright, and beautiful present for her brand new brother. This expedition takes Lily from the bedroom to a busy downtown department store. Escalators, elevators, and revolving doors move in finely detailed, colored drawings where Lily confronts clerks, grandly deals with charges and returns, and finally finds the perfect present for her baby brother. *Russell Clark Award for Illustration. eb*

**2.131** Ross, Tony. **I Want My Potty**. Illustrated by the author. Kane/-Miller, 1986. Originally published by Andersen Press in 1986. ISBN 0-916291-08-1. 24 p. (1-3). Picture book. **Great Britain**.
The trials and tribulations of toilet training, featuring a determined little princess, are presented with humor, understanding, and a few mistakes along the way to ultimate success. A book to be enjoyed by parents and children alike. *cmt*

**2.132** Scheffler, Ursel. **The Stranger**. Translated by Rosemary Lanning. Illustrated by Jutta Timm. North-South Books, 1994. Originally published as *Alle nannten ihn Tomate* by Nord-Sud Verlag AG in 1994. ISBN 1-55858-312-2. 27 p. (4-6). Picture book. **Switzerland**.
A stranger is ridiculed by villagers because of his big, red nose. He is then mistaken for a thief and hides all winter in a brokendown house. Meanwhile, it is proven that he had nothing to do with the crimes. When he is discovered, he is given work to do about town. He finds his true happiness when he is offered a job caring for children at the orphanage. Loving him for his kindness, the children never notice his nose. Illustrations provide a glimpse of European village life. *cmt*

**2.133** Schermbrucker, Reviva. **Charlie's House**. Illustrated by Niki Daly. Viking, 1991. Originally published by Songololo Books in 1989.

ISBN 0-670-84024-6. 25 p. (4-9). Picture book. **Republic of South Africa**.

From the mud and flotsam around him in a crowded township near Cape Town, Charlie Mogotsi builds his dream house with ingenuity and make-believe. Bright, dancing watercolors evoke both sympathy for Charlie's poverty and awareness of the warmth of his family's love and the laughter and anger bursting from the rows of houses around him. *hr*

**2.134** Seed, Jenny. **Ntombi's Song**. Illustrated by Anno Berry. Beacon Press, 1987. (paperback: Beacon, 1989). ISBN 0-8070-8318-6. (paperback: 0-8070-8319-4). 46 p. (7-9). Picture book. **Republic of South Africa**.

Six-year-old Ntombi is on her first solo venture to the store to buy sugar. She successfully negotiates a busy road and a scary forest, but on the way home she accidentally drops the sugar. She is determined to find a way to earn the money to buy more. Zulu words are interspersed, sometimes with translations. When there is no translation, their meaning is made clear by the context. Watercolor illustrations extend the cheerful mood of the story and depict customs of Zulu villagers. *bkn*

**2.135** Shalev, Meir. **My Father Always Embarrasses Me**. Translated by Dagmar Herrmann. Illustrated by Yossi Abolafia. Originally published as *Aba 'oseh bushot* by Keter Publishing House in 1988. ISBN 0-922984-02-6. 32 p. (4-7). Picture book. **Israel**.

Mortimer's father, a writer, is unorthodox in every way. Even though he is a loving and attentive parent, his behavior causes Mortimer intense embarrassment. That is, until his father's unorthodox surprise cake wins a school baking contest, and Mortimer learns that his father's father was a baker who always embarrassed *his* son. Illustrations show that, although Mortimer is embarrassed by his father's jolly ways, most other people smile at him. *cmt*

**2.136** Škutina, Vladimír. **Nobody Has Time for Me**. Translated by Dagmar Herrmann. Illustrated by Marie-José Sacré. Wellington Publishing, 1991. Originally published as *Kde bydlí čas* by Bohem Press in 1988. ISBN 0-922984-07-7. 28 p. (4-7). Picture book. **Czechoslovakia**.

No one has time for Karin, and so she wants to know more about time. Having literally interpreted what she has heard about time, she looks for it in the village clock tower. There she meets the kindly old caretaker who takes time to explain a few things and agrees to hold the clock back until she can get home in time. Karin agrees to tell her story, if her parents make a little time for her. *cmt*

**2.137** Soya, Kiyoshi. **A House of Leaves**. Illustrated by Akiko Hayashi. Philomel, 1987. Originally published by Fukuinkan Shoten, 1986. ISBN 0-399-21422-4. 24p. (4-6). Picture book. **Japan**.
When it begins to rain, Sarah seeks shelter under a roof of leaves. There she is joined by a praying mantis, a butterfly, a beetle, a ladybug, and an ant, who occupy her attention until the rain stops and they all head back to their real houses. Appealing watercolor illustrations give a universal quality to the story. *jg*

**2.138** Spanner, Helmut. **Mouse in the Kitchen**. Illustrated by the author. Boyds Mills, 1995. Originally published as *Die Küchen maus* by Ravenburger Buchverlag Otto Maier in 1986. ISBN 1-56397-474-6. Unpaginated. (1-3). Picture book/fold-out book. **Germany**.
Twelve bright, uncomplicated drawings show a furry mouse playing with common kitchen utensils such as a timer, a hotpad, and a nutcracker. Foodstuffs rather than utensils are featured in one illustration. Sturdy cardboard in a fold-out, wordless format. *cmt*

**2.139** Spanner, Helmut. **My Little Zoo**. Illustrated by the author. Boyds Mills, 1995. Originally published as *Mein kleiner Zoo* by Ravensburger Buchverlag Otto Maier in 1991. ISBN 1-56397-476-2. Unpaginated. (1-3). Picture book/fold-out book. **Germany**.
Twelve animals often found in zoos are presented in easily distinguished drawings on sturdy cardboard in a fold-out, wordless format. Soft, toy-like appearance of the animals will add to their appeal for very young children. *cmt*

**2.140** Sundvall, Viveca. **Mimi and the Biscuit Factory**. Translated by Eric Bibb. Illustrated by Eva Eriksson. R&S Books, 1989. Originally published as *Mimmi och Kexfabriken* by Rabén & Sjögren, 1988. ISBN 91-29-59142-2. 25 p. (4-7). Picture book. **Sweden**.
On the very day that Mimi gets her first loose tooth, she and her fellow first-graders go on an antic-filled field trip to Henry's Bread and Biscuit (cookie) Factory. Humorous illustrations add details, physical reactions, and minor visual narratives, greatly enriching the story. *cmt*

**2.141** Sundvall, Viveca. **Mimi Gets a Grandpa**. Translated by Richard E. Fisher. Illustrated by Eva Ericksson. R&S Books, 1990. Originally published as *Mimmi Får en Farfar* by Rabén & Sjögren in 1990. ISBN 912-959-8648. 29 p. (4-9). Picture book. **Sweden**.

In an effort to prove that the local shoeseller is a bandit, high-spirited Mimi and her sidekick Roberta instead discover that the man is lonely and offer to take him on as their "grandpa." Humorous illustrations provide a glimpse of village life. *cmt*

**2.142** Tejima, Keizaburo. **Owl Lake**. Illustrated by the author. Philomel, 1987. Originally published as *Shimafurō no mizuumi* by Fukutake Publishing in 1982. ISBN 0-399-21426-7. 38 p. (4-7). Picture book. **Japan**.

As evening falls on an isolated mountain lake, a family of owls awaken and start to look for food. Oversized, beautifully balanced, and graceful woodcut illustrations capture the unspoiled natural beauty of the setting and the fierce confidence of the owls and give a subtle hint of their Japanese origins. Text is held to a minimum. *cmt*

**2.143** Thiele, Colin. **Farmer Schulz's Ducks**. Illustrated by Mary Milton. Harper & Row, 1988. Originally published by Walter McVitty Books in 1986. ISBN 0-06-026182-X. 32 p. (7-9). Picture book. **Australia**.

When Farmer Schulz's ducks—the most beautiful in the world—are threatened by traffic as they cross the road to go to the river, it is young Anna who offers the solution to the problem. Beautiful, simile-rich language and glowing, realistic watercolor illustrations enhance this low-key, rural drama. *cmt*

**2.144** Tomioka, Chiyoko. **Rise and Shine, Mariko-chan!** English adaptation by Lauren Stevens, based on translations by Cathy Hirano and Jennifer Riggs. Illustrated by Yoshiharu Tsuchida. Scholastic, 1992 (paperback). Originally published as *Itterasshai* by Fukutake in 1986. ISBN 0-590-45507-9. 32 p. (3-6). Picture book. **Japan**.

Young Mariko rises in the morning, has breakfast with her family, sees various family members off for the day, and boards a bus for preschool. This glimpse into Japanese family life concludes with a pronunciation guide and an explanation of some of the references to Japanese culture, such as forms of address, food, and childhood customs. *jy*

**2.145** Törnqvist. Rita. **The Christmas Carp**. Translated by Greta Kilburn. Illustrated by Marit Törnqvist. R&S Books/Farrar, 1990. Originally published as *Julkarpen* by Rabén & Sjögren in 1989. ISBN 91-29-59794-6. 33 p. (7-9). Picture book. **Sweden**.

This is Grandpa's first Christmas without Grandma, and Thomas has been sent to Prague to keep him company during the holidays. When they go to the market, Thomas assumes Grandma's job of buying the carp. By the time he gets it home to put in the bathtub, he has already named it Peppo. The next day, Thomas grows increasingly worried as he and Grandpa make preparations for the evening celebration, but when Peppo is placed on the table, it is in an aquarium, not on a platter. Törnqvist's muted watercolor illustrations present a timeless picture of Prague's architecture and street life as well as the warm interior of Grandpa's home. *ss*

**2.146** Trottier, Maxine. **The Tiny Kite of Eddie Wing**. Illustrated by Al Van Mil. Kane/Miller, 1996. Originally published by Stoddart Publishing, Toronto, in 1995. ISBN 0-916291066-9. 22 p. (4-9). Picture book. **Canada**.

Eddie loved kites, but was so poor that he had to fly an imaginary one. Old Chan was rich, but he, too, had a secret desire—to become a poet. At the annual Festival of Kites, Old Chan set the rule: the smallest kite wins. Eddie did not win the contest with his imaginary kite, but his efforts did catch Old Chan's attention. Inspired by the boy's determination, Old Chan gave him materials to make a fine kite, and then, for the first time, wrote down a poem. Illustrations show details of the Asian-Canadian culture. *cmt*

**2.147** Tsuchiya, Yukio. **Faithful Elephants: A True Story of Animals, People, and War**. Translated by Tomoko T. Dykes. Illustrated by Ted Lewin. Houghton Mifflin, 1988. Originally published as *Kawaisō na zō* by Kin-no-Hoshi-Sha Co. in 1951. ISBN 0-395-46555-9. 32 p. (7-12). Picture book. **Japan**.

Because officials at Ueno Zoo in Tokyo during World War II were afraid that bombs might free the animals to run through the city, they decided to poison the large, dangerous ones. The zoo's three elephants, however, resisted all efforts to put them to death quickly and painlessly. Instead, they slowly starved. Their pitiful begging for food until their deaths two weeks later broke the zoo keepers' hearts, and their story reminds all who hear it of the waste and tragedy of war. *cmt*

**2.148** Tsutsui, Yoriko. **Anna's Secret Friend**. Illustrated by Akiko Hayashi. Viking, 1987. Originally published by Fukuinkan Shoten in 1986. (paperback: Puffin). ISBN 0-670-81670-1. 32 p. (5-9). Picture book. **Japan**.

When Anna moves to a new town, she misses her old friends. One day, someone mysteriously leaves violets in the letter box on her front door. Then it is dandelions, then a letter, and finally a beautifully folded paper doll. Anna is sure that a new friend must be nearby. See also: *Anna In Charge* (Puffin, 1991). *jy*

**2.149** Valgardson, W.D. **Winter Rescue**. Illustrated by Ange Zhang. McElderry Books, 1995. Originally published as *Thor* by Groundwood Books in 1994. ISBN 0-689-80094-0. 40 p. (7-9). Picture book. **Canada**.

Thor, visiting his grandparents on Lake Winnipeg for the Christmas holidays, helps Grandfather set the nets on the ice and collect fish from previously set nets. Coming back to shore, they encounter a snowmobiler who has fallen through the ice, and only Thor, because he is light, is able to crawl out on the cracked ice to save the man. Thus Thor, usually a passive viewer of television action programs, becomes a hero in his own right. This satisfying contemporary story provides a fascinating look at the process of ice fishing, made clear in Grandfather's instructions to Thor and Valgardson's detailed illustrations. *ss*

**2.150** Vincent, Gabrielle. **Ernest and Celestine**. Illustrated by Gabrielle Vincent. Greenwillow, 1982. Originally published as *Ernest et Célestine ont perdu Siméon* by Duculot Paris-Gembloux in 1981. (paperback: Morrow, 1986). ISBN 0-688-00855-0. 28 p. (4-6). Picture book. **Belgium**.

Ernest and Celestine go out for a walk with Gideon, Celestine's stuffed bird. When Gideon is lost, Celestine is heartbroken, despite Ernest's efforts to find a replacement. Finally he makes a new Gideon for Celestine, and she is happy once again to have her Gideon back. They have a Christmas and slumber party to celebrate. *SLJ Best Books; Booklist Reviewers' Choices. jk*

**2.151** Vulliamy, Clara. **Blue Hat Red Coat**. Illustrated by Clara Vulliamy. Candlewick Press, 1994. Originally published by Walker in 1994.

ISBN 1-56402-361-3. 12 p. (1-3). Board book. **Great Britain**.
The narrative of this deceptively simple concept book is contained in the illustrations, which depict a toddler undressing. Under each picture, two words label each garment by kind and color. Outer garments are shed to reveal new ones underneath, until on the final spread, the bare toddler and the ten items of clothing are pictured on facing pages. Teddy bear's subtle actions in the background allow young children to create their own story a second time through. Other books in this series: *Bang and Shout; Boo Baby Boo!; Yum Yum!* (all 1994). *ss*

**2.152** Waddell, Martin. **Amy Said**. Illustrated by Charlotte Voake. Little, Brown, 1990. Originally published by Walker in 1989. ISBN 0-316-911636-6. Unpaginated. (4-6). Picture book. **Great Britain**.
*Editor's note: Author is Irish.*
A young boy and his slightly older, "big" sister Amy visit their grandma and have a wonderful time. He wants to bounce on the bed, and Amy, liking the idea herself, said he could! For the same reason, Amy also said they could swing on the curtains, give their lunch to the dog, pick Gran's flowers and help in the muddy garden. But when Gran said, "That's enough! Please try to be good," Amy said "We should," and they were! Illustrations capture the children's impetuousness and their loving Gran's patience. *djg*

**2.153** Wagener, Gerda. **A Mouse in the House!** Translated by Rosemary Lanning. Illustrated by Uli Waas. North-South, 1995. Originally published as *Fertzer jagt die Maus* by Nord-Süd Verlag in 1995. ISBN 1-55858-507-9. 47 p. (6-8). Beginning reader. **Switzerland**.
A mouse is loose in the house. Mother is appalled, but the children are delighted. They secretly leave food for the mouse, finally catch him, and return him to the woods. All are happy, except the cat. Delicate illustrations add to the gentle humor and provide predictability. *mew*

**2.154** Wallace, Ian. **Chin Chiang and the Dragon's Dance**. Illustrated by the author. McElderry/Atheneum, 1984. Originally published by Groundwood in 1984. ISBN 0-689-50299-0. Unpaginated. (7-9). Picture book. **Canada**.
Young Chin Chiang is sure that he will stumble and fall when he dances the dragon dance, disgrace himself, and anger the dragon spirit. He runs away to the library and there meets an old woman who tells him that

she's too old to dance anymore. He dances with her and they both end up performing a magnificent dragon dance, much to the delight of all. Ancient tradition and modern life are intertwined in this story set in Vancouver. *Amelia Frances Howard-Gibbon Award. lg*

**2.155** Walsh, Jill Paton. **Lost and Found.** Illustrated by Mary Rayner. Andre Deutsch, 1984. ISBN 0-233-97672-8. Unpaginated. (7-9). Picture book. **Great Britain**.

Young Ag, a Stone-Age boy, takes an arrowhead to his grandfather but loses it while playing in the river shallows. Centuries later, a young girl loses a jug in the woods, but finds the arrowhead. Centuries pass, and a boy loses his sixpence, but finds the jug. Finally, a girl of the present is sent to her grandmother's with a pair of scissors. She loses the scissors but finds the ancient sixpence. An observant reader will notice all the objects, now treasured in the home of the present-day grandmother. A simple, yet intriguing, way to connect past to present. *djg*

**2.156** Widerberg, Siv. **The Big Sister.** Translated by Birgitta Sjöquist. Illustrated by Cecilia Torudd. Farrar, 1989. Originally published as *Den Stora Systern* by Rabén & Sjögren in 1989. ISBN 9-129-59186-4. 36 p. (4-6). Picture book. **Sweden**.

Being a big sister appears ideal in the eyes of a little sister, until she realizes that being a younger sister is one thing that her older sister can never be. Lively illustrations complement this witty look at contemporary family life in Sweden, life very much like that in North America. *clb*

**2.157** Wild, Margaret. **Let the Celebrations Begin!** Illustrated by Julie Vivas. Orchard, 1991. Originally published by Omnibus Books in 1991.(paperback: Orchard, 1996). ISBN 0-531-05937-5. 32 p. (7-10). Picture book. **Australia**.

Set in a concentration camp in Poland toward the end of World War II, this story tells how women secretly made toys out of scraps (often the sleeves or hems of their only garments) for the children in the camp who have never even seen a toy. The illustrator's exuberant artistic style reflects the women's enduring spirit, and the drab, washed-out colors of camp life contrast with the bright colors of the prisoners' childhood memories. A passage from a collector's book on antique toys precedes the story to anchor it in history. *ss*

**2.158** Wild, Margaret. **Our Granny.** Illustrated by Julie Vivas. Ticknor & Fields, 1994. Originally published by Omnibus in 1993. ISBN 0-395-67023-3. 32 p. (3–6). Picture book. **Australia.**
Grannies live in different places, have varied looks and clothes, are active in many ways, have friends and pets, husbands and grandchildren. The text tells of all kinds of grannies, but the illustrations assert that every child's granny is special. Watercolor illustrations depict grannies of different shapes, but mostly round, as are the happy-faced children. *jsn*

**2.159** Wildsmith, Brian. **Brian Wildsmith's ABC.** Illustrated by the author. Star Bright, 1996. Originally published by Oxford in 1963. (paperback: Millbrook, 1995). ISBN 1-887734-02-3 (paperback: 1-56294-906-3). Unpaginated. (3-5). Picture book. **Great Britain.**
Stunning color combinations and bold brush strokes depict things ordinary and extraordinary, from a kettle to a unicorn. Differing perspectives and energy levels from page to page turn this alphabet book into a work of art. *Kate Greenaway Medal. al*

**2.160** Williams, Susan. **I Went Walking.** Illustrated by Julie Vivas. Harcourt Brace Jovanovich, 1990. Originally published by Omnibus in 1989. (paperback: Harcourt, 1992). ISBN 0-15-200471-8. (paperback: 0-15-238011-6). 32 p. (1–3). Beginning reader. **Australia.**
A child goes walking and sees a black cat, a brown horse, a red cow, a green duck, a pink pig, and a yellow dog who all follow the youngster. A few words repeated in simple rhyme teach about colors and domestic animals. Large, clearly defined illustrations of child and animals against a white background are appropriate for a very young audience. *California Children's Book, Video, and Software Award. jsn*

**2.161** Williams, Susan. **Poppy's First Year.** Illustrated by the author. Four Winds, 1989. Originally published by Marilyn Malin in association with Andre Deutsch in 1988. ISBN 0-02-793031-9. 32 p. (4-6). Picture book. **Great Britain.**
Sam and his parents eagerly await the birth of a new baby. His new sister is named Poppy. Over the course of her first year, as she grows and learns, Poppy and Sam become fast friends. The pastel watercolor illustrations capture facial features and emotions while the text describes in detail the many stages of the siblings' first year together. An appeal-

ing and substantial book about the positive side of having a new sibling. *mb*

**2.162** Winter, Susan. **A Baby Just Like Me**. Dorling Kindersley, 1994. Originally published by Dorling Kindersley Limited in 1994. ISBN 1-56458-668-5. 32 p. (4-6). Picture book. **Great Britain**.
Martha expects her new baby sister to be just like her, because that is what her mother has said. But Martha and her friend Sam discover that the baby ignores their puppet show, sleeps through their favorite tune, and frightens away a bird they are watching. Martha's mother explains that Martha herself was once just like that, and that the baby, too, will grow and develop. Patience pays off, and Martha and Sam eventually gain a playmate. A universal setting and strong theme of family love make this a reassuring book for all children with infant siblings. *jg*

**2.163** Wojciechowski, Susan. **The Christmas Miracle of Jonathan Toomey**. Illustrated by P.J. Lynch. Originally published by Walker in 1995. ISBN 1-56402-320-6. 34 p. (4-9). **Great Britain**. *Editor's note: This book is a British-American co-publication with an American author and an Irish illustrator. It was designed in Great Britain.*
Having never recovered from his grief at losing his wife and child, Jonathan Toomey, a woodcarver, has developed over the years a reputation for being mirthless and grumpy. He agrees to carve figures for a nativity scene for a widow and her son, and later agrees to let the child learn woodcarving by watching him carve. Gradually, the woodcarver responds to these two warm hearts, is able to end his mourning, and begins to live again. Lynch's warm, brown palette helps to place the setting in the past, to lend emotional warmth to the story, and to suggest the warmth of wood. *Kate Greenaway Medal. cmt*

**2.164** Yerxa, Leo. **Last Leaf First Snowflake to Fall**. Illustrated by the author. Orchard Books, 1994. Originally published by Groundwood Books in 1993. ISBN 0-531-06824-2. 32 p. (5-8). Picture book. **Canada**.
Change from autumn to winter is masterfully evoked in this story, set long ago in North America. Lyrical text first creates a primordial world and sets the scene for the book's narrative, which traces the first full day of a canoe voyage through the forest. The trip is recounted from the point of view of a native adult and child, who at once witness this

change and are part of it. Tissue-paper collage illustrations view the humans from a height, set in a vast context, a perspective in tune with the Native American recognition of themselves as part of nature. *Amelia Frances Howard-Gibbon Award. ss*

**2.165** Zak, Monica. **Save My Rainforest**. Translated by Nancy Schimmel. Illustrated by Bengt-Arne Runnerström. Harcourt/Volcano, 1992. Originally published as *Rädda Min Djungel* by Bokförlaget Opal in 1989. ISBN 0-153-02234-5. 32 p. (7-9). Picture book. **Sweden**.
Eight-year-old Omar Castillo hears of rainforests from his father, then learns that the Lancandon Rainforest in southern Mexico, the country's last, is endangered. He convinces his father to walk there with him to protest the cutting of the forest. They arrive after thirty-nine days and 870 miles. Later, back in Mexico City, Omar pickets the President's home until he gets an audience. The President of Mexico promises to stop the destruction, but breaks his promise. This inspiring story of youth activism is based on actual events. Afterword updates Omar's efforts. *CCBC Choices. jl, cmt*

**2.166** Zhitkov, Boris. **How I Hunted the Little Fellows**. Translated by Djemma Bider. Illustrated by Paul Zelinsky. Dodd, Mead, 1979. Originally published in Leningrad. ISBN 0-396-07692-0. 64 p. (7-9). Picture book. **Russia**.
During a childhood visit to his grandmother, Boria became infatuated with an intricate and valuable model ship, but was forbidden to touch it. Convinced that it contained little, living sailors, Boria contrived to stay at home to investigate. The result: no sailors and a ruined, dismantled ship. Distraught, Boria can only wait in agony until his grandmother discovers what he has done. Extensive translator's end note about the author. *cmt*

## Fantasy Picture Books

**3.1** Ahlberg, Janet and Ahlberg, Allan. **Each Peach Pear Plum**. Illustrated by Janet Ahlberg. Penguin, 1979. Originally published by Kestrel in 1978. (paperback: Viking, 1986). ISBN 0-670-28705-9 (paperback: 0-14-050639-X). Unpaginated. (2-6). Picture book. **Great Britain.**
Simple rhymes ("In this book, with your little eye, take a look and play I spy") lead the reader from one character to another in a visual hide-and-seek, culminating in a surprise ending. Detailed illustrations depict well-known characters from nursery rhymes and fairy tales as they interact unwittingly with one another. *Kate Greenaway Medal. al, djg*

**3.2** Ahlberg, Janet and Ahlberg, Allen. **The Jolly Christmas Postman**. Illustrated by Janet Ahlberg. Little, Brown, 1991. Originally published by Heinemann in 1991. ISBN 0-316-02033-8. Unpaginated. (4-7). Picture book. **Great Britain.**
It is Christmas, and all our favorite folk- and fairy tale characters are exchanging humorous messages, delivered by the Jolly Postman. Pull-out letters, post-cards, and games in a variety of media complement the interactive text. *Kate Greenaway Medal. al*

**3.3** Ahlberg, Janet and Ahlberg, Allan. **The Jolly Postman or Other People's Letters**. Illustrated by Janet Ahlberg. Little, Brown, 1986. Originally published by Heinemann in 1986. ISBN 0-316-02036-2. Unpaginated. (4-6). Picture book/engineered book. **Great Britain.**
A postman cycles from house to house delivering various articles of mail to various fairytale characters. Each letter is housed in an addressed, stamped envelope and is removable. Rhyming text, embedded humor, charming watercolor illustrations, and excellent examples of common types of mail are highlights. *Kurt Maschler Award. cmt*

**3.4** Anno, Mitsumasa. **Anno's Magic Seeds**. Translated by Dowaya Publishing Co. Illustrated by the author. Philomel, 1995. Originally published as *Fushigina Tane* by Dowaya Publishing Co. in 1992. ISBN 0-399-22538-2. 32 p. (7-9). Picture book. **Japan.**
A wizard gives Jack two seeds and tells him that if he eats one seed and plants the other, he will not be hungry for a year and will harvest two seeds. For years, Jack follows this cycle, but then risks hunger in order to plant both seeds. Within a few years of following this plan, Jack

harvests many seeds, takes a wife, has a child, and builds a bigger house. A hurricane washes away all but ten seeds, and Jack and his family start over again. Simple illustrations and distinct, golden seeds make counting easy. Author's afterword explains the social significance of the story. *sl*

**3.5** Anno, Masaichiro and Anno, Mitsumasa. **Anno's Mysterious Multiplying Jar.** Translated by Dowaya Publishing Co. Illustrated by Mitsumasa Anno. Philomel, 1983. Originally published as *Tsubo No Naka* by Dowaya Publishing Co. in 1982. ISBN 0-399-20951-4. 44 p. (7-12). Picture book. **Japan**.
In glowing illustrations the contents of a jar are shown: one island, two countries, in each country three mountains, on each mountain four walled kingdoms, and so on, ending with, "Within each box there were 10 jars. But how many jars were in the boxes altogether?" In this way the author sets the stage for explaining about factorial numbers, and then does so using dots. From one tiny dot in the middle of the page, he shows how this soon grows, in factorial terms, to stupendous numbers. An afterword gives more information about factorials. *cmt*

**3.6** Asare, Meshack. **Cat in Search of a Friend.** Translated by the publishers. Illustrated by the author. Kane/Miller, 1986. Originally published as *Die Katze sucht sich einen Freund* by Verlag Jungbrunnen in 1984. ISBN 0-916291-07-3. 32 p. Picture book. (4-9). **Austria**.
A cat searched the jungle for a strong friend who would protect her. Each animal gave way to a more powerful one, until the elephant proved strongest. Then, the elephant showed fear of man, man showed fear of woman, and woman showed fear of a mouse. At this, the cat decided that there was no one stronger than herself and that she alone was her own master. *cmt*

**3.7** Baillie, Allan. **Drac and the Gremlin.** Illustrated by Jane Tanner. Dial, 1989. Originally published by Viking Kestrel in 1988. ISBN 0-803-70628-6 (paperback: Puffin, 1992, ISBN 01-40545-425). 32p. (4-8). Picture book. **Australia**.
The imaginative play of two siblings comes to life as vibrant illustrations transform the children's backyard into the setting of their heroic quest through "quivering jungles" and "poisonous fumes of the black volcano." Drac, the fearless Warrior Queen (the sister), enlists the aid of the Gremlin of the Groaning Grotto (her little brother), to save their planet

from General Min and the Terrible Tongued Dragon (their cat and dog). When they return triumphantly to the palace of the wise White Wizard (their mother), they are awarded the planet's highest honor, the Twin Crimson Cones (pink ice cream). *Australian Children's Picture Book of the Year Award (joint winner). bt*

**3.8** Barbot, Daniel. **A Bicycle for Rosaura**. Illustrated by Morella Fuenmayor. Kane/Miller, 1991. Originally published as *Rosaura en bicicleta* by Ediciones Ekaré-Banco del Libro in 1990. (paperback: Kane/Miller, 1994). ISBN 0-916291-34-0. 24 p. (4-6). Picture book. **Venezuela**.

Señora Amelia loves her many animals, and when it is almost time for her pet hen Rosaura's birthday, she asks the hen what she would most like as a present. A bicycle, says Rosaura, so Señora Amelia tries to make her wish come true. A stranger comes to town, selling all manner of things, and with his help, Rosaura has a birthday surprise. *CCBC Choices. jl*

**3.9** Base, Graeme. **Animalia**. Illustrated by the author. Abrams, 1986. Originally published by Viking Kestrel in 1986. ISBN 0-8109-1868-4. (7-14). Picture book. **Australia**.

Intricately drawn, full-page illustrations provide a thousand items to find and name in this alphabet I-Spy book for the connoisseur. A vocabulary stretcher, this book will challenge people of all ages. *cmt*

**3.10** Base, Graeme. **The Eleventh Hour: A Curious Mystery.** Illustrated by the author. Abrams, 1989. Originally published by Penguin Books Australia Limited in 1988. ISBN 0-8109-0851-4. 32 p. (8-14). Picture book. **Australia**.

Horace celebrates his eleventh birthday by cooking a sumptuous feast and inviting his friends for fun and games. Sometime during the games someone eats the birthday food, and to discover who did it, readers must search the minutely detailed illustrations for clues. A coded "Notes for Detectives" and a full explanation of the clues are included at the end. *Co-winner: Australia's Picture Book of the Year Award. cmt*

**3.11** Berndt, Catherine. **Pheasant and Kingfisher.** Illustrated by Arone Raymond Meeks. Mondo, 1994. Originally published by Bookshelf in 1987. (paperback: Mondo, 1994). ISBN 1-879531-65-8. 24 p. (6-10). Picture book. **Australia**.

In this Aboriginal creation tale, pheasant and kingfisher were once human, but changed into their present shapes to escape a band of men who were attacking them, while their enemies turned into the familiar craggy stone shapes that are part of the Australian landscape. The author credits Nganalgindja, the Aborigine who told it to her, on the title page. Meeks's illustrations reflect his Aboriginal culture. Includes a guide to interpretation of the symbolism and imagery of the illustrations. *ss*

**3.12** Blundell, Tony. **Beware of Boys**. Illustrated by the author. Greenwillow, 1992. Originally published by Viking Children's Books, 1991. ISBN 0688-10924-1. Unpaginated. (4-9). Picture book. **Great Britain**.
A little boy takes a shortcut through the woods and is captured by a wolf, who threatens to eat him up! Appalled at being eaten raw, the boy offers the wolf three outrageous recipes: Boy Soup, Boy Pie and Boy Cake. The clever boy omits salt from each list of ingredients and makes the silly wolf think that he forgets to add the salt each time. Absolutely outwitted, the wolf collapses into an exhausted heap. A wickedly clever book perfectly enhanced by the humorous watercolor illustrations. *djg*.

**3.13** Boujon, Claude. **Bon Appétit, Mr. Rabbit!**. Illustrated by the author. Margaret K. McElderry, 1987. Originally published as *Bon appétit! Monsieur Lapin* by L'école des Loisirs in 1985. ISBN 0-689-50425-X. 24 p. (4-6). Picture book. **France**.
Mr. Rabbit is not too crazy about having carrots to eat, so he goes out to see what everyone else is eating. He soon realizes that carrots are not so bad after all. The sketchy, colorful illustrations suggest that all the other animals are happy with their lot in life as well. *CCBC Choice. jl*

**3.14** Briggs. Raymond. **The Bear**. Illustrated by the author. Random House, 1994. Originally published by Julia MacRae in 1994. ISBN 0-679-86944-1. 40 p. (4-6). Picture book. **Great Britain**.
Tilly is awakened when a huge polar bear climbs through the window into her bedroom. She helps him into bed, then spends the day with him, finding that caring for and cleaning up after this new friend is a chore. Her parents humor her as she tells them about the bear, assuming that she has imagined it. The next night the bear leaves, with the last illustration showing him returning to his arctic home. *jg*

**3.15** Briggs, Raymond. **The Man**. Random House, 1995. Originally published by Julia MacRae Books in 1992. ISBN 0-679-87643-X. 62 p. (9-14). Picture book. **Great Britain**.

On Monday, a boy awakens to find a visitor in his room—a bedraggled, naked man, about 10 inches tall! For the next four days, the boy provides for the demanding little man. Their relationship includes equal measures of caring and frustration, patience and impatience, and understanding and annoyance, calling to mind the responsibilities of parenthood, the concept of power and powerlessness, the social responsibilities of the enfranchised for the disenfranchised, and the concepts of self and homelessness. *Kurt Maschler Award. cmt*

**3.16** Browne, Anthony. **Changes**. Illustrated by the author. Knopf, 1990. Originally published by Julia MacRae/Walker in 1990. ISBN 0-679-91029-3. 32 p. (7-9). Picture book. **Great Britain**.

Joseph, with no context for interpreting his father's parting remark that things are going to change, takes the statement literally and observes everything around him for signs of change. Browne's illustrations, rendered in a realistic style, contain surrealistic images that represent Joseph's imagination. A teapot develops cat-like characteristics, a slipper sprouts wings, an armchair grows gorilla claws. Joseph's lonely confusion is apparent and is resolved only when his parents come home with a new baby sister. *ss*

**3.17** Browne, Anthony. **Gorilla**. Illustrated by the author. Random House, 1985. Originally published by Julia MacRae in 1983. (paperback: Knopf, 1989). ISBN 0-394-97525-1 (paperback: 0-394-82225-0). Unpaginated. (4-7). Picture book. **Great Britain**.

Since Hannah's father is too busy to do anything but work, she has never been to the zoo to see a real gorilla, her favorite animal. The night before her birthday, she receives a toy gorilla, which, during the night, becomes real. Hannah and the gorilla spend an adventurous evening together, eating out, dancing, and visiting the zoo before returning home. But the most magical birthday present occurs the next day, when Hannah's father proposes a trip to the zoo. *Kate Greenaway Medal. al*

**3.18** Browne, Eileen. **Tick-Tock**. Illustrated by David Parkins. Candlewick, 1993. Originally published by Walker in 1993. ISBN 1-56402-300-1. 28 p. (4-6). Picture book. **Great Britain**.

Skip Squirrel and her friend Brainy knock the valuable cuckoo clock off the wall and break it. A bicycle repairman patches the clock as though it were a bicycle. A cobbler repairs it as though it were a shoe. Mr. Owl, the Fix-It man, fixes the clock, but the children have to take it back home before he can adjust the cuckoo. Mother returns, and at four o'clock they all get a big surprise. Illustrations contain much incidental humor. *cmt*

**3.19** Burningham, John. **Mr. Gumpy's Outing**. Illustrated by the author. Holt, 1971. Originally published by Jonathan Cape in 1970. (paperback: Holt, 1990). ISBN 0-03-089733-5 (paperback: 0-8050-3854-X). Unpaginated. (3-7) Picture book. **Great Britain**.
One summer day Mr. Gumpy takes his boat out on the river. As he rows along, he attracts many human and animal companions. Full-color pages introduce each new character and predict the natural result of too many bodies in a boat. The summer day reaches a perfect conclusion, nonetheless. *Kate Greenaway Medal. al*

**3.20** Burningham, John. **Hey! Get Off Our Train**. Illustrated by the author. Crown, 1989. Originally published by Jonathan Cape in 1989. (paperback: Dragonfly, 1994). ISBN 0-517-57638-4. (paperback: 0-517-88204-3). 48 p. (4-6). Picture book. **Great Britain**.
After being tucked into bed, a little boy takes an imaginative train trip with his stuffed dog. A parade of animals plead to be allowed on the train rather than face death or destruction from hunters or loss of habitat. Although the boy and his dog shout "Hey! Get off our train," the train is soon full of animals. Burningham has a political message, but his story is very much aware of its young audience. The art is free-spirited, childlike, and very appealing. *bb*

**3.21** Calders, Pere. **Brush**. Translated by Marguerite Feitlowitz. Illustrated by Carme Solé Vendrell. Kane/Miller, 1986. Originally published as *Cepillo* by Ediciones Hymsa in 1981. (paperback: Kane/Miller, 1988). ISBN 0-916291-05-7. 24 p. (4-6). Picture book. **Spain**.
Little Sala is very sad after his puppy is taken away (for eating his father's hat). He searches high and low in the house for a substitute, until he founds a lovely brush which starts to seem pretty doglike. Sala's family thinks he is silly, until Brush bites a would-be burglar on the leg. Using the imagination is good for children and adults alike. *jl*

**3.22** Cohen, Peter. **Olson's Meat Pies**. Translated by Richard E. Fisher. Illustrated by Olof Landström. R&S, 1989. Originally published as *Olssons Pastejer* by R&S, Stockholm in 1988. ISBN 91-29-59180-5. 36 p. (4-6). Picture book. **Sweden**.

Mr. Olson is well-known for the quality of his meat pies. But when his trusted bookkeeper, Strom, runs off with the company's money, Mr. Olson is forced to buy cheaper ingredients, then odd fillers (like gloves and potted plants) to keep selling his pies. The situation worsens when Mr. Olson tries putting an interesting object, such as a wind-up monkey, in each pie to compensate for the terrible taste. Luckily, the conscience-ridden Strom returns with enough money to return Olson's meat pies to their former glory. *New York Times Best Illustrated Children's Books of the Year. jl*

**3.23** Cousins, Lucy. **Za-Za's Baby Brother**. Illustrated by the author. Candlewick, 1995. Originally published by Walker in 1995. ISBN 1-56402-582-9. Unpaginated. (2-5). Picture book. **Great Britain**.

Za-Za the Zebra's mother is going to have a baby, and there is not much room left on her lap for a hug. When the baby brother arrives, even less attention is paid to poor Za-Za, or so it seems at first. While the theme is adequately treated, the real attraction here is the striking art. Hand-lettered text, bold, flat colors, and abstract shapes outlined in thick black line, lend a modern charm. *cw*

**3.24** Crew, Gary. **The Watertower**. Illustrated by Steven Woolman. Originally published in Australia by Era in 1994 (distributed in U.S. by Publishers' Distribution Service). ISBN 1-86374-200-X. 32p. (8-12). Picture book. **Australia**.

To get relief from the blistering summer heat, Spike and Bubba go for a swim in the murky, green depths of the town's old watertower. Left alone when Spike goes to get him fresh shorts to replace those that have mysteriously disappeared, Bubba's fear of the spooky tower intensifies. The text's foreboding ambiguity challenges older readers to seek clues in the dark, surreal illustrations. Woolman invites multiple interpretations by using visual subplots, repeated symbols, and red herrings. The book's unique format heightens the intrigue, beginning sideways, and slowly spiralling like the rotating sphere of the watertower as the plot thickens. *Australian Children's Picture Book of the Year Award. bt*

**3.25** Cutler, Ivor. **Herbert: Five Stories**. Illustrated by Patrick Benson. Lothrop, 1988. Originally published by Walker Books in 1988. ISBN 0-688-08147-9. 42 p. (4-6). Picture book. **Great Britain**.

Each day Herbert wakes up as a different animal and his mother finds the appropriate breakfast, his teacher accepts him, and his friend Annie plays with him. In the last story, Herbert remains "a Herbert," and Annie becomes an anaconda. *jg*

**3.26** Damjan, Mischa, pseud. [Dimitrije Sidjanski]. **Atuk**. Illustrated by József Wilkon. North-South, 1990. Originally published as *Atuk, der Eskimojunge* by Nord-Süd Verlag, in 1990. (paperback: North-South, 1996). ISBN 0-55858-091-3. 26 p. (7-9). Picture book. **Switzerland**.

Atuk, an Inuit boy, is five when a wolf kills his pet husky. From that point on, the desire for revenge shapes his life. Fox, himself a great hunter, encourages Atuk to seek friendship rather than revenge, but Atuk is unmoved. When Atuk finally does kill the wolf, he feels curiously sad and dissatisfied. Like the fox, he has become feared and isolated. His salvation comes in the form of a flower he can care for. Wilkon's impressionistic drawings underscore the meaning of this literary tale by reflecting the sparseness of the tundra, the dark winter days, and the glimmer of hope that arrives with spring. *ss*

**3.27** Damjan, Mischa, pseud. [Dimitrije Sidjanski]. **December's Travels**. Translated by Anthea Bell. Illustrated by Dušan Kállay. Dial, 1986. Originally published as *Dezember und seine Freunde* by Otto Maier Verlag Ravensburg in 1986. ISBN 0-8037-0257-4. 30 p. (7-9). Picture book. **Germany**.

December, alone and cold, is given a chance by the North Wind to visit three other months in the three other seasons. He makes fast friends and wonderful memories with March, June, and October. Back in his own time he decides to make his month a time of giving and friendship, leading up to Christmas. Inventive illustrations help to characterize the seasons and underscore the theme of friendship. *cmt*

**3.28** Davies, Andrew and Davies, Diana. **Poonam's Pets**. Illustrated by Paul Dowling. Viking, 1990. Originally published by Methuen in 1990. ISBN 0-670-83321-5. 24 p. (4-6). Picture book. **Great Britain**.

Class One is planning a Special Pets Assembly. What a surprise when Poonam, who is so quiet and shy that she only whispers in the teacher's ear, arrives with her six enormous lions! Her classmates are scared until Poonam shows the tricks the lions can do and invites the children to have a ride. After Pet Assembly day, Poonam is still quiet, but speaks up loudly when she has something important to say. The lions are never seen again. *CCBC Choices. jl*

**3.29** de Beer, Hans. **Little Polar Bear**. Translated by J. Allison James. Illustrated by the author. North-South, 1988, 1996. Originally published as *Kleiner Eisbär, wohin fährst du?* by Nord-Süd Verlag in 1988. ISBN 1-55858-024-7. Unpaginated. (5-8). Picture book. **Switzerland**.

On his first hunting trip with his father, little Lars the polar bear loses his father, drifts off on an iceberg, ends up in a jungle, and is rescued by a hippopotamus who brings him home. Softly contoured illustrations fit the gentle nature of this story. In each book of this series, Lars becomes lost, has an adventure, and is rescued by another animal. Other books in the series: *Ahoy there, Little Polar Bear*; *Little Polar Bear Finds a Friend*; *Little Polar Bear and the Brave Little Hare*; *Little Polar Bear, Take Me Home! mew*

**3.30** de Vries, Anke. **My Elephant Can Do Almost Anything**. Translated by the publishers. Illustrated by Ilja Walraven. Front Street/ Lemniscaat, 1995. Originally published as *Mijn olifant kan bijna alles* by Lemniscaat in 1995. ISBN 1-886910-06-5. 28 p. (1-3). Picture book. **Netherlands**.

This elephant, a child's trusty companion and the product of his imagination, is shown going through his paces—from balancing on a coffeepot to sleeping at the foot of his master's bed. Illustrations confirm that this elephant is not only multitalented and inventive, but also a very good friend, sad when its owner is away at school and happy when he comes home again. *jl, djg, cmt*

**3.31** Denton, Terry. **Felix and Alexander**. Illustrated by the author. Houghton Mifflin, 1988. Originally published by Oxford in 1985. ISBN 0-395-48661-0. 32p. (4-8). Picture book. **Australia**.

When Alexander gets lost walking in the city near his apartment, his faithful toy dog, Felix, bravely sets out to find him. As night falls, the buildings seem to grow taller and more menacing, but when Felix finds Alexander, the beam of his flashlight stills the monsters of the night. The friends remain hopelessly lost, however, until Alexander notices a trail of Felix's stuffing that has been leaking ever since he ripped his side on a nail when leaving through their backyard fence. The warm conclusion sees them tucked up safely in bed, Felix's side replenished and re-stitched. *Australian Children's Picture Book of the Year Award. bt*

**3.32** Diaz, Jorge. **The Rebellious Alphabet.** Translated by Geoffrey Fox. Illustrated by Øivind S. Jorfald. Holt, 1993. Originally published as *Alfabeto rebelde* by Carlsen Forlag. Text copyright, 1977. ISBN 0-8050-2765-3. 32 p. (7-14). Picture book for older readers. **Norway.**
An illiterate dictator, wishing to control people's minds, bans all reading and writing in the village. But Plácido, an old man who loves to express his thoughts freely, uses his pet birds (with letters on their toes) and an ink pad as his own secret printing press. Thanks to Plácido, free thought vanquishes the dictator. Scraps of newspapers from around the world integrated into the illustrations reinforce the theme of the power of the printed word to combat political repression. The author was born in Chile and was in exile in Spain where *The Rebellious Alphabet* was first performed as a play. *jl, djg*

**3.33** Dische, Irene and Enzensberger, Hans Magnus. **Esterhazy: The Rabbit Prince.** Illustrated by Michael Sowa. Creative Editions, 1994. Originally published by Verlag Sauerländer in 1993. ISBN 1-56846-091-0. 32 p. (7-10). Picture book. **Switzerland.**
An old rabbit, Lord Esterhazy, sends his grandchildren abroad from Vienna to seek very large spouses to stem his family's dwindling size. His youngest grandson he sends to Berlin, describing for him the wall that separates the city. Young Esterhazy has a series of adventures in Berlin, and finally gets to see the wall and observe its dismantling. He finds a wife, and thus there are medium-sized rabbits with slight Austrian accents living in Berlin today. While a knowledge of European history enriches the reading experience, enjoyment of the story does not depend on it. *jg, ss*

**3.34** Duquennoy, Jacques. **The Ghosts' Trip to Loch Ness.** Translated by Kathryn Nanovic. Illustrated by the author. Harcourt, 1996. Originally published as *Fantômes au Loch Ness* by Albin Michel Jeunesse in 1996. ISBN 0-15-201440-3. 52 p. (4-6). Picture book. **France.**
Henry the Ghost reads an article in the newspaper about a new sighting of the Loch Ness Monster. He and his three ghost friends travel to

Scotland in hopes of seeing the creature and are befriended and helped in their search by a local spook, MacGhost. They believe that the creature has eluded them until they return home and find him in the background of many of their photos, something that young readers, with the help of humorous, cartoon-style illustrations, will already know. Sequel to *The Ghosts' Dinner* (1994). *djg, mew*

**3.35** Eco, Umberto. **The Three Astronauts**. Translated by William Weaver. Illustrated by Eugenio Carmi. Harcourt Brace Jovanovich, 1989. Originally published as *I Tre Cosmonauti* by Gruppo Editoriale Fabbri in 1989. ISBN 0-15-286383-4. 32 p. (7-12). Picture book. **Italy**. Astronauts from the United States, Russia, and China land on Mars at the same time. At first they distrust one another because of their differences, but become friends after realizing that they share the same feelings. They encounter a monsterlike Martian and think that it must be bad, because it looks and sounds different from themselves. But then the Martian comforts a little bird, and the astronauts again realize that on earth and on other planets, too, a little understanding can pave a path to peace. Torn-paper collage illustrations use well-known icons of each country to symbolize astronauts (U.S.= Chicklets box). *cmt*

**3.36** Fischer, Hans. **Pitschi**. Translated by Marianne Martens. Illustrated by the author. North-South, 1996. Originally published by Nord-Süd Verlag in 1959. ISBN 1-55838-644-X. 32 p. (4-6). Picture book. **Switzerland**.
Pitschi, the smallest of five kittens in Lisette's household, is not quite certain of her place. She wanders off and decides that she wants to be just like each animal she meets...until something changes her mind. She tries swimming like the ducks, but almost drowns. Lisette's joy in finding Pitschi and her loving care in nursing her back to health convinces the kitten that she is loved for what she is. *ss*

**3.37** Foreman, Michael. **Grandfather's Pencil and the Room of Stories**. Illustrated by the author. Harcourt, 1994. Originally published by Andersen Press in 1993. ISBN 0-15-200061-5. 32 p. (4-7). Picture book. **Great Britain**.
A retired sailor tells his visiting grandson Jack of a pencil he had that wrote its memoirs and those of the other wood products in his bedroom—the paper, the door, and the floorboards. The boy returned to the

family home, retrieved the pencil from a crack in the floor, and thus enabled it to continue its story. Illustrations establish the early twentieth-century setting of the grandfather's youth and the present-day setting for Jack. Excellent model for stories of the creation of other manufactured products. *cmt*

**3.38** Fort, Patrick. **Redbird**. Illustrated by the author. Orchard Books, 1988. Originally published by Editions Laurence Olivier Four, Caen and Chardon Blue Editions, 1987. ISBN 0-531-05746-1. Unpaginated. (5-9). Text in Braille, raised illustrations - thermoform technique. **France**.
Redbird, an airplane, meets bad weather and cannot land. While waiting for clearance, he meets other planes, a flock of ducks, and a kite. Simple text, in clear black type and Braille, and colorful raised illustrations invite the reader, both sighted and blind, to enjoy the story. (An Eyes on the Ends of Your Fingers Book) *djg*

**3.39** Fox, Mem. **Feathers and Fools**. Illustrated by Nicholas Wilton. Harcourt, 1996. Originally published by Ashwood House in 1989. ISBN 0-15-200473-4. Unpaginated. (7-14). Picture book. **Australia**.
Long ago in a distant garden, a pride of magnificent peacocks lived near a flock of elegant swans. For no reason other than their different appearance and habits, the birds began to fear one another and built sharpened arrows to defend themselves. The more arrows they amassed, the more terrified the birds became, until, inevitably, a bloody battle ensued. There were no survivors. Hatchlings from both groups, untainted by their parents' paranoia, meet and go off together in peace. There is always hope for a better future. Vivid acrylic paintings illustrate this didactic fable. *djg*

**3.40** Fox, Mem. **Hattie and the Fox**. Illustrated by Patricia Mullins. Bradbury, 1987. Originally published by Ashton Scholastic in 1986. (paperback: Aladdin, 1992). ISBN 0-02-735470-9. (paperback: 0-68-971611-7). 32 p. (3–6). Picture book. **Australia**.
Hattie the black hen sees something in the bushes and warns the goose, pig, sheep, horse, and cow. They respond nonchalantly until she cries that it is a fox. The cow's moo frightens the fox away. The tale builds cumulatively in Hattie's sightings from the fox's nose and eyes to its legs and tail, and repetitively in the other animals' responses. Humorous expressions on the barnyard animals are reassuring compared to the

fox's hungry look. *jsn*

**3.41** Fox, Mem. **Possum Magic.** Illustrated by Julie Vivas. Omnibus Books, 1983. (paperback: Harcourt, 1991). ISBN 0-949641-05-7. (paperback: 0-152632-24-7). 32 p. (4-6). Picture book. **Australia.**
Grandma Poss, who had made Hush invisible in order to keep her safe, is having trouble turning her back into a visible little possum. She tries everything, till she remembers that Hush must eat some special kind of human food and takes her on a grand bicycle tour of Australia in search of the right food. The softly flowing watercolor illustrations humorously portray the possums as well as other Australian animals and foods. *Children's Book Council of Australia Highly Commended Picture Book; IBBY Honour List. jvl*

**3.42** French, Fiona. **Snow White in New York.** Illustrated by the author. Oxford, 1987. Originally published by Oxford in 1986. (paperback: Oxford, 1990). ISBN 0-19-279808-1 (paperback: 0-19-272210-7) Unpaginated. (7-12) Picture book for older readers. **Great Britain.**
A modern revision of Snow White casts the familiar characters as wealthy socialites, jazz club musicians, and the Queen of the Underworld in New York City in the 1920s. Art deco illustrations capture the vitality and glamour of New York in the Jazz Age. *Kate Greenaway Medal. al*

**3.43** Fromenthal, Jean-Luc. **Broadway Chicken.** Translated by Suzi Baker. Illustrated by Miles Hyman. Hyperion, 1995. Originally published as *Le Poulet de Broadway* by Editions du Seuil in 1993. ISBN 0-7868-0061-5. 32 p. (5-9). Picture book. **France.**
Charlie, the Dancing Chicken, makes it all the way from the humble arcade in New York City to Hollywood movie studios in a rags-to-riches story. Soon, however, his money and glory are gone, and Charlie is back at the arcade telling his story to all who will listen. He always ends with this advice: "Learn to cultivate your flaws. It's your defects that win applause." Puns, clichés, and illustrations provide much humor. *mew*

**3.44** Furtado, Jo. **Sorry, Miss Folio.** Illustrated by Frédéric Joos. Kane/Miller, 1992. Originally published by Andersen Press Ltd. in 1987. ISBN 0-916291-18-9. 32 p. (7-9). Picture book. **Great Britain.**
Around Christmas, a little girl checks out a book at her local library.

Members of her family read it to her over and over. In January, when the book is due, the little girl explains to the librarian why she can't return the book (the book is at her grandfather's, and he has developed terrible spots!). With each succeeding month, the excuses grow more fantastical and amusing. A year later, the book is finally returned...a fitting Christmas gift for the librarian. Excellent model for yet another writing form for young writers to explore—the excuse. *cmt*

**3.45** Gardam, Jane. **Through the Dolls' House Door**. Illustrated by the author. Greenwillow, 1987. Originally published by Julia MacRae in 1987. (paperback: Dell, 1991) ISBN 0-688-074472. 121 p. (10-12). Novel. **Great Britain**.

An oddly mismatched collection of dolls are now squashed into an old doll house, abandoned and nearly forgotten by their owners, who have grown up. To pass the time, the dolls tell one another stories, until they are rediscovered by the next generation of playmates. The characters are well drawn, the plot is low key, and the tone is gentle. *mb*

**3.46** Gay, Marie-Louise. **Moonbeam on a Cat's Ear**. Illustrated by the author. Silver Burdett, 1986. Originally published by Stoddart in 1986. ISBN 0-382-09162-0. Unpaged. (4-6). Picture book. **Canada**.

Two young children and a fluffy white cat capture the moon and set sail for adventure in this brief story of a dream. *Amelia Frances Howard-Gibbon Award. lg*

**3.47** Gay, Marie-Louise. **Rainy Day Magic**. Illustrated by the author. Albert Whitman, 1989. Originally published by Stoddart in 1987. ISBN 0-8075-6767-1. Unpaginated. (4-6). Picture book. **Canada**.

A young boy and girl imagine their way into an adventure in the dark basement on a rainy day, returning only when Mom calls them for supper. *Amelia Frances Howard-Gibbon Award. lg*

**3.48** Graham, Bob. **First There Was Frances**. Illustrated by the author. Bradbury, 1986. Originally published by Lothian in 1985. ISBN 0-02-737030-05. 30 p. (4-6). Picture book. **Australia.**

First there was just Frances in her beach house, but soon her family multiplied as her husband Graham found Teak, a dog, then the children, Marisol and Frances, were born, then Grandma came to live on the beach in her trailer, then Kathy the goat took up residence in the laundry room, and then assorted other animals joined them, had young, and wreaked havoc. Still, everyone managed to live together. Cartoon-style characters and settings add details and further humor to this cumulative story. *IBBY Honour List for Illustration. jvl*

**3.49** Gray, Nigel. **A Balloon for Grandad**. Illustrated by Jane Ray. Orchard Books, 1988. ISBN 0-531-05755-0. 30 p. (4-6) Picture book. Originally published by Orchard Books, London, in 1988. **Great Britain**.
When Sam's balloon flies out of the window, he is comforted by his father as they imagine together that it is winging across the ocean to North Africa where Sam's grandfather, Abdualla, lives. Vibrant watercolor illustrations depict what they imagine the balloon sees on its journey, such as snow-topped mountains and hot yellow sands. Colorful patterned borders enhance the pages as the balloon avoids punctures from sandgrouse, hawks, falcons and vultures. The balloon manages to reach the river near grandfather Abdualla's baked-mud hut where they imagine that he retrieves it and instantly realizes that it is from his grandson Sam. A charming story, especially for children who live far away from their grandparents. *cb*

**3.50** Gutiérrez, Douglas. **The Night of the Stars**. Translated by Carmen Diana Dearden. Illustrated by María Fernández Oliver. Kane/Miller, 1988. Originally published as *La Noche de las Estrellas* by Ediciones Ekaré-Banco del Libro in 1987. ISBN 0-916291-17-0. 24 p. (7-9). Picture book. **Venezuela**.
A man loves the daytime when he works and plays, but he hates the night, for the unrelieved darkness makes him sad. One night he goes out and pokes holes in the darkness so that the light hiding behind shines through. Now, anyone can look up into the night sky and see the moon and the stars. The weight of the dark early in the story is emphasized by the use of sad blue-grays. *jl*

**3.51** Haarhof, Dorian. **Desert December**. Illustrated by Leon Vermeulen. Clarion, 1992. Originally published by Songololo Books/David Philip in 1990. ISBN 0-395-61300-0. Unpaginated. (5-8). Picture book. **Republic of South Africa**.
This Christmas story is set in the Namibian desert. The illustrations evoke a strong sense of place. *hr*

**3.52** Hadithi, Mwenye. **Crafty Chameleon**. Illustrated by Adrienne Kennaway. Little, Brown, 1987. Originally published by Hodder & Stoughton in 1987. (paperback: Little, Brown, 1995). ISBN 0-316-33723-4 (paperback: 0-316-33771-4). 32p. (3-6). Picture book. **Great Britain**.
Tired of being bullied by Leopard and Crocodile, a clever Chameleon threatens to tie each bully up by a rope—"just like a dog." While the bullies laugh, he ties them together, and watches as each unknowingly tries to out-pull the other. Vivid watercolors depict the Chameleon in various shades as it watches Leopard and Crocodile struggle. *Kate Greenaway Medal. al*

**3.53** Hadithi, Mwenye. **Hungry Hyena**. Illustrated by Adrienne Kennaway. Little, Brown, 1994. Originally published by Hodder & Stoughton in 1994. ISBN 0-316-33715-3. 32 p. (3-6). Picture book. **Great Britain**.
Retaliating against Hyena for tricking him out of his fish, Eagle tricks every single one of the hyenas into thinking that they can eat the moon. Instead of juicy meat, the hyenas get a nasty fall into the lake and a bite on the tail from Crocodile. Ever since then, the greedy hyenas have had to slink around the great African plain. Brilliant double-page panoramas and interesting perspectives capture the vastness and drama of the African veldt. See also: *Hot Hippo; Lazy Lion; Baby Baboon. cmt*

**3.54** Harley, Rex. **Mary's Tiger**. Illustrated by Sue Porter. Harcourt Brace Jovanovich, 1990. Originally published by Orchard, London, in 1990. ISBN 0-15-200524-2. 24 p. (4-6). Picture book. **Great Britain**.
Mary paints a tiger with a huge head, and gives it a great big smile. Each person she shows her masterpiece to wonders why he is so happy, but she gives them no help. Unable to find a comfortable way to sleep in the picture on the wall that night, the tiger slips off the paper onto Mary's pillow. *mb*

**3.55** Hastings, Selina. **Sir Gawain and the Loathly Lady**. Illustrated by Juan Wijngaard. Lothrop, 1985. Originally published by Walker in 1985. (paperback: Morrow, 1987). ISBN 0-688-05823-X (paperback: 0-688-07046-9). 29p. (6-12). Picture book for older readers. **Great Britain**.
King Arthur enlists the aid of a hideously misshapen woman in order to save himself from the Black Knight. In exchange for her wisdom, King Arthur, with great misgivings, allows his youngest knight, Sir Gawain,

to honor his part of the bargain by marrying the woman at her request. Sir Gawain's chivalrous behavior breaks a spell, and the loathly lady becomes a great beauty. Luminous paintings and ornate borders depict King Arthur and his court in this dramatic retelling. *Kate Greenaway Medal. al*

**3.56** Heine, Helme. **The Marvelous Journey Through the Night**. Translated by Ralph Manheim. Illustrated by the author. Farrar, 1990. Originally published as *Reise durch die Nacht* by Gertraud Middelhauve Verlag in 1989. LCCN 90-55191. 23 p. (4-6). Picture book. **Germany**.
Going to sleep, sleeping, and dreaming are described through words and illustrations. Decidedly romantic and fanciful, these explanations and large, slightly humorous illustrations will satisfy young listeners. Includes several thought-provoking ways to know that one is in the paradise of dreamland. *cmt*

**3.57** Heine, Helme. **Mr. Miller The Dog**. Translation by the publisher and Dent & Sons, London. Illustrated by the author. McElderry/ Atheneum, 1980. Originally published by Friedrich W. Heye Verlag GmbH in 1979. ISBN 0-689-50174-9. 55 p. (7-9). Picture book. **Germany**.
Over the years, Mr. Miller and his devoted dog Murphy came to look more and more like one another. Secretly, each envied the other's life. Eventually, they agreed to change places, and the transformation from dog to person and person to dog continued. Will the complete transformation bring the same dissatisfactions and yearnings as before? Wonderfully simple line and watercolor drawings capture the characters' devotion, their gradual transformation, and humorous details of their lives. *cmt*

**3.58** Hughes, Ted. **The Iron Giant: A Story in Five Nights**. Illustrated by Dirk Zimmer. Harper & Row, 1988. Originally published as *The Iron Man* in 1988. ISBN 0-060-22638-2. 58 p. (8-12). Picture book for older readers. **Great Britain**.
An iron giant challenges a huge space monster that threatens the earth. Once feared by the people, the giant becomes a hero for his brave actions. *Kurt Maschler Award. cmt*

**3.59** Hürlimann, Ruth (reteller). **The Cat and Mouse Who Shared a House**. Translated from the German by Anthea Bell. Illustrated by the author. Walck, 1975. Originally published as *Katze und Maus in Gesellschaft* (from Grimms' *Kinder- und Hausmärchen*) by Atlantis Verlag AG Zürich in 1973. ISBN 0-8098-1214-2. 24 p. (4-6). Picture book. **Switzerland.**

In an unlikely domestic arrangement, a cat convinced a mouse to do her housework if she agreed to provide food for them both. The partnership seemed to develop into friendship. One day the cat and mouse laid aside a pot of butter for winter provisions, but the greedy, devious cat sneaked off to the hiding place and soon ate the butter all up. When winter revealed the cat's deceit, the mouse denounced her as a false friend. Angered, the cat ate the mouse, too. Cat and mouse can never really be friends. *Mildred Batchelder Award. cmt*

**3.60** Ichikawa, Satomi. **Nora's Duck.** Illustrated by the author. Philomel, 1991. Originally published as *Doctor John No Doubutsuen* by Kaisei-Sha Publishing in 1990. ISBN 0-399-21805-X. 33 p. (4-6). Picture book. **Japan.**

Nora, about five, finds an abandoned duckling in the woods. She takes it to her friend, Dr. John, a retired medical doctor and friend of all animals needing care. Dr. John helps revive the duckling and gives Nora, her doll, teddy bear, and dog a tour of his animal menagerie and a lesson in caring for injured animals. Beautifully precise watercolor illustrations present Nora's perspective, combining the fantasy of a living doll and teddy bear in an otherwise realistic setting. Other books in the *Nora* series: *Nora's Stars*; *Nora's Surprise. cmt*

**3.61** Ishii, Momoko. **The Tongue-cut Sparrow.** Translated by Katherine Paterson. Illustrated by Suekichi Akaba. Dutton, 1987. Originally published as *Shita-kiri Suzume* by Fukuinkan Shoten in 1982. ISBN 0-525-67199-4. 40 p. (4-8). Picture book. **Japan.**

When his spiteful wife snipped his pet sparrow's tongue for drinking her starch, a kindly old man searched for his pet to apologize, doing good deeds along the way. The sparrow, once found, rewarded the man with a small box of great riches. The wife, greedy for even greater riches, made her way to the sparrow, but was rewarded with a box of goblins. Distinctly Japanese illustrations use traditional motifs and symbolic colors. Translator's Note to the Reader is a pronunciation guide to onomatopoeic words found in the story. *cmt*

**3.62** Iwamura, Kazuo. **The 14 Forest Mice and the Harvest Moon Watch**. Translated by Mary Lee Knowlton. Illustrated by the author. Gareth Stevens, 1991. Originally published as *Juyonhiki No Otsukimi* by Doshin-sha in 1988. ISBN 0-8368-0497-X. 32 p. (7-9). Picture book. Japan.

The Forest Mouse family enjoys an evening of gazing at the setting sun and the rising of the "harvest full moon." They encounter a variety of interesting creatures as they climb a tree to gain a good vantage point. This book is part of a series, of which four, in addition to the featured title, have been translated into English: *The 14 Forest Mice*; *The 14 Forest Mice and the Spring Meadow Picnic*; *The 14 Forest Mice and the Summer Laundry Day*; and *The 14 Forest Mice and the Winter Sledding Day*. *jy*

**3.63** Jorgensen, Gail. **Crocodile Beat**. Illustrated by Patricia Mullins. Bradbury, 1994. Originally published by Omnibus Books in 1988. (paperback: Aladdin, 1994) ISBN 002-748-010-0. 32 p. (4-6). Picture book. **Australia**.

As crocodile snoozes, animals of all types gather by the river to play. When crocodile is awakened by their noise, he thinks that he will make a meal of the revelers, but King Lion saves the day. Rhyming couplets and highly textural torn-paper collage illustrations make the text predictable. Young readers can provide the animal sounds. *cmt*

**3.64** Joubert, Jean. **White Owl and Blue Mouse**. Translated by Denise Levertov. Illustrated by Michel Gay. Zoland, 1990. Originally published as *Hibou blanc et souris bleue* by L'École des Loisirs in 1978. ISBN 0-944072-13-5. 63 p. (7-9). Beginning reader. **France**.

White Owl hunts mice for food, but Blue Mouse is too smart for him. As a result, White Owl finds himself caught, put in a cage, and made part of a circus. Blue Mouse now becomes Owl's eyes beyond the cage, going out to see the world and returning to relieve his new friend's boredom. When the cage is left open one night, White Owl and Blue Mouse fly free together into the night sky. *CCBC Choices*. *jl*

**3.65** Kharms, Daniil. **First, Second**. Translated by Richard Pevear. Illustrated by Marc Rosenthal. Farrar, 1996. Originally published as *Vo pervykh i vo vtorykh*. ISBN 0-374-32339-9. Unpaginated. (5-9). Picture book. **Russia**.

First published in a Russian children's magazine in 1930, this cumulative story details the slapstick journey of a young adventurer who steps out singing a song and is joined along the way by several fellow travelers, each presenting an obstacle to progress, but adding to the hilarity of this journey. Each traveler is numbered and, hence, the title. Line and bold watercolor illustrations are reminiscent of Katzenjammer cartoons and are perfectly suited to this wacky story. *djg*

**3.66** Kipling, Rudyard. **The Beginning of the Armadillos**. Illustrated by John A. Rowe. North-South Books, 1995. Originally published as *Die Entstehung der Gürteltiere* by Michael Neugebauer Verlag AG in 1995. ISBN 1-55858-482-X. Unpaginated. (6-8). Picture book. **Switzerland.**

In this beautifully told pourquoi tale of how the armadillo came to have qualities of both a hedgehog and a tortoise, John Rowe's illustrations add mystery, interest, and a suitable sense of quirkiness. Kipling's rhythmic, inventive use of language and his gentle humor make this story appropriate for read-aloud. *Rowe: 1996 Bratislava Grand Prix for Illustration*. *cmt*

**3.67** Kitamura, Satoshi. **When Sheep Cannot Sleep. The Counting Book**. Farrar, 1986. Originally published by Black, London, in 1986. (paperback: Sunburst, 1988) ISBN 0-374-38311-1. 32 p. (4-6). Picture book. **Great Britain**.

Woolly, a sheep, cannot sleep, so he goes for a leisurely walk down the meadow, finds an interesting house, looks at the paintings, cooks a light supper, takes a bath, and lies down in a little bed. Each illustration reveals a discovery made by Woolly. These 22 items are listed at the back. Kitamura uses color and design to depict the long process of getting ready to fall asleep. *New York Academy of Sciences: Children's Science Book Awards, Younger Category. Kitamura: Winner of Mother Goose Award (UK) for a picture book newcomer. mb*

**3.68** Kitchen, Bert. **Tenrec's Twigs**. Illustrated by the author. Philomel, 1989. Published simultaneously by Lutterworth in 1989. ISBN 0-399-21720-7. 26p. (3-6). Picture book. **Great Britain**.

Tenrec, a cross between a shrew and a hedgehog, is doing what he loves best—twig building. He is perfectly happy until hedgehog comes along and tells him that this is a perfect waste of time. Tenrec then asks a variety of unusual animals what they think of his twig-building, but they all dismiss him. Tenrec finally finds support from the Milky Eagle Owl who gives him good reasons to twig-build. Detailed watercolor illustrations underscore the theme of the value of difference. A glossary provides descriptions of each animal. *Redbook Children's Picturebook Award. mja*

**3.69** Koralek, Jenny. **The Cobweb Curtain: A Christmas Story.** Illustrated by Pauline Baynes. Holt, 1989. Originally published by Methuen Children's Books. ISBN 0-8050-1051-3. Unpaginated. (4-9) Picture book. **Great Britain.**
Soon after the birth of Christ, the Holy Family is led away from Bethlehem by a shepherd to a remote cavern to escape the wrath of Herod's soldiers. During the night a spider spins a web over the entrance of the cavern convincing the passing soldiers that the cave is long deserted. As the family leaves the cave the next morning, the shepherd takes the sparkling web and drapes it over a nearby tree, thus creating the first Christmas tree. This legend was first told by William Barclay as "The Legend of the Spider's Web" for The Daily Study Bible (Saint Andrew Press). *cb*

**3.70** Laird, Elizabeth. **The Road to Bethlehem. A Nativity Story from Ethiopia.** Foreword by Terry Waite. Holt, 1987. Originally published by Collins in 1987. ISBN 0-8050-0539-0. 32 p. (7-12). Picture book. **Great Britain.**
This retelling of the Christian nativity story is based on 200-year-old Ethiopian manuscripts held at the British Library, accompanied by reproductions of their illustrations. The nativity story is told from the birth of the Virgin Mary through Herod's death and the return of the child Jesus to Nazareth. In captions, Laird provides a commentary on Ethiopian art styles and customs. *mb*

**3.71** Lawson, Julie. **The Dragon's Pearl.** Illustrated by Paul Morin. Clarion, 1993. Originally published by Oxford Canada, 1992. ISBN 0-395-63623-X. Unpaginated. (7-9). Picture book. **Canada.**
This retelling of a Chinese tale captures the myth and wonder of a dragon's power. Xiao Sheng loved to sing, and even though he and his mother were poor, he sang at his work. When he discovered a magic pearl, their fortunes improved, but they remained the happy, kind folk

they had always been. When two wicked men try to steal the pearl, Xiao Sheng swallows it, turning into a dragon and ending the punishing drought that had been plaguing Szechuan. *Amelia Frances Howard-Gibbon Award. lg*

**3.72** LeCain, Errol. **Hiawatha's Childhood**. Illustrated by the author. Farrar, 1984. Originally published by Faber in 1984. (paperback: Farrar, 1994). ISBN 0-374-33065-4. (paperback: 0-374-42997-9). 32p. (5-7). Picture book. **Great Britain**.
Richly stylized watercolors depict the young Hiawatha as he explores the native beauty of the land, shown to him by his nurse, Nokomis. Spiritual presence radiates from every page in this rhythmic passage from Longfellow's "The Song of Hiawatha." *Kate Greenaway Medal. al*

**3.73** Lindenbaum, Pija. (Retold by Gabrielle Charbonnet). **Boodil My Dog**. Illustrated by the author. Holt, 1992. Originally published as *Boken om Bodil* by Bonniers Juniorförlag in 1992. ISBN 0-8050-2444-1. Unpaginated. (4-6). Picture book. **Sweden**.
Wryly humorous illustrations tell the tale of Boodil the bull terrier and are in direct contrast to her young master's loving, and obviously biased, commentary. "Boodil's guard is never down," says her master. The illustration shows Boodil lounging on a chair! Nighttime is when the decidedly quirky Boodil gets frisky. *N.Y. Times Best Illustrated Picture Book Award; BCCB Blue Ribbon Book. djg*

**3.74** Lindenbaum, Pija. (Adapted by Gabrielle Charbonnet). **Else-Marie and Her Seven Little Daddies**. Illustrated by the author. Holt, 1991. Originally published as *Else-Marie och Småpapporna* by Bonniers Junior Förlag in 1991. ISBN 0-8050-1752-6. 32 p. (7-9). Picture book. **Sweden**.
Everybody else has one big daddy, but Else-Marie has seven little ones. One day when her daddies, instead of her mother, are scheduled to pick her up from school, Else-Marie worries. She can only imagine that the worst will happen, when the other children and her teacher see her daddies. To her surprise, no one seems to notice the difference. The illustrations abound with humor and help to show that families come in all shapes and sizes. *CCBC Choices. jl, djg*

**3.75** Lindgren, Barbro. **A Worm's Tale**. Translated by Dianne Jonasson.

Illustrated by Cecilia Torudd. R&S, 1988. Originally published as *Sagan om Karlknut: En Masks Historia* by Rabén & Sjögren in 1985. ISBN 91-29-59068-X. 32 p. (4-6). Picture book. **Sweden**.

Arthur is an impeccably dressed, well-mannered gentleman, but he is very lonely and has no friends. One day, while walking in the park, he strikes up a friendship with a worm. He takes the worm home, names him Charles (after his father), gets him some tailor-made clothes, and they do many things together that friends do. A town bully tries to spoil their friendship, but the children accept Charles for the worm that he is and throw the bully out of town. *CCBC Choices*.

**3.76** Lively, Penelope. **Good Night, Sleep Tight**. Illustrated by Adriano Gon. Candlewick, 1995. Originally published by Walker, 1994. ISBN 1-56402-417-2. Unpaginated. (4-6). Picture book. **Great Britain**.

A little girl takes very good care of all of her stuffed animals. At the end of the day she washes their faces, reads them a book, and takes them to bed. But someone who is not ready to go to sleep keeps "kicking and jiggling around." The animals all want to take the little girl on an adventure; and so she goes off, first with frog, then with lion, until at last it is time to sleep. Illustrations provide an appropriate nighttime setting for this bedtime fantasy. *djg*

**3.77** Lobato, Arcadio. **Paper Bird**. Illustrated by Emilio Urberauga. Carolrhoda, 1994. Originally published as *Der Papiervogel* by Bohem Press in 1993. ISBN 0-87614-817-8. 26 p. (5-8). Picture book. **Switzerland**.

One evening before he goes to bed, an artist draws a picture of a bird for his daughter's birthday. That night, the bird, still in its flat paper form, asks the resident cat to help it fly and is tossed out of the window. Ravens, swallows, and other birds all try unsuccessfully to teach the paper bird to fly, but it can only float downward. On one such trip, the cat retrieves the bird and returns it to the artist's studio. The bird's wish comes true the next morning, when the artist returns to the studio to turn the paper bird into a kite. Stylized illustrations rendered in a cartoon style portray the birds' nighttime activities against the backdrop of a sleeping city. *ss*

**3.78** Lunn, Janet. **Amos's Sweater**. Illustrated by Kim LaFave. Groundwood/Douglas & McIntyre, 1988. ISBN 0-88899-074-X.

Unpaginated. (4-6). Picture book. **Canada**.

Amos the sheep is old, cold, and tired of giving away his wool, so when Hattie shears him and knits a sweater for Henry, Amos bites it every chance he gets. He finally gets himself literally wound up in the sweater, and Hattie and Henry decide that maybe Amos needs his own sweater. Content, Amos isn't cold any more. *Amelia Frances Howard-Gibbon Award; Canada Council Award for Illustration.* lg

**3.79** Macourek, Miloš. **Max and Sally and the Phenomenal Phone**. Translated by Dagmar Herrmann. Illustrated by Adolf Born. Wellington, 1989. Originally published as *Mach a Šebestová* by Artia in 1980. ISBN 0-922984-00-X. 84 p. (4-9). Picture book. **Czechoslovakia**.

Third-graders Max and Sally help a man find his glasses in the park and are rewarded with an old telephone receiver that turns out to be magic. It grants whatever wish the children speak into it. Because of this, Max and Sally and their neighbor's dog Jonathan have several unforgettable adventures, and, thanks to the telephone, everything works out well. Illustrations project good humor through exaggeration. *cmt*

**3.80** Mahy, Margaret. **17 Kings and 42 Elephants**. Illustrated by Patricia MacCarthy. Dial, 1987. Originally published by J. M. Dent in 1972. (paperback: Dial, 1990). ISBN 0-8037-0458-5. (paperback: 0-1405-4597-2). 26 p. (4–7). Picture book. **New Zealand**.

Seventeen kings and forty-two elephants journey in the jungle on a wild wet night and see crocodiles, hippos, tigers, large birds, baboons, and gorillas. The text consists of thirty-two lines of highly rhythmic verse, with internal alliteration and wordplay reminiscent of Edward Lear. The double-page illustrations are reproduced from gorgeous batik paintings on silk. *New York Times Best Illustrated Book Award. jsn*

**3.81** Manton, Denis. **Wolf Comes to Town**. Illustrated by the author. Dutton, 1993. Originally published by Hutchinsons Children's Books in 1993. ISBN 0- 525-45281-8. 32 p. (4-6). Picture book. **Great Britain**.

Wolf loves to shop. He comes to town in disguise, because he knows that people do not like wolves, especially wolves that simply take what they want. He cleverly manages to take cats, dogs, ducks, and even a child for his dinner. The humor of this clever wolf's ruses, and his philosophy expressed in the refrain, "I like it, I want it, and I'LL TAKE

IT" make this decidedly immoral tale delightful. *jg*

**3.82** Matura, Mustapha. **Moon Jump.** Illustrated by Jane Gifford. Knopf, 1988. Originally published by Heinemann in 1988. ISBN 0-394-81976-4. 32 p. (4-6). Picture book. **Great Britain.**
Cayal and his teddy bear love to jump on the bed before going to bed at night. One night, they jump higher than ever and land on the moon where they meet the moon man and have a bit to eat before returning home to be tucked into bed by Father. Illustrations portray a nonwhite child and his very lifelike teddy bear—a lively duo with whom children can identify. *mb*

**3.83** McBratney, Sam. **Guess How Much I Love You.** Illustrated by Anita Jeram. Candlewick, 1995. Originally published by Walker in 1994. ISBN 1-56402-473-3. 32 p. (1-3). Picture book. **Great Britain.**
Father and son hares compete at demonstrating their love for each other. As the little hare spreads his arms to show the breadth of his love, the big hare spreads his even wider. Again and again they show with hare-like skills how far their love reaches until a very sleepy little hare is given the last word by a doting father as he puts him to bed. Gently comical and subtly tinted watercolor and ink illustrations capture perfectly the affection these two share. *bb*

**3.84** McKee, David. **The Sad Story of Veronica Who Played the Violin.** Illustrated by the author. Kane/Miller, 1991. Originally published by Andersen Press Ltd. in 1987. ISBN 0-916291-37-5. 25 p. (4-6). Picture book. **Great Britain.**
Veronica played the violin beautifully, but her music was so sad that everyone who heard it cried. Bored with stardom, she took a trip to the jungle. For days she was unable to play the violin, but when she did, her music had changed. It made the listeners happy! What glorious prospects! At that moment an old lion leapt upon Veronica and ate her up. He was deaf. That is why the world is not full of happy, dancing people. *cmt*

**3.85** McKee, David. **Tusk Tusk.** Illustrated by the author. Kane/-Miller, 1990. Originally published by Andersen Press Ltd. in 1978. ISBN 0-916291-28-6. 29 p. (4-12). Picture book. **Great Britain.**
White elephants and black elephants wage war until all are dead.

Fortunately, the peace-loving elephants fled deep into the jungle before the war, and when their grandchildren emerge years later, all of them are grey. Is the problem solved? Perhaps not, as some have small ears and some have large ears. An allegory of human strife based on insignificant differences. Bold, humorous illustrations suggest the human connection. *cmt*

**3.86** McNaughton, Colin. **Guess Who's Just Moved In Next Door?** Illustrated by the author. Random House, 1991. Originally published as *Have You Seen Who's Just Moved In Next Door to Us?* by Walker Books in 1991. ISBN 0-679-81802-2. 32 p. Picture book. **Great Britain**.

Everyone in the neighborhood is concerned about the new arrivals: they are *different*! Will it ruin the neighborhood? As this neighborhood consists of fairytale characters, movie monsters, larger-than-life historical and literary figures, and nightmares, one wonders what these new neighbors can be like to cause such concern. A double fold-out spotlights these "ugly customers"—an average, white, middle class family! A story told in verse. *Kurt Maschler Award. cmt*

**3.87** McNaughton, Colin. **Oops!** Illustrated by the author. Harcourt, 1997. Originally published by Andersen in 1996. ISBN 0-152-01588-4. Unpaginated. (4-7). Picture book. **Great Britain**.

A confused wolf and a clumsy pig named Preston meet. Their story contains elements of "Little Red Riding Hood" and "The Three Little Pigs." (FirstSearch) *Smarties Prize. cmt*

**3.88** Mennel, Wolfgang. **Henry and Horace Clean Up**. Translated by Marianne Martens. Illustrated by Gisela Dürr. North-South, 1996. Originally published as *Franz & Wolke* by Michael Neugebauer Verlag in 1996. ISBN 1-55858-658-X. 25 p. (4-6). Picture book. **Switzerland**.

Horace's house is spic and span, but Henry's house next door is a mess. To clean his house, Henry gets poor Horace to lug every stick of furniture out and dump it into his own once-neat home. Horace finally breaks down, and Henry realizes how he has imposed on his friend. To make amends, Henry suggests that they camp out and share the contents of his treasure chest, which is full of books! Illustrations reveal that Horace is an elephant and Henry is a pig. *cmt*

**3.89** Mollel, Tololwa M. **The Orphan Boy**. Illustrated by Paul Morin. Clarion, 1990. Originally published by Oxford, Canada in 1990. (7-9). Picture book. **Canada**.

This retelling of a Maasai legend explains why the planet Venus is known to them as the orphan boy. Kileken, an orphan, appears at the camp of a childless old man who is delighted to have a son at last. Kileken makes the old man's life easier, although it becomes more and more difficult for the old man to accept what appear to be magical powers. When the old man spies on him, Kileken turns back into the planet Venus. *Amelia Frances Howard-Gibbon Award. lg*

**3.90** Moore, Inga. **The Sorcerer's Apprentice**. Illustrated by the author. Macmillan, 1989. Originally published by Walker in 1989. ISBN 0-02-767645-5. 32 p. (4-6). Picture book. **Great Britain**.

When a meddling young Franz inadvertently unleashes magic that he has no power to stop, he discovers that there is more to sorcery than creating a spell. In this fanciful rendition of a familiar folktale, the illustrator supplies tension with an ever-increasing number of dancing brooms that eerily sway their way through a craggy medieval castle. *be*

**3.91** Munsch, Robert and Kusugak, Michael. **A Promise Is a Promise.** Illustrated by Vladyana Krykorka. Annick Press, 1988. (paperback: Annick Press, 1988) ISBN 1-55037-009-X. (paperback: 1-55037-008-1). 30 p. (7-9). Picture book. **Canada.**

Allashua goes fishing on the sea ice and is captured by the Qallupilluits, who capture human children and hold them under the ice. She promises that, if they will let her go, she will bring her brothers and sisters instead. When her parents find out, they devise a way to trick the sea creatures without Allashua breaking her promise. In the end, the whole family goes fishing on the sea ice together without fear of the Qallupilluits. Though the story is told in the style of a folktale, the colorful illustrations depict a modern Inuit family. *Vicky Metcalf Award* (Canada). *bkn*

**3.92** Murphy, Jill. **The Last Noo-Noo**. Illustrated by the author. Candlewick, 1995. Originally published by Walker in 1995. ISBN 0-744-53228-0. Unpaginated. (2-4). Picture book. **Great Britain**.

Marlon's grandmother thinks that he is too big to have a pacifier, and his mother agrees. The other children make fun of him, but Marlon will not give up his "noo-noo" until he is ready. FirstSearch. *Smarties*

*Prize. cmt*

**3.93** Nesbit, Edith. **The Deliverers of Their Country.** Illustrated by Lisbeth Zwerger. Picture Book Studio, 1985. Originally published by Michael Neugebauer in 1985. ISBN 0-88708-005-7. Unpaginated. (7-12). Picture book. **Switzerland.**
Effie and her brother Harry are the first to discover the dragons that soon descend like a plague and wreak havoc in the land. As the beasts grow larger and larger, daily life is disrupted. Effie and Harry set forth on a mission to rid the land of dragons. They get help from St. George and eventually discover the universal tap room. There they restore nature's balance and banish the dragons, thus becoming the deliverers of their country. *djg*

**3.94** Niland, Kilmeny. **A Bellbird in a Flame Tree.** Illustrated by the author. Tambourine Books, 1991. Originally published by Angus & Robertson in 1989. ISBN 0-688-10798-2. 28 p. (7-9). Picture book. **Australia.**
In this Australian version of "The Twelve Days of Christmas," the giver sends Australian birds and animals, such as dingoes, wallabies, and koalas. The colorful illustrations advance the story by showing each "gift animal" contributing to the party atmosphere. For example, the crocodiles sing carols in front of a beach at sunset, the dingoes dance around in a desert, and the numbats knit by a fireplace with knitted stockings hanging from the mantle. As a finale, all the birds and animals form a Christmas tree. Music to the song is included. *bkn*

**3.95** Nilsson, Ulf. **Little Bunny & the Hungry Fox.** Illustrated by Eva Eriksson. Chronicle, 1989. Originally published as *När lilla syster Kanin blev jagad av en räv* by Bonniers in 1987. ISBN 0-87701-605-4. 24 p. (1-3). Picture book. **Sweden.**
Even though Little Bunny has been told not to, she decides to go out by herself one day to take a walk. She has fun whistling and rolling down the hill, until she meets up with a hungry fox. Good advice and fast hopping get her home safely. The carefree illustrations lend a light-hearted, optimistic mood. *CCBC Choices. jl*

**3.96** Nilsson, Ulf. **Little Bunny at the Beach.** Illustrated by Eva Eriksson. Chronicle, 1989. Originally published as *När Lilla Syster Kanin*

*Bade i det Stora Havet* by Bonniers in 1987. ISBN 0-87701-610-0. 24 p. (1-3). Picture book. **Sweden.**
Little Bunny goes to the beach with Big Brother Rabbit. She is having so much fun that she ignores his warnings and starts to be carried away by the current. Big Brother saves her, but she does not appreciate it until she notices how deep and wide the ocean really is. Then Little Bunny realizes how nice it is to have Big Brother Rabbit with her after all. The whimsical background action in the illustrations adds to the fun of being at the beach. *CCBC Choices. jl*

**3.97** Nygren, Tord. **The Red Thread.** Illustrated by Tord Nygren. R&S, 1988. Originally published as *Den Röda Tråden* by Rabén & Sjögren, 1987. ISBN 91-29-59005-1. 28 p. (7-9). Picture book. **Sweden.**
In this wordless picture book, a red thread winds through colorful scenes of fantasy and dreams. The thread leads the reader through lush forests and night skies, baboons and harlequins, puppet shows and storybook characters. Where the red thread, or our imagination, ends, no one can tell. *jl*

**3.98** Offen, Hilda. **Nice Work, Little Wolf.** Illustrated by the author. Dutton, 1992. Originally published by Hamish Hamilton in 1991. ISBN 0-525-44880-2. 25 p. (4-7). Picture book. **Great Britain.**
Little Wolf fell into the Porker family's garden and was mistaken for a little puppy. Brian, the youngest in this lazy, pass-the-buck family of pigs was delighted to have someone to pass his chores along to, and the industrious little wolf did it all. Over time, he created a paradise for the insatiable pigs, but as they wallowed in their good fortune, Little Wolf was getting bigger and bigger. Finally losing his temper, he chased the pigs away and invited his poor mother to live in the beautiful home that he had built. Sweet justice and lots of humor. *Smarties Book Prize. cmt*

**3.99** Ormerod, Jan. **The Story of Chicken Lickin.** Illustrated by the author. Lothrop, 1985. Originally published by Walker in 1985. ISBN 0-688-06058-7. 26 p. (3–7). Picture book. **Australia.**
Children perform the folktale of Chicken Lickin, who involves Henny Penny, Cock Lock, Duck Luck, Drake Lake, Goose Loose, Gander Lander, and Turkey Lurkey on her way to tell the king that the sky is falling...before Foxy Woxy eats them all. Double-page illustrations show eleven costumed children on stage across the top of each page. Across

the bottom of each page appears (mostly in silhouette) the parent-grandparent-sibling audience, including a dozing dad, a talkative toddler, and a baby who explores the contents of a purse and crawls from basket to stage. A story within a story. *jsn*

**3.100** Oxenbury, Helen. **It's My Birthday.** Illustrated by the author. Candlewick Press, 1994. Originally published by Uitgeverjj J.H. Gottmer/H.J.W. Becht B.V. in 1993. ISBN 1-56402-143-2. 26 p. (7-9). Picture book. **Netherlands.**
In this cumulative story, a young child enlists animals to help gather the ingredients needed to bake a birthday cake. A chicken supplies the eggs, a bear some flour, a cat the butter and milk, a pig a pinch of salt, a dog the sugar, and a monkey the cherries for the top. All repair to the child's kitchen to help in the preparation and, finally, the eating. Oxenbury's muted watercolor illustrations show each of the animals procuring their contributions and deliberately leave the gender of the child unclear to promote baking as an activity all children can enjoy. *ss*

**3.101** Oyono, Éric. **Gollo and the Lion.** Illustrated by Laurent Corvaisier. Hyperion, 1994. Originally published as *Gollo et le Lion* by Albin Michel Jeunesse in 1994. ISBN 0-7868-0041-0. Unpaginated. (5-9). Picture Book. **France.**
Every morning when Gollo leaves to go hunting, he warns his sister Kaye not to open the door until she hears him sing his special song. Every evening Kaye waits to hear his sweet voice. Polgozom, a fierce lion, manages to change his raspy voice, tricks Kaye into opening the door, and devours her. With advice from the Soothsayer and the help of all the animals, Gollo is able to force the lion to return Kaye unharmed. Bright acrylic illustrations enliven this retelling of a folktale from Cameroon. *djg*

**3.102** Pacovská, Květa. **The Little Flower King.** Translated by Anthea Bell. North-South/Michael Neugebauer, 1996. Originally published as *Der Kleine Blumenkönig* by Michael Neugebauer Verlag AG in 1991. ISBN 1-55858-532-X. 36 p. (1-4). Picture book. **Switzerland.**
In order to make his life complete, the tiny king of the flowers searches for and finds a queen. This simple tale is told using few words, large, intensely colored abstract illustrations, and simple cutouts and flaps. *Pacovská winner of Hans Christian Andersen Medal for Illustration,*

*1992.* cmt

**3.103** Pacovská, Květa. **Midnight Play**. Translated by Andrew Clements. North-South Books, 1994. Originally published as *Mitternachtsspeil* by Michael Neugebauer Verlag AG in 1992. ISBN 1-55858-252-5. 36 p. (4-6). Engineered book. **Switzerland**.
Actors put on a play at midnight for their special guest, the moon. Cutouts, a moon shape mounted on a string, and split pages allow readers to interchange characters' names and costumes. Childlike artistic style and sophisticated design combine to intrigue readers of all ages. *Pacovská: Hans Christian Andersen Medal for Illustration.* cmt

**3.104** Pallandt, Nicholas van. **The Butterfly Night of Old Brown Bear**. Illustrated by the author. Farrar, 1992. Originally published by Lemniscaat in 1990. ISBN 0-374-31009-2. Unpaginated. (4-6). Picture book. **Netherlands**.
Old Brown Bear collected butterflies and moths. One day the brightest, most brilliant blue moth that he had ever seen landed on his toe. Away he went, net in hand, in hot and happy pursuit of the moth who led him up a tree, past the clouds, into the night, to the tip of the crescent moon. Returning from his adventure, he freed the butterflies in his collection, realizing that the fun is in the chasing, not the catching. *djg*

**3.105** Pelgrom, Els. **Little Sophie and Lanky Flop**. Translated by Arnold Pomerans. Illustrated by The Tjong Khing. Farrar, 1988. Originally published as *Kleine Sofie en Lange Wapper* by Em. Querido's Uitgeverij B.V. in 1984. ISBN 0-374-34624-0. 88 p. (9-12). Picture book for older readers. **Netherlands**.
Sickly and long confined to bed, Sophie yearns to know all that life has to offer. Her cat puts on a play that soon seems real, and Sophie finds herself caught up in a wild adventure, giving her tastes of both happiness and misery and a glimpse of many facets of the human condition. She and her dolls, Lanky Flop, Mr. Bear, and Annabella are main characters. Having seen something of life, Sophie dies, only to begin an endless, happy journey with her three faithful friends. Expressive and sensitive black and white illustrations reflect Sophie's delirium. *German Children's Book Prize; Dutch Golden Pencil and Golden Brush Awards.* cmt

**3.106** Pfister, Marcus. **The Rainbow Fish.** Translated by J. Alison James. Illustrated by the author. North-South, 1992. Originally published as *Der Regenbogenfisch* by Nord-Süd Verlag in 1992. ISBN 1-55858-009-3. 25 p. (4-7). Picture book. **Switzerland.**

The rainbow fish, with its shimmering silver scales, was the most beautiful fish in the sea...and the haughtiest. Without friends and unhappy, Rainbow Fish consulted the wise octopus who told him that he would find happiness in sharing his scales with other fish. Following this advice, Rainbow Fish discovered that sharing and friendship are more valuable than beauty. *Christopher Award; American Booksellers Book of the Year. mew, cmt*

**3.107** Place, François. **The Last Giants.** Translated by William Rodarmor. Illustrated by the author. David R. Godine, 1993. Originally published as *Les Derniers Géants* by Editions Casterman, 1992. ISBN 0-87923-990-5. 74 p. (10-12). Picture book for older readers. **Belgium.**

The picture book format belies the complex and sophisticated nature of this story. Told in the first person, it is the account of an English explorer who discovers nine gentle giants, the last of their race, living in a remote mountain kingdom. During the year he lives with them, he studies their elaborate language and culture and is awed by their knowledge and wisdom, which he shares in a book when he returns home. The sensation it causes has a tragic outcome, spelling the end of these unique people who are sought out and destroyed in the name of science. *Grand Prize for Children's Literature; The Totem Prize; The Golden Circles Prize for Children's Literature (all French awards). ss*

**3.108** Popov, Nikolai, **Why?** Illustrated by the author. North-South, 1996. Originally published as *Warum?* by Michael Neugebauer in 1996. ISBN 1-098-765432-1. Unpaginated. (7-14). Picture book. **Switzerland.**

As Frog peacefully contemplates, Mouse suddenly bursts in and takes away his flower. Retaliative action quickly escalates, and the once serene mood becomes sinister, represented by the darkening tone of the illustrations. The final illustration in this wordless fable shows mouse and frog with their tattered and useless spoils of war, prompting the reader to ask, "Why?" The author's note tells of a terrible childhood memory of a friend who found a shiny "treasure" while collecting shrapnel in the streets of post-World War II Moscow. The "treasure" flashed and exploded, leaving the boy crippled and impressing upon

Popov the senselessness of war. *djg*

**3.109** Preussler, Otfried. **The Tale of the Unicorn**. Translated by Lenny Hort. Illustrated by Gennady Spirin. Dial, 1989. Originally published as *Das Märchen vom Einhorn* by K. Thienemanns Verlag in 1988. (paperback: Puffin, 1992). ISBN 0-8037-0583-2. 32 p. (4-6). Picture book. **Germany**.
Three brothers set out to capture the unicorn with the horn of ivory, hooves of gold, and a diamond star on its forehead. The two elder brothers are distracted along the way and abandon the search. When the younger brother finds the unicorn, he is so struck by its beauty that he stands and gazes, becoming an old man. Gennady Spirin's exuberant miniaturist illustrations convey the human capacity to appreciate beauty. *jl*

**3.110** Prokofiev, Sergei. **Peter & the Wolf**. Knopf, 1986. Illustrated by Jörg Müller. Originally published as *Peter und der Wolf: Ein Musikalische Märchen* by Sauerlander, Aarau, in 1985. ISBN 0-394-88417-5. 24 p. (7-12). Picture book. **Switzerland**.
This oversized picture book version of the well-known orchestra piece (written and composed in 1936) incorporates the music and staging by beginning with an introduction of the main characters and their musical motifs and ending with their final curtain call. Müller paces the story by using different sized illustrations in comic book style on each page. Appropriately, the animals are portrayed in a slightly exaggerated, humorous style. *Critici in Erba Prize, Bologna, Italy; Müller: Hans Christian Andersen Award Winner for Illustration. mb*

**3.111** Rascal. **Oregon's Journey**. Illustrated by Louis Joos. Bridgewater/Troll, 1994. Originally published by Pastel, L'Ecole des Loisirs in 1993. ISBN 0-8167-3305-8. 33 p. (4-7). Picture book. **France**.
Because he is a lonely captive of sorts himself, Duke, a circus dwarf, agrees to help Oregon, a circus bear, return to the freedom of his forest home in the state of Oregon. Leaving the grime of Pittsburgh, they hitchhike west, leaving their pasts behind. Their journey is often difficult, but ultimately rewarding, as they slowly exchange unnatural for natural, sordid for beautiful. Having returned Oregon to his home, Duke is ready to face the world as himself, a clown no longer. *cmt. Editor's note: Author and illustrator are Belgian.*

**3.112** Rascal. **Orson**. Illustrated by Mario Ramos. Lothrop, 1995. Originally published by L'Ecole des Loisirs in 1993. ISBN 0-688-13462-9. 26 p. (4-7). Picture book. **France**.
Because Orson is the biggest bear in the forest, all of the other animals are afraid of him, and this leaves him sad and lonely. Then one spring he emerges from hibernation to find a small teddy bear outside his cave. He makes the toy his friend and surrogate son. In the fall, Orson leaves the teddy bear where he found it; but as he steps into his cave, he hears the toy call to him and knows that it will not be a lonely winter. *jg*

**3.113** Reeves, James. **Mr. Horrox and the Gratch**. Illustrated by Quentin Blake. Wellington Publishing, 1991. Originally published by Abelard-Schuman in 1969. ISBN 0-922984-08-5. 32 p. (4-7). Picture book. **Great Britain**.
Mr. Horrox painted very predictable and lifelike pictures. His art dealer encouraged him to expand his repertoire, so Mr. Horrox moved to Scotland. He was warned to provide his Gratch, the wee spirit that lived in his house, with string, but he forgot. Soon, his very predictable and lifelike paintings were being overpainted in wild, squiggly lines, which turned out to be exactly what his art dealer and the art dealer's clients wanted. Mr. Horrox quickly adopted the Gratch's style, rewarded the Gratch with string, and became rich. *cmt*

**3.114** Richard, Françoise. **On Cat Mountain**. Translated by Arthur A. Levine. Illustrated by Anne Buguet. Putnam, 1994. Originally published as *La Montagne aux Chats* by Albin Michel Jeunesse in 1993. ISBN0-399-22608-7. 30 p. (7-12). Picture book. **France**.
Sho, a servant girl in Japan, coped with her hate-filled employer by pouring out her dreams and hopes to Secret, her cat. When the cat was thrown out, kind Sho went to Cat Mountain, despite warnings that she would never return. Because of her kindness, Sho was protected from danger and given gold by the strange cat-humans on Cat Mountain.The evil mistress, greedy for gold, met an altogether different, though well-deserved, fate, when she came to the mountain. Highly textured paper in sumptuous collages featuring figures in traditional Japanese dress and poses provide a suitable setting for this Japanese folktale. *cmt*

**3.115** Rondón, Javier. **The Absent-Minded Toad**. Translated by Kathryn Corbett. Illustrated by Marcela Cabrera. Kane/Miller, 1994. Originally published as *Sapo Distraído* by Ediciones Ekaré-Banco del Libro in 1988. ISBN 0-916291-53-7. 32 p. (3-6). Picture book. **Venezuela**. This good-natured story in verse follows a toad as he surveys his pantry, outfits himself very snazzily and goes off to the market. So overwhelmed is he by all the activity that he forgets to bring home anything on his list. The lively market illustrations include many details of clothing, animals, and foodstuffs indigenous to Venezuela. *jl*

**3.116** Rose, Deborah Lee. **The People Who Hugged the Trees. An Environmental Folk Tale.** Illustrated by Birgitta Saflund. Roberts Rinehart, 1990. Originally published by Roberts Rinehart International in 1990. (paperback: Roberts Rinehart, 1994). ISBN 0-911797-80-7. 32 p. (7-12). Picture book. **Ireland**.
Long ago in Rajasthan, India, a village people lived in a desert and prized their trees for shade and protection, especially during sand storms. When a greedy majarajah ordered the trees to be cut down and used for his fortress, a brave young woman risked her life to defy the orders. Her whole village then rallied around her and the Majarajah, impressed with her courage, let the trees stand. The values conveyed in this beautifully illustrated folktale—respect for nature and civil disobedience—are still valid today. *mb*

**3.117** Rowe, John A. **Baby Crow.** Illustrated by the author. North-South Books, 1994. Originally published as *Raben-Baby* by Michael Neugebauer Verlag AG in 1994. ISBN 1-55858-277-0. 32 p. (4-6). Picture book. **Switzerland.**
Since he is descended from a long line of illustrious singers, Baby Crow is expected to have a wonderful voice, but he can only make a weak, "Beep." Grandfather Crow solves this problem when he removes a cherry pit from Baby Crow's throat, but creates another problem when Baby Crow, whose voice is indeed enormous, sings around the clock. Father Crow finds a solution—more cherries! Glowing illustrations provide droll humor. *cmt*

**3.118** Rowe, John A. **Jack the Dog.** Illustrated by the author. Picture Book Studio/Simon & Schuster, 1993. Originally published by Michael Neugebauer Verlag in 1993. (paperback: North-South, 1996). ISBN 0-88708-266-1. 32 p. (4-6). Picture book. **Switzerland.**
Jack, an appealing floppy-eared dog, is enveloped by a thick London fog

and ends up on a freighter to Japan. In the process of finding a cup of hot tea, he partakes of the culture of Japan, including a deep tub bath and lessons in Japanese etiquette and garb. Just as he is finally ready for that tea, he is jerked out of his dream and back to reality, where his owner has fixed him (what else?) a cup of tea. Rowe's illustrations abound with deft allusions to Japanese culture and quirky details. *ss*

**3.119** Rowe, John A. **Peter Piglet**. Illustrated by the author. North-South, 1996. Originally published as *Ferkel Ferdinand* by Nord-Süd Verlag in 1996. ISBN 1-5585-660-1. Unpaginated. (4-6). Picture book. **Switzerland**.
Strolling through the woods, Peter finds a pair of beautiful golden shoes. He learns to walk in them and in time grows to love them. When he wakes one morning to discover that his golden shoes have vanished, he begins a search which leads to a tortoise, who has recently come into possession of a golden palace to replace his lost shell. Thus begins a cumulative tale in which Piglet learns that happiness cannot be found in possessions, but in bringing happiness to others. The illustrator's use of black background accentuates the gold metallic paint used for the shoes. *djg*

**3.120** Sato, Satoru. **I Wish I Had a Big, Big Tree**. Translated by Hitomi Jitodai and Carol Eisman. Illustrated by Tsutomu Murakami. Lothrop, 1989. Originally published as *Ōkina ki ga hoshii* by Kaisei-sha in 1984. ISBN 0-688-07303-4. 38 p. (4-7). Picture book. **Japan**.
Kaoru wishes that he had a tree to climb, but his yard just has a few bushes. Kaoru imagines his tree into a towering daydream, complete with a hollow center, a tree house, and lots of friendly squirrels and birds that will keep him company throughout the year. During Kaoru's dream, the illustrations rotate to allow the vast trunk to grow "up" through each double-page spread. *cmt*

**3.121** Scammell, Ragnhild. **Buster's Echo**. Illustrated by Genevieve Webster. Willa Perlman Books, 1993. Originally published as *Woof! Woof!* by All Children's Company Ltd. ISBN 0-06-022883-0. Unpaginated. (4-6). Picture book. **Great Britain**.
When Buster the dog, a rooster, and a cow hear woofs, cock-a-doodle-do's, and moos from across the valley, they decide to chase away their challengers. They are joined by a mouse who wants to chase away a

mean rat (though no one hears him). When the group gets to the other side of the valley, they find no one, but still hear those challenging replies to their woofs, cock-a-doodle-do's, and moos. Believing that they have scared their challengers over to *their* hill, they return home, find no one, and are convinced that they have chased the interlopers away. Only the mouse realizes that there were never any foes. The bright paintings with bold black outlines feature the "echoes" in large bold type that decreases in size to symbolize the fading sound. *cb*

**3.122** Scammell, Ragnhild. **Three Bags Full.** Illustrated by Sally Hobson. Orchard, 1993. Originally published by ABC in 1993. ISBN 0-531-05486-1. 26 p. (3-5). Picture book. **Great Britain.**
Millie, a sheep, is generous to a fault. She gives away all her wool to bird, badger, and rabbit in the early spring and is left shivering, until Mrs. Farmer knits her a new sweater. Soon, however, the sweater begins to unravel and the giving cycle starts over. Millie's gamboling and humorous expressions, the saturated greens and blues of the early spring scenes, and the rounded shapes of hills and animals create a gentle, warm mood for this circular story. *jvl*

**3.123** Schami, Rafik. **Fatima and the Dream Thief.** Translated by Anthea Bell. Illustrated by Els Cools and Oliver Streich. North-South, 1996. Originally published as *Fatima und der Traumdieb* by Neuer Malik Verlag in 1992. ISBN 1-55858-653-9. Unpaginated. (7-9). Picture book. **Germany.**
Hassan sets out to find work to provide for his widowed mother and younger sister, Fatima. Desperation drives him to work for an evil giant who offers a gold coin for a week's toil. Hassan must agree to keep his temper or lose the coin as well as his dreams. Worked to the bone and purposely provoked, Hassan loses his bargain and returns home emptyhanded and dreamless. Spunky Fatima sets off to redress this injustice and outwits the giant. Lavish watercolor illustrations add humor and life. *djg, mew*

**3.124** Schubert, Ingrid and Schubert, Dieter. **The Magic Bubble Trip.** Translated by Kane/Miller Book Publishers. Illustrated by the authors. Kane/Miller, 1985. Originally published as *Helemaal Verkikkerd* by Limniscaat b. v. Rotterdam in 1981. (paperback, Kane/Miller, 1985). ISBN 0-916291-02-2 (paperback: 0-916291-03-0). 24 p. (4-6). Picture

book. **Netherlands.**
James loves frogs, but his parents will not have them in their apartment. Sad, James resorts to blowing soap bubbles, but is suddenly enveloped in a bubble and transported to a land of giant, grassy-backed, playful frogs. A friendly inventor, Mr. Odds-and-Ends, takes James home in his Heli-plane, and there James finds his parents happily playing with several giant grass frogs. James's future looks brighter. *cmt*

**3.125** Sheldon, Dyan. **The Whales' Song**. Illustrated by Gary Blythe. Dial, 1991. Originally published by Hutchinson in 1990. ISBN 0-8037-0972-2. 32p. (4-6). Picture book. **Great Britain.**
Luminous oil colors and lyrical text tell the story of Lilly, a young girl enchanted with her grandmother's stories of the whales she used to see off the pier near her home. Though the whales no longer inhabit the ocean in that area, Lilly brings them a flower and waits all day for them to appear. They do not, but late that night she wakes up to find them, leaping and singing in the moonlight, just as her grandmother described. *Kate Greenaway Medal. al. Editor's note: Author is American, illustrator is British.*

**3.126** Siekkinen, Raija. **Mister King**. Translated by Tim Steffa. Illustrated by Hannu Taina. Carolrhoda, 1987. Originally published as *Herra Kuningas* by Otava Publishing Company Ltd. in 1986. ISBN 0-87614-315-X. 32 p. (7-9). Picture book. **Finland.**
A king with no subjects became so sad that he could not appreciate the wondrous beauty of his home and its surroundings. Then a cat moved in, and the little king regained his joy of living through caring for the cat. Later, a village grew up around the castle. The king, happy to have subjects (and neighbors) at last, was generous and benevolent to all. The villagers, unaware that the kind little man was a king, thought of him as just a neighbor named King, but all were content. *Biennale of Illustrations Bratislava Grand Prix. cmt*

**3.127** Simmonds, Posy. **Fred.** Illustrated by the author. Knopf, 1987. Originally published by Jonathan Cape Limited in 1987. ISBN 0-394-88627-5. 24p. (4-6). Picture book. **Great Britain.**
Sophia and Nick are sad that their cat, Fred, has died. They bury Fred in the backyard and go to bed, but are awakened by meowing. It is Ginger,

a neighbor's cat, soon joined by many cats, all dressed in formal attire for the funeral of their friend, "Famous Fred." Nick and Sophia's memories of their pet are expanded when they learn that Fred sang with the band, "The Heavy Saucers," at night. Dialogue in speech balloons and illustrations help convey the story and add humor. *jg*

**3.128** Simmonds, Posy. **Lulu and the Flying Babies.** Illustrated by the author. Knopf, 1988. Originally published by Jonathan Cape Limited in 1988. ISBN 0-394-89597-5. 24 p. (4-6) Picture book. **Great Britain**.

Lulu's anger at having to do what is best for her baby brother reaches its climax when she must visit the art museum rather than play in the snow because it is too cold for the baby outside. As she stubbornly sulks on a sofa, two cherubs leave their picture and join her. They transport Lulu from painting to painting, entering each for an adventure. On the way home, Lulu's father listens to her tales; likewise, the museum curator listens to the cherubs' stories, while escorting them back to their painting. *jg*

**3.129** Smith, Helen (adapter). **Inch Boy**. Illustrated by Junko Morimoto. Viking, 1986. Originally published by William Collins Pty. Ltd., in 1984. ISBN 0-14-050677-2. (4-8). Picture book. **Australia**.

Buddha answered the prayers of an old couple and sent them a miraculous child only one inch long, but with the heart of a lion and the determination of a giant. Determined to become a Samurai warrior, Inch Boy made his way to Kyoto and there became a special bodyguard to the princess. When a huge Demon threatened the princess, Inch Boy, using his wits and his needle-sized sword, saved the day and was transformed into General Horikawa, a Samurai whose size and gallantry matched Inch Boy's bravery and indomitable spirit. Glowing watercolors reminiscent of Japanese calligraphy provide a sense of the story's origins. *Highly Commended: Australian Picture Book of the Year Award, 1985.* *cmt*

**3.130** Smith, Helen. **Kojuro and the Bears**. Freely adapted from a story by Kenji Miyazawa. Illustrated by Junko Morimoto. HarperCollins (paperback), 1991. ISBN 0-7322-7228-9. 32p. (6-10). Picture book. **Australia**.

Kojuro and the bears he hunts on Mt. Nametoko live in mutual respect of each other, realizing that life inevitably will permit each a turn at the top. Kojuro begs forgiveness of a huge bear he has trapped, saying, "I have no hate for you, but I must kill you...the choice is not mine." Years later, he hears the same words from the massive bear that kills him. As Kojuro lies lifeless, encircled by bears in silent vigil over his body, his spirit intones, "The wheel has turned. Forgive me, bears." The multiple layers of this adaptation of a classic Japanese children's story are enriched by the haunting illustrations of the Japanese-Australian artist. *Australian Children's Picture Book of the Year Award. bt*

**3.131** Steiner, Jörg. **The Animals' Rebellion**. Translated by Susan Leubuscher and Tadzio Koelb. Illustrated by Jörg Müller. Atomium, 1990. Originally published as *Aufstand der Tiere oder Die neuen Stadmusikanten* by Sauerländer in 1989. ISBN 156-182-025-3. 32 p. (7-12). Picture book. **Switzerland**.

Four much-used animal logos (such as the alligator on Izod shirts) hear that they are about to be discarded. Making the first move, they leave their corporate employer to seek their fortune in this contemporized version of *The Brementown Musicians*. Only at the end do careful readers realize that the characters have been watching a film of their story, making this a complex story within a story within a story. *German Children's Literature Picture Book Prize. cmt*

**3.132** Steiner, Jörg (from an idea by Frank Tashlin). **The Bear Who Wanted to Be a Bear**. Illustrated by Jörg Müller. Atheneum, 1977. Originally published as *Der Bär der ein Bär bleiben wollte* by Sauerländer AG, Aarau, in 1977. ISBN 0-689-50079-3. 32p. (8-14). Picture book. **Switzerland**.

Upon awakening one spring to find that his cave has been completely overbuilt by a factory during his winter hibernation, a bear is drummed into the work force! His protestations ("I am a bear!") are to no avail, and he must live the dreary, confined life of a factory worker for months. But, as the next winter approaches and his bearish instincts assert themselves, he falls asleep on the job, is fired, and regains his freedom. Müller's surreal paintings contribute both humor and a stark and chilling contrast between nature and technology in this parody of modern life. *Müller: Hans Christian Andersen Award for Illustration. cmt*

**3.133** Steiner, Jörg. **Rabbit Island**. Translated by Ann Conrad Lam-

mers. Illustrated by Jörg Müller. Harcourt, 1978. Originally published as *Die Kaninchininsel* by Verlag Sauerländer in 1977. ISBN 0-15-265034-2. 32 p. (10-14). Picture book. **Switzerland.**
Big Gray Rabbit lives in a sanitized, orderly rabbit factory with all the food he wants to eat and the hope of eventually being taken to a rumored place where good rabbits are forever "protected." In truth, these rabbits are being fattened for slaughter. Little Brown Rabbit, a newcomer to the factory, convinces Big Gray to escape with him. But unaccustomed to the perils of the wild, Big Gray soon decides that he prefers the "security" of his cage to the responsibilities that come with freedom and returns to the factory. *Mildred Batchelder Award, 1979; Müller: Hans Christian Andersen Award for Illustration, 1994. mew*

**3.134** Storm, Theodor. **Little Hobbin**. Translated by Anthea Bell. Illustrated by Lisbeth Zwerger. North-South Books, 1995. Originally published as *Der kleine Häwelmann* by Michael Neugebauer Verlag AG in 1995. ISBN 1-55858-460-9. 15 p. (4-6). Picture book. **Switzerland.**
Hobbin slept in a crib on wheels and loved to be wheeled around. In fact, he could never get enough of it, so he wore his poor mother out. Hobbin then rolled his crib out of his room, out onto the street, and up into the sky. The kind moon followed him, but Hobbin rolled the crib over Moon's nose. At this, Moon gave way to Sun, who soon dampened Hobbin's wild escapade. This cautionary tale was written in 1849. *mja*

**3.135** Sundvall, Viveca. **Santa's Winter Vacation**. Translated by Kjersti Board. Illustrated by Olof Landström. R&S Books, 1995. Originally published as *Ruben* by Rabén & Sjögren in 1994. ISBN: 91-29-62953-5. (4-9). Picture book. **Sweden.**
Reuben Stormfoot and his wife, Hosannah, met the Sandworm family while vacationing in the Canary Islands. Johannes, the youngest of the three Sandworm brothers, thinks that Reuben is nice; his brothers think that the tango-dancing, bearded old man is wacky. Reuben next meets the Sandworms on Christmas Eve when he arrives with gifts, and an especially large one for Johannes. Is Reuben really Santa? Resting somewhere between reality and fantasy, this story makes an important statement about the Christmas spirit. Cartoon-style illustrations add many humorous details. *cmt*

**3.136** Sutcliff, Rosemary, reteller. **Black Ships Before Troy**. Illustrated by Alan Lee. Delacorte, 1993. Originally published by Frances Lincoln in 1993. ISBN 0-385-31069-2. 128p. (10-14). Picture book for older readers. **Great Britain**.

Taken from *The Iliad*, this retelling begins with Helen's flight with Paris and ends with the destruction of Troy. Alternately dreamy and minutely detailed, the watercolor paintings heighten the power of this moving myth. *Kate Greenaway Medal. al*

**3.137** Sutcliff, Rosemary. **The Minstrel & the Dragon Pup**. Illustrated by Emma Chichester Clark. Candlewick, 1993. (paperback: Candlewick, 1996). Originally published by Walker in 1993. ISBN 1-56402-098-3. 48 p. (7-9). Picture book. **Great Britain**.

A wandering minstrel encounters a dragon pup hatching from a lost egg, and the two become inseparable. The minstrel finds that having something to love and care for inspires him to sing and play more beautifully than ever. When the dragon pup is stolen, the minstrel must rely on the power of his music to recover his companion. Clark's muted pastel illustrations create a lush medieval backdrop for this original tale. *ss*

**3.138** Taylor, C. J. (reteller) **How Two-Feather Was Saved from Loneliness**. Illustrated by the reteller. Tundra, 1990. ISBN 0-88776-254-9. Unpaginated. (4-9). Picture book. **Canada**.

In this retelling of "The Origin of Corn," the Corn Goddess leads Two-Feather to a vast meadow, shows him how to start a fire, and with her hair plants corn so that the Abenaki people can settle down. *dd*

**3.139** Tejima, Keizaburo. **Fox's Dream**. Translated by Susan Matsui. Illustrated by the author. Philomel, 1987. Originally published as *Kitakitsune no yume* by Fukutake Publishing in 1985. ISBN 0-399-21455-0. 40 p. (5-9). Picture book. **Japan**.

In a snow-covered, moonlit landscape a lone fox hunts. Chasing a snow hare leaves him in unfamiliar territory, and ice-covered trees take on the appearance of various animals. The fox recalls scenes from its brief life, walks on, and, as day dawns, meets a mate. Gorgeously rendered woodcuts in black, white, and pale blues provide a frosty, mysterious nighttime setting. *New York Times Best Illustrated Books Award. See also: Ho-Limlim: A Rabbit Tale from Japan. cmt*

**3.140** Toye, William. **The Loon's Necklace**. Illustrated by Elizabeth

Cleaver. Oxford, 1977. ISBN 0-19-540278-2. 24 pp. (7-9). Picture book. **Canada**.
This traditional tale explains why the loon wears a white necklace around his black throat. An old man, his wife, and young son are starving because the man is blind and can't hunt. When the boy helps his father kill a bear, an evil hag takes the meat from them. The old man goes in despair to sing of his misery to the wise loon, who restores his sight. In return, the old man flings a necklace of beads around the loon's neck, thus gracing that bird forever with his distinctive white markings. *Amelia Frances Howard-Gibbon Award*. *lg*

**3.141** Trezise, Percy and Roughsey, Dick. **Gidja the Moon**. Illustrated by Dick Roughsey. Gareth Stevens, 1988. Originally published by William Collins in 1984. ISBN 1-55532-948-9. 32 p. (7-9). Picture book. **Australia**.
In this Aboriginal folk tale, Gidja the Moon marries Yalma, the Evening Star girl. When their child, Lilga the Morning Star, is killed accidentally, the people try to kill Gidja for bringing death into their midst. When he survives, they throw him into the sky where he dies but comes back to life. Yalma and Lilga also get places in the sky. The illustrator is an Aboriginal man whose primitive style of paintings lends authenticity. U.S. edition includes an introduction by Kathy Keller, a map, and a glossary. *bkn*

**3.142** Trezise, Percy and Roughsey, Dick. **Turramulli the Giant Quinkin**. Illustrated by Dick Roughsey. William Collins, 1982. ISBN 0-00-184343-5. 32 p. (4-6). Picture book. **Australia**.
Turramulli the Giant Quinkin is an aboriginal mythical being. Its name meant thunder and it ate children, and so it was feared by all back in Dream Time. Then, one day Turramulli tumbled to his death as he chased two children, Moonbi and Leeanlin. Illustrations show indigenous Australian people, animals, and plants, as well as the mythical creatures, the Quinkins, and their cave painting representations. The clay-red and golden tones, with refreshing blues for a pond and flowers reflect the Australian wilderness. *Children's Book Council of Australia. Highly Commended Picture Book*. *jvl*

**3.143** Trinca, Rod, and Argent, Kerry. **One Woolly Wombat**. Illustrated by Kerry Argent. Kane/Miller, 1985. Originally published by Omnibus

Books in 1982. (paperback: Kane/Miller, 1987). ISBN 0-916291-00-6 (paperback: 0-916291-10-3). 29 p. Picture book. **Australia**.

The numbers one through fourteen are introduced by animals indigenous to Australia. Large, humorous, personified illustrations, rhyme, and alliteration make the sparse text of this counting book predictable and appropriate for beginning readers. *cmt*

**3.144** Trivizas, Eugene. **The Three Little Wolves and the Big Bad Pig**. Illustrated by Helen Oxenbury. Simon & Schuster, 1993. Originally published by Heinemann in 1993. ISBN 0-689-50569-8. 32p. (4-6). Picture book. **Great Britain**.

This parody on "The Three Little Pigs" pits cuddly, lovable little wolves against a ferocious pig. The pig sumarily destroys the wolves' houses of bricks and armor plates. They then build a house of flowers. As the relentless Pig inhales to blow the house down, he sniffs the wonderful aroma of the flowers, and "his heart grows tender." The three little wolves, convinced that the pig has indeed had a change of heart, offer to let him stay with them, and they all live happily ever after. Illustrations add to the humor of the story. *American Library Association Notable Books for Children; School Library Journal Best Book of the Year. mja*

**3.145** Troughton, Joanna (reteller). **The Quail's Egg: A Folktale from Sri Lanka**. Illustrated by Joanna Troughton. Bedrick/Blackie, 1988. Originally published as *The Quail's Egg* by Blackie and Son, London in 1988. ISBN 0-87226-185-9. 24 p. (4-6). Picture book. **Great Britain**.

In this cumulative tale, a quail goes looking for assistance when her egg rolls and lodges in a rock crevice. No one will help her—not the stonemason, not the pig, not the thorny creeper, not the fire, not the water pool—until she talks to the cat, who readily agrees to chase the mouse, who runs up the elephant's leg who muddies the water pool, and so on, until the stonemason agrees after all to free the egg. *CCBC Choices. jl*

**3.146** Vá, Leong. **A Letter to the King**. Translated by James Anderson. Illustrated by the author. HarperCollins, 1991. Originally published as *Brevet til Kongen* by Det Norske Samlaget in 1987. ISBN 0-06-020079-0. 29 p. (4-9). Picture book. **Norway**.

Chinese tradition holds that sons are more desirable than daughters, since they will care for their parents better in old age. In this ancient tale, a village doctor was jailed unjustly. The youngest of his five daughters,

Ti Ying, wrote a letter to the emperor asking for mercy and offering to serve her father's sentence for him. The king was so moved that he freed the doctor and sent them both home. From then on, the doctor was glad that he had daughters. The colorful and exuberant illustrations, executed when the artist was a child, are distinctly Chinese. *cmt. Editor's note: The author is Chinese and lives in Norway.*

**3.147** Velthuijs, Max. **Frog and the Stranger**. Illustrated by the author. Tambourine, 1994. Originally published by Andersen Press in 1993. ISBN 0-688-13267-7. 25 p. (2-6). Picture book. **Netherlands**.
When a rat moves into the forest neighborhood, many animal residents want him to leave, because rats are thieving and dirty. First Frog, and then others, find out that Rat is actually nice, clever, and helpful. They are disappointed when he eventually decides to move on. Large, simple, richly colored illustrations will help nonreaders to enjoy this story independently. *American Booksellers Pick of the Lists. cmt*

**3.148** Velthuijs, Max. **Frog in Love**. Translated by Anthea Bell. Illustrated by the author. Farrar, 1989. Originally published by Andersen Press in 1989. ISBN 0-374-32465-4. 24 p. (4-6). **Netherlands**.
Frog feels strange, and Hare diagnoses his condition. He is in love! Frog realizes that this is true. He is in love with Duck! Pig avows that frogs cannot love ducks, but Frog nearly kills himself showing Duck how he feels. As Duck nurses the injured Frog, their feelings for one another come out. Love knows no boundaries. *cmt*

**3.149** Vivas, Julie. **The Nativity**. Illustrated by the author. Harcourt, 1988. Originally published by Omnibus Books in 1986. ISBN 0-15-200535-8. 36 p. (4-9). Picture book. **Australia**.
With excerpts from the King James version of the Bible and large, expressive watercolor illustrations, the illustrator tells the story of the birth of Jesus. Using humor and visual hyperbole, Vivas recreates the well-known characters of Mary and Joseph, presenting them as innocent peasants. Very accessible to young children. *cmt*

**3.150** Voake, Charlotte. **Mrs. Goose's Baby**. Illustrated by the author. Little, 1989. Originally published by Walker in 1989. (paperback: Dell, 1992). ISBN 0-316-90511-9. 24 p. (4-6) Picture book. **Great Britain**.
Mrs. Goose adopts an egg and lovingly dotes on her hatchling, even

when it prefers grain to grass, cheeping to honking, and pecking to swimming. Pastel watercolor pictures set against a white background explain all. This story of mother love and the acceptance of differences is well suited for read-aloud story hours. *mb*

**3.151** Waddell, Martin. **Can't You Sleep, Little Bear?** Illustrated by Barbara Firth. Candlewick Press, 1992. Originally published by Walker in 1988. (paperback: Candlewick Press, 1994). ISBN 1-56402-007-X (paperback: 1-56402-262-5). Unpaginated. (3-6). Picture book. **Great Britain**.
When a wakeful Little Bear has trouble falling asleep, Big Bear tries a variety of comforting activities to ease Little Bear's fear of the dark. Tender pastels depict both the comforting closeness of the bears' cave and the vast, silent night sky as the two bears leave the cave to confront the dark outside. *Kate Greenaway Medal. al*

**3.152** Waddell, Martin. **Farmer Duck**. Illustrated by Helen Oxenbury. Candlewick Press, 1992. Originally published by Walker Books Ltd. in 1991. ISBN 1-56402-009-6. 34 p. (4-6). Picture book. **Great Britain**.
While a lazy farmer lounged in bed all day, his industrious duck did all the work. Eventually reduced to a sleepy, weepy state, the duck collapsed. The barnyard animals took charge, chased the farmer away, and joined the duck in caring for *their* farm. Effective use of light and shadow in the illustrations helps to establish mood, as in the wonderfully contrasting endpages. *cmt*

**3.153** Waddell, Martin. **The Park in the Dark**. Illustrated by Barbara Firth. Lothrop, 1989. Originally published by Walker Books in 1989. ISBN 0-688-08516-4. 27 p. (1-6). Picture book. **Great Britain**.
Three stuffed animals leave their owner's bedroom at night for a romp in the playground. They brave the scary shadows and enjoy the park. The THING that eventually scares them back to their owner's bed is revealed in the illustrations—a train. Verse and repetition help make the text predictable. Soft colors evoke an urban nighttime setting. *Kurt Maschler Award. cmt*

**3.154** Wagner, Jenny. **The Bunyip of Berkeley's Creek**. Illustrated by Ron Brooks. Bradbury, 1977. Originally published by Kestrel in 1973. (paperback: Viking, 1980). ISBN 0-87888-122-0. (paperback: 0-14050-

126-6). 32 p. (6–8). Picture book. **Australia.**
A creature emerges from the mud of Berkeley's Creek. It learns from a platypus that it is a bunyip. A wallaby and an emu tell it that it looks horrible, and a man tells it that it doesn't really exist. Coming to a billabong pond, the bunyip is happy to find another bunyip when she crawls from the mud. Belittled and scorned by others, he gains identity and happiness with his friend. Illustrations are mainly earthtone brown and green; the ugly beast is not nearly so threatening as the man's complex machine. *Australian Picture Book of the Year. jsn*

**3.155** Weninger, Brigitte. **Ragged Bear.** Translated by Marianne Martens. Illustrated by Alan Marks. North-South, 1996. Originally published as *Teddybär* by Michael Neugebauer Verlag in 1996. ISBN 1-55858-662-8. 25 p. (3-6). Picture book. **Switzerland.**
An old teddy bear became more and more ragged until his owners discarded him in the park in the rain. There, he was rescued by someone else, taken home, washed, repaired, and loved again. Large, soft watercolor illustrations give the bear much appeal. *cmt*

**3.156** Wensell, Ulises. (Adapted from a poem, *El Pessebre*, by Joan Alavedra, 1943). **They Followed a Bright Star.** Illustrated by Ulises Wensell. G.P. Putnam, 1994. Originally published as *Sie folgten einem hellen Stern* by Ravensburger Buchverlag Otto Maier GmbH in 1993. ISBN 0-399-22706-7. 40 p. (4-6). Picture book. **Germany, Spain.**
In this retelling of the Nativity story, the shepherds, as they follow the star, encounter a well-tender, a fisherman, a plowman, and winemakers. They cannot accompany the shepherds, because they have been instructed by angels to prepare water, fish, bread, and wine for when it is needed. These instructions presage events in Jesus's life. Full-page, jewel-tone watercolor illustrations underscore the characters' wonder at this event. *jl, cmt*

**3.157** Wild, Margaret. **Going Home.** Illustrated by Wayne Harris. Scholastic, 1994. Originally published by Ashton Scholastic in 1993. ISBN 0-590-47958-X. 30 p. (4-7). Picture book. **Australia.**
While Hugo is in the hospital, he looks out at the zoo next door and daydreams of traveling to far-off wildernesses with various animals. Detailed illustrations help compare Hugo's confined hospital environment and the zoo cages with the wide, unspoiled animal habitats around

the world. All creatures want to be in their own homes. *cmt*

**3.158** Wild, Margaret. **The Very Best of Friends.** Illustrated by Julie Vivas. Harcourt Brace, 1990. Originally published by Margaret Hamilton Books, 1989. ISBN 0-15-200077-1. 32p. (4-9). Picture book. **Australia.**
Jessie and James had many animals on their farm, but William the cat was James's favorite and his constant companion. Then James died, and Jessie shut herself away in sorrow, rejecting William's attempts to comfort her. Forgotten and unloved, William became wild and mean until Jessie was startled into realizing how much William needed her love. In learning to love one another, Jessie and William begin to recover. Vivas's expressive illustrations capture the rough-hewn Australian Outback and track William's progression from gentle companion to fearsome feral beast, and back again. *Australian Picture Book of the Year Award. cmt*

**3.159** Wormell, Mary. **Hilda Hen's Search.** Illustrated by the author. Harcourt, Brace, 1994. Originally published by Victor Gollancz in 1994. ISBN 0-15-200069-0. 32 p. (3-5). Picture book. **Great Britain.**
Since the henhouse is full, Hilda searches the farmyard to find the perfect spot to lay her eggs. Text and illustrations both carry the story forward, as Hilda dialogues with herself each time she nestles into a new place. The close-up illustrations portray each place as perfect...until the page is turned. Then the spot is revealed for what it is: a bicycle basket, a laundry tub, a horse's feeding bin, all currently in use. Colorful linocut illustrations suit this timeless and satisfying story of the search for a place of one's own. Sequel: *Hilda Hen's Happy Birthday* (Harcourt, Brace, 1995). *ss*

**3.160** Wynne-Jones, Tim. **Zoom Away.** Illustrated by Ken Nutt. Groundwood/ Douglas & McIntyre, 1985. ISBN 0-88899-042-1. (4-6). Picture book. **Canada.**
Zoom the Cat takes an imaginary journey to the North Pole to search for his uncle who has yet to return from his journey there. Zoom's daring gets him to the Pole and back without mishap, returning to the safety and warmth of Maria's fireplace. *Amelia Frances Howard-Gibbon Award. lg*

**3.161** Yagawa, Sumiko. **The Crane Wife.** Translated by Katherine

Paterson. Illustrated by Suekichi Akaba. Morrow, 1981. Originally published as *Tsuru-nyobo* by Fukuinkan Shoten in 1979. (paperback: Mulberry, 1987). ISBN 0-688-07048-5. 32 p. (7-9). Picture book. **Japan.**
Soon after Yohei, a poor young peasant, helps an injured crane, a woman appears at his door and asks to be his wife. She mysteriously weaves exquisite cloth that provides for their needs, but Yohei's curiosity about how the cloth is woven and his desire for more wealth results in his wife's departure. Includes pronunciation guide to Japanese names and onomatopoeic words. *Akaba: Hans Christian Andersen Medalist for Illustration; Paterson: Newbery Medalist. jy*

**3.162** Zeman, Ludmila. **Gilgamesh the King**. Illustrated by the author. Tundra, 1992. ISBN 0-88776-283-2. Unpaginated. (4-9). Picture book. **Canada.**
Set in ancient Mesopotamia, the legend of Gilgamesh, the cruel king of Uruk, is simply told with bold illustrations reminiscent of Egyptian paintings. After a fight, Enkidu and Shamhat persuade the king to make Uruk a happy place instead of a violent one. *dd*

**3.163** Zeman, Ludmila. **The Revenge of Ishtar**. Illustrated by the author. Tundra, 1993. ISBN 0-88776-315-4. Unpaginated. (4-9). Picture book. **Canada.**
The monster Humbaba destroys the city of Uruk and Shamhat is killed. The Goddess Ishtar is rejected by Gilgamesh, and she returns to take her revenge. Enkidu dies of a fatal illness and Shamhat comes as a bird to take his spirit away. Evil seems to have won in this, the second book of the Gilgamesh trilogy. *dd*

## Informational Picture Books

**4.1** Anno, Mitsumasa. **Anno's Math Games**. Translated by Fred Balin and Jane Elliot. Illustrated by the author. Philomel, 1987. Originally published as *Hajimete Deau Sugaku No Ehon* by Fukuinkan Shoten in 1982. ISBN 0-399-21151-9. 103 p. (7-9). Picture book. **Japan.**

Fundamental mathematical concepts are presented through words, games, and clearly-drawn illustrations gauged to encourage thinking and looking at things in a new way. Sets, combining, sequence, and measurement are introduced. Afterword for parents, teachers and other older readers explains the author's motives. See also: *Anno's Math Games II* (1989, ISBN 0-399-21615-4, concepts of relationships, comparisons, the structure of matter, symbols, and units of measure); *Anno's Math Games III* (1991, ISBN 0-399-22274-X, concepts of space and dimensions, triangles and geometry, mazes and electric circuits, and left- and right-handedness). *cmt*

**4.2** Anno, Mitsumasa. **Anno's Medieval World**. Translated by Ann Beneduce. Illustrated by the author. Philomel, 1980. Originally published as *Kuso Kobo* by Fukuinkan Shoten in 1979. ISBN 0-399-20742-2. 46 p. (7-12). Picture book. **Japan.**

During the Middle Ages the general population gradually changed from one view of the universe to another. Using antique-toned, double-page spreads, the author provides glimpses of the era during which one mode of thinking dominated by superstition and guesswork was replaced by a mode of thinking based on science. *cmt*

**4.3** Armstrong, Carole. **Lives and Legends of the Saints**. Simon and Schuster, 1995. Originally published by Frances Lincoln Limited in 1995. ISBN 0-689-80277-3. 45 p. (10-12). Informational book. **Great Britain.**

Paintings from art museums around the world portray each of the twenty Christian saints described in the text. In the section on St. Francis of Assisi, for example, the author notes that the painting by Giotti is just one of several of Assisi that the artist did. She comments that St. Francis chose a simple monastic life over his monied inheritance and that he loved people and animals. Information about the art is given in each case. For example, symbols within the painting by Giotti are explained.

*jg*

**4.4** Cousins, Lucy. **Country Animals**. Illustrated by the author. Tambourine, 1991. Originally published by Walker in 1990. ISBN 0-688-10070-8. Unpaginated. (1-3) Board book. **Great Britain**.
*Country Animals* is part of an appealing board book set of four which also includes *Farm Animals*, *Garden Animals*, and *Pet Animals*. Each of the books presents ten animals, eight on square, single pages and two on double-page spreads. Animals are identified by a single hand-lettered word on each page. The animals are illustrated in bold colors with wide black outlines. With childlike illustrations, these titles have much child appeal and provide an alternative and pleasing style of art in the board book format. *cb*

**4.5** Ekoomiak, Normee. **Arctic Memories**. Illustrated by the author. Holt, 1990. Originally published in Canada in 1988 by NC Press. ISBN 0-8050-1254-0. 32 p. (4-9). Informational book. **Canada**.
This informational book is about life in the Arctic as lived by the Inuit people. The author illustrates this book with his paintings and wall hangings. He describes shelters, fishing, travel, games, and the Nativity. Text is in both English and Inuktitut. *dd*

**4.6** Epple, Wolfgang. **Barn Owls**. Translated by Amy Gelman. Photographs by Manfred Rogl. Carolrhoda, 1992. Originally published as *Die Schleiereule* by Kinderbuchverlag Reich Luzern in 1988. ISBN 0-87614-742-2. 48 p. (7-9). Informational book. **Switzerland**.
A family of barn owls is followed from nest building to mating to raising five young over a period of two months. Facts about the physical features, hunting techniques, food preferences, and family life of these owls are given in well-written text and startlingly clear and detailed photographs. Glossary and index provided. *cmt*

**4.7** Fischer-Nagel, Heiderose and Fischer-Nagel, Andreas. **The Housefly**. Photographs by the authors. Carolrhoda, 1990. Originally published as *Stubenfliege* by Kinderbuchverlag KBV in 1988. ISBN 0-876-14374-5. 48 p. (7-9). Picture book. **Switzerland**.
With revealing photographs and lively text, the authors manage to put the common housefly in a positive light and may convince young readers to pay closer attention to this pesky insect. The housefly's physical

characteristics (very clean!), habits, natural environment, and relationship with humans are described. *cmt*

**4.8** Gomi, Taro. **Seeing, Saying, Doing, Playing**. Illustrated by the author. Chronicle, 1991. Originally published as *Kotoba Zukan 1— Ugoki no Kotoba* by Kaisei-sha in 1985. ISBN 0-87701-859-6, 25 p. (4-6). Informational book. **Japan**.
Humorous and interesting scenes of a neighborhood, schoolroom, street, farm, swimming pool, campground, zoo, park, market, amusement park, and ice skating rink fill this book. Participants' activities are labelled with an action word describing what they are doing, such as singing, fighting, tickling, and fleeing. *jy*

**4.9** Gryski, Camilla. **Cat's Cradle, Owl's Eyes: A Book of String Games**. Illustrated by Tom Sankey. Morrow, 1984. Originally published by Kids Can, Toronto, in 1983. (paperback: Beech Tree, 1984). 78 p. (7-12) Informational book. **Canada**.
This is the first of a series of books done by Gryski which intends to pass along the lore of string games. They come, like folktales, from different countries and cultures, which she cites in short introductions. Twenty-one figures are presented with easy-to-follow, step-by-step illustrations including the internationally famous and centuries-old "Cat's Cradle." Sequels include *Many Stars & More String Games* (1985) and *Super String Games* (1988). *mb*

**4.10** Gryski, Camilla. **Friendship Bracelets**. Illustrated by the author. Morrow Junior Books, 1993. Originally published by Kids Can Press in 1992. ISBN 0-688-12435-6. 48 p. (10-12). Informational book. **Canada**.
The author describes, in step-by-step instructions, how to make 14 friendship bracelets using different colors of embroidery threads. The instructions are numbered, have clear illustrations, and are easy to follow. *dd*

**4.11** Harvard, Christian. **The Wolf: Night Howler**. Photographs by the author. Charlesbridge, 1996. Originally published as *Le Loup, Brigand des Bois* by Éditions Milan in 1994. ISBN 0-88106-436-X (paperback). 26 p. (7-9). Picture book. **France**.
Distinguished by abundant, high-quality photographs and clear, fact-filled text and captions, this book covers the life cycle of the wolf.

Sections at the back provide information about efforts to protect the wolf, a look at the extended canine family, and sources for further information. Part of the *Animal Close-Ups* series that features bees, cheetahs, deer, elephants, foxes, giraffes, hippopotamuses, penguins, polar bears, seals, and whales. *cmt*

**4.12** Jin, Xuqi and Kappeler, Markus. **The Giant Panda.** Translated by Noel Simon. Putnam, 1986. Originally published as *Der Grosse Panda: Bedrohtes Leben im Bambuswald* by Kinderbuchverlag KBV Luzern in 1986, in collaboration with Xinhua Publishers, Bejing. ISBN 0-399-21389-9. 48 p. (10-12). Informational photo essay. **Switzerland.**
With simple yet detailed text and marvelous pictures, a present-day portrait of the panda is rendered. Main topics include natural habitat in China, habits, threats to the animal's existence, and efforts to save and breed the species. Especially well presented is the series of photographs of the panda from newborn to near adult size. *CCBC Choices. jl, djg*

**4.13** Kaizuki, Kiyonori. **A Calf Is Born.** Translated by Cathy Hirano. Illustrated by the author. Orchard, 1990. Originally published as *Koushi Ga Umareta yo* by Fukutake Publishing in 1988. ISBN 0-531-05862-X. Unpaginated. (5-7). Picture book. **Japan.**
One cold winter night a calf is born. Full double-page oil paintings chronicle the first day of the calf's life as it nurses, takes its first steps, ventures out of doors, is treated by a veterinarian, investigates the barnyard, and returns to the barn for the night. Just enough of the birthing process is shown to stimulate interest and good questions. Gold, brown and white palette enhances the feel of a crisp winter's day in the country. *cmt*

**4.14** Kindersley, Barnabas and Kindersley, Anabel. Sue Copsey, compiler. **Children Just Like Me.** Photographs by Barnabas Kindersley. Dorling Kindersley, 1995. Originally published by Dorling Kindersley Limited in 1995. ISBN 0-7894-0201-7. 82 p. (7-12). Picture book. **Great Britain.**
Each of five sections introduces individual children from the Americas, Europe, Africa, Asia, and Southeast Asia and Australasia. Crisp photographs of the children and their families, homes, schools, communities, foods, and favorite things are surrounded by informative captions and quotes from the children. Emphasis is on similarities of children around

the world. Includes authors' travel diary, details on joining the UNICEF-endorsed "Children Just Like Me Penpal Club," table of contents, and index. Related title by same authors: *Celebrations. cmt*

**4.15** Klinting, Lars. **Bruno the Carpenter**. Translated by the publisher. Illustrated by the author. Holt, 1996. Originally published as *Castor Snickrar* by Alfabeta Bokförlag AB. ISBN 0-8050-4501-5. 32 p. (7-9). Picture book. **Sweden**.
Bruno the Beaver's workshop is messy, and so he builds a toolbox to hold his tools. The step-by-step procedure, illustrations of each tool used, and an accurate set of toolbox plans all show that work can be satisfying, when done right. Watercolor illustrations show how each tool is used. In *Bruno the Tailor* (Holt, 1996) the beaver makes an apron. *cmt*

**4.16** Les Chats Pelés. **Long Live Music!** Translated by Carol Volk. Illustrated by the authors. Harcourt, 1995. Originally published as *Vive la Musique!* ISBN 0-15-201310-5. 46 p. (8-14). Informational book. **France**.
A history of musical instruments and forms of music, beginning with the bone flute in neolithic times (40,000 B.C.) and continuing to the 20th century are presented in innovative text and illustrations. Facts are strung on a story of Phil and Pippo the dog who are being chased by Silence the Giant. Silence is trying to destroy them and all musical instruments, but when the heroes build and play a washtub bass, Silence is defeated and music reigns again. *mew*

**4.17** Lucht, Irmgard. **The Red Poppy**. Translated by Frank Jacoby-Nelson. Illustrated by the author. Hyperion, 1995. Originally published as *Roter Mohn* by Ravensburger Buchverlag in 1994. ISBN 0-786-80055-0. 27 p. (5-9). Picture book. **Germany**.
The miracle of a flower and the many forms of life connected to it are captured in large, striking acrylic illustrations. The text describes how a red poppy grows, unfolds, and reproduces during the summer. End Notes provide further explanations of aspects of the illustrations. Author's Note gives a glimpse of the author's inspiration and techniques for creating her work. *cp*

**4.18** Massin. **Fun With Numbers**. Translated by Carol Volk. Illustrated by Les Chats Pelés. The Creative Company/Harcourt Brace, 1995.

Originally published as *Jouons avec les chiffres* by Editions du Seuil in 1993. ISBN 0-15-200962-0. 32 p. (7-9). Picture book. **France.**

Phil and his dog, Pippo, visit ancient civilizations to learn how counting and measuring systems began and how they influence our lives today. Wacky illustrations demonstrate how numbers can be made to look like people or animals. *cmt, djg*

**4.19** Michels, Tilde. **At the Frog Pond.** Translated by Nina Ignatowicz. Illustrated by Reinhard Michl. Lippincott, 1989. Originally published as *Am Froschweiber* by Deutscher Tascherbuch Verlag in 1987. ISBN 0-397-32314-X. Unpaginated. (4-6). Informational picture book. **Germany.**

The warm days of spring bring signs of life to a secluded frog pond. The cycle of life is explained in simple terms as tadpoles emerge from wobbly clusters of frog eggs, night gives way to dawn, and spring becomes summer. Detailed watercolor illustrations enhance the descriptive text. *djg*

**4.20** Micklethwait, Lucy. **I Spy a Lion: Animals in Art.** Greenwillow, 1994. Originally published by HarperCollins Ltd. in 1994. ISBN 0-688-13230-8. 46 p. (4-9). Picture book. **Great Britain.**

In each of twenty full-color reproductions of works of fine art an animal appears. On the facing page the animal's name is prefaced with the words, "I spy with my little eye." Readers are at first challenged to find the featured animals, but invariably the paintings, selected for their narrative quality, are then enjoyed for their beauty, the stories they tell, or their variation in style. Artist and title for each work are given. In a summary at the end, the owner of each work of art is given. *cmt*

**4.21** Morozumi, Atsuko. **One Gorilla: A Counting Book.** Illustrated by the author. Farrar, 1990. Originally published by Bodley Head in 1990. (paperback: Sunburst, 1993). ISBN 0-374-35644-0. 26 p. (4-6). Picture book. **Great Britain.**

Elaborate, pastel, double-page spreads count 10 animals commonly known to preschool children. The wealth of detail in the different landscape scenes in which the animals are hidden deserve many readings. *A New York Times Best Illustrated Children's Book of the Year. mb*

**4.22** Muller, Gerda. **Around the Oak.** Illustrated by the author. Dutton,

1994. Originally published as *Unser Baum* by Ravensburger Buchverlag in 1991. ISBN 0-525-45239-7. 39 p. (7-9). Picture book. **Germany**.
Nick and his visiting cousins explore the forest where he lives, noting plants, animals, and seasonal changes. Detailed drawings and paintings provide clear identification of the life and activity in this temperate zone hardwood forest. *jg*

**4.23** Nanao, Jun. **Contemplating Your Bellybutton**. Illustrated by Tomoko Hasegawa. Kane/Miller, 1995. Originally published as *Oheso Ni Kiite Goran* by Akane Shobo Company in 1985. ISBN 0-916291-60-X. 32 p. (3-6). Picture book. **Japan**.
This engaging look at the origin, reason for, and care of the bellybutton features Tettchan, who asks, "Why do I need a bellybutton anyway?" Large, uncomplicated pastel drawings give cutaway views of Tettchan developing in the womb and being born. Excellent for parent-child reading and discussion. *cmt*

**4.24** Onyefulu, Ifeoma. **Ogbo: Sharing Life in an African Village**. Photographs by the author. Harcourt, 1996. Originally published by Frances Lincoln, 1996. ISBN 0-15-200498-x. Unpaginated. (7-9). Picture book. **Great Britain**.
Six-year-old Obioma tells about the Ogbo, groups of same-age village children to which all children in Obioma's tribe belong. Members of the Ogbo work and play together sharing the tasks and responsibilities, joys and celebrations of village life. Obioma tells about her Ogbo. The author grew up in this village and was herself a member of an Ogbo. *djg*

**4.25** Peach, Susan. (Ed.). **The DK Geography of the World**. DK Publishing, 1996. Originally published by Dorling Kindersley Ltd. in 1996. ISBN 0-7894-1004-4. 304 p. (7-14). Illustrated resource book. **Great Britain**.
Each of six continental sections begins with an overview of the continent and peoples. Details about life in individual countries follow, heavily illustrated with photographs, maps, and illustrations. The reference section contains subjects of general interest, such as world religions or political systems. Includes glossary, gazetteer, and index. *cmt*

**4.26** Petit, Geneviève. **The Seventh Walnut**. Translated by Dagmar Herrmann. Illustrated by Joëlle Boucher. Wellington Publishing, 1992.

Originally published as *La Septième Noix* by Editions Didier in 1991. ISBN 0-922984-10-7. 32 p. (7-9). Picture book. **France.**

A boy takes seven walnuts to school, but loses one in the woods on the way. The walnut is a potential meal for a squirrel, a magpie, a dormouse, and a water rat, but each time, some predator intervenes, demonstrating several simple food chains. Uneaten, the walnut takes root and grows into a majestic tree. The boy, now a grown man with a son of his own, wonders how the tree came to grow there. Large illustrations clearly identify each animal. Further information on the plants and animals mentioned in the story and a walnut cake recipe are provided. *cmt*

**4.27** Schmid, Eleonore. **The Air Around Us.** Translated by J. Alison James. Illustrated by the author. North-South, 1992. Originally published as *Winde wehen, vom Lufthauch bis zum Sturm* by Nor-Süd Verlag in 1992. ISBN 1-55858-165-0. 26 p. (6-9). Picture book. **Switzerland.**

In spare text and full double-page spread landscape illustrations, the varying conditions and uses of air are effectively explained. Subtle environmental warnings are included. *NCSS-CBC Notable Children's Trade Book in the Field of Social Studies.* See also: *The Water's Journey. cmt*

**4.28** Schmid, Eleonore. **The Living Earth.** Illustrated by the author. North-South, 1994. Originally published as *Die Erde lebt* by Nord-Süd Verlag in 1994. ISBN 1-55858-298-3. 26 p. (7-9). Informational picture book. **Switzerland.**

Double-page spreads offering panoramic scenes and cutaway views dominate this presentation of Earth's complex ecosystem. Paragraphs of text placed at the bottom of each page provide a clear explanation of the layers that comprise the earth and detail the roles played by animals, plants, and other living organisms, including humans, in renewing Earth's valuable resources. *ss*

**4.29** Scholes, Katherine. **Peace Begins with You.** Illustrated by Robert Ingpen. Sierra Club, 1990. Originally published by Hill of Content Publishing in 1989. ISBN 0-316-77436-7. 37 p. (7-12). Picture book. **Australia.**

In easy to understand language, the concept of peace is explained. Discussion of the nature of conflict, conflict resolution, and ways to be a peacemaker increase the value of this book. Muted color pencil drawings will help readers understand that it is people like themselves who make or disturb peace. *Ingpen: Hans Christian Andersen Medalist for Illustration. cmt*

**4.30** Schubert, Ingrid and Schubert, Dieter **Amazing Animals**. Translated and adapted by Leigh Sauerwein. Illustrated by Dieter Schubert. Front Street/Lemniscaat, 1995. Originally published as *Van Mug tot Olifant* by Lemniscaat in 1994. ISBN 1-886910-05-7. 32 p. (4-9). Picture book. **Netherlands**.
Through sumptuous illustrations assisted by spare, rhyming text, assorted animals of the world are presented, though not named. The focus is on these animals' natural behavior, habits, and life cycles. Best used as a stage for further explanation or investigation. *National Parenting Publications Award. mew, cmt*

**4.31** Sellier, Marie. **Cézanne from A to Z**. Translated by Claudia Zoe Bedrick. Peter Bedrick Books, 1996. Originally published as *C comme Cézanne* by Réunion des Musées nationaux in 1995. ISBN 0-87226-476-9. 59 p. (9-YA). Informational book. **France**.
The life of the French artist, Cézanne, is presented in an alphabetical sequence of words that focus on key elements of his life and works. Each letter of the alphabet is accompanied by a reproduction of one of the artist's paintings to help tell his story. The location of each painting is provided in the Acknowledgments. Learn about other artists (e.g., Chagall, Matisse) in the *Artists from A to Z* series. *mew*

**4.32** Shemie, Bonnie. **Houses of Bark: Tipi, Wigwam and Longhouse**. Illustrated by the author. Tundra Books of Northern New York, 1990. Originally published by Tundra Books in 1993. ISBN 0-88776-246-8. 24 p. (7-12). Picture book. **Canada**.
In alternating double-page spreads of text and colored pencil illustrations, three types of dwellings of the Native American tribes of the northern woodlands are described. Materials, architectural features, and construction procedures are included. Pencil sketches provide additional information. Native Dwellings Series includes six titles, plus Teacher's Kit. *cmt*

**4.33** Svedberg, Ulf. **Nicky the Nature Detective**. Translated by Ingrid

Selberg. Illustrated by Lena Anderson. R&S Books, 1988. Originally published as *Maja Tittar på Naturen* by Rabén & Sjögren in 1983. ISBN 91-29-58786-7. 50 p. (10-12). Informational book. **Sweden**.

Accompanied by cheerful illustrations of Nicky, an inquisitive, bespectacled girl, elements of nature and the four seasons are explored. Topics include trees, flowers, insects, birds, and mammals. The text encourages observation, experimentation, and curiosity about the wonders of the natural world. *jl*

**4.34** Tracqui, Valérie. **My Home Is the Desert. Who Am I?** Translated by Timothy Froggatt. Photographs by the author. Charlesbridge, 1996. Originally published as *Les Animaux du Désert* by Éditions Milan in 1990. ISBN 0-88106-934-5. Unpaginated. (1-3). Picture book/board book. **France**.

Interesting and unusual desert-dwelling animals are presented, one per page, in large, clear, glossy photographs. Each photograph is accompanied by the animal's name and one fact about it. After several readings, these could become naming books. Others in the Little Nature Board Book series: *My Home Is the Mountains*; *My Home Is the Polar Regions*; *My Home Is the Sea*. *cmt*

**4.35** Vyner, Sue. **Arctic Spring**. Illustrated by Tim Vyner. Viking, 1993. ISBN 0-670-84934-0. Unpaginated. (4-9). Picture book. Originally published by Gollancz in 1992. **Great Britain**.

With the long winter over, a polar bear and her two cubs begin to explore their world above the Arctic Circle. A narwhal, an Arctic fox, a ringed seal, and an Arctic hare are shown as they, too, forage for food. Large watercolor illustrations show the animals in their natural habitat and show the transition of the landscape from winter to spring. The brief text tells more about the region than about the animals found there. Concluding pages give information about each animal and a map of the area. *cb*

**4.36** Wardley, Rachel, Ed. **The Big Book of Animals**. DK, 1997. Originally published by Dorling Kindersley Ltd. in 1997. ISBN 0-7894-1485-6. 48 p. (6-9). Picture book. **Great Britain**.

Habitat types and animal groups are summarized before animals unique to each continent are introduced by region. Text and beautiful photographs are given approximately equal space. With only one or two facts about each animal, the text gives just enough information to encourage further investigation. Includes table of contents and index and brief sections on the coral reef, the ocean, and domestic animals. *cmt*

# TRANSITIONAL BOOKS

**5.1** Blades, Ann. **Mary of Mile 18**. Illustrated by the author. Tundra, 1971. ISBN 0-88776-059-7. Unpaginated. (7-9). Transitional book. **Canada**.

This day in the life of a young Mennonite girl in northern British Columbia in the mid-twentieth century promises to be special for she heard the northern lights sing during the night. She finds a puppy by the roadside, and is certain that this is her special thing. At first, her father refuses to let her keep an animal that does not work for its keep, but when the puppy warns the family of a coyote in the chicken house, it earns a warm place in Mary's bed. *Canadian Children's Book of the Year Award. lg*

**5.2** Bojunga-Nunes, Lygia. **The Companions**. Translated by Ellen Watson. Illustrated by Larry Wilkes. Farrar, 1989. Originally published as *Os Colegas* by J. Olympio in 1972. ISBN 0-374-31465-9. 62 p. (7-9). Transitional book. **Brazil**.

Stony, a street rabbit, Crystal-Voice, an escaped circus bear, and Fleur, a fed-up poodle belonging to a rich, fancy woman, meet each other, become friends and decide to live together. When Crystal-Voice is captured and returned to the circus, and Fleur is caught and returned to her superficial lifestyle, Stony must find a way to rescue his companions. After all, friends stick together. *Bojunga-Nunes: Hans Christian Andersen Medalist for Writing. jk*

**5.3** Bröger, Achim. **The Day Chubby Became Charles**. Translated by Renée Vera Cafiero. Illustrated by Emily Arnold McCully. J.B. Lippincott, 1990. Originally published as *Oma und Ich* by Verlag Nagel & Kimche AG in 1986. ISBN 0-397-32144-9. 90 p. (7-9). Transitional book. **Switzerland.**

Julia is usually annoyed that the silent Chubby follows her and her friend Jacob around. One day, when she arrives home, she finds that her beloved grandmother is sick and maybe dying. Having no one else to tell, she confides in Chubby (whose real name is Charles) and finds that a real friend has been under her nose all along. *IBBY Honour List; German State Prize for Young Adult Literature; CCBC Choice. jl*

**5.4** Crossley-Holland, Kevin. **Storm**. Illustrated by Alan Marks. Originally published by Heinemann in 1985. ISBN 0-434-93232-6. 42p. (7-10). Transitional book. **Great Britain.**

When Annie's sister falls ill, Annie is led to the doctor by the ghost of a farmer who had been murdered while defending himself against two highwaymen. An appropriately eerie house in a vast marsh provides the setting for this spare drama. *Carnegie Medal. al*

**5.5** Disher, Gary. **The Bamboo Flute**. Ticknor & Fields, 1993. Originally published by Angus & Robertson in 1992. ISBN 0-395-66595-7. 82p. (7-9). Transitional book. **Australia.**

In 1932 Australia is in the grip of the Great Depression. Desperate men, "swaggies", roam the countryside working for food or stealing it. Paul, twelve, dreams of the past, when music and laughter were part of his life. Then a swaggie teaches him how to build a wooden flute. This, and Paul's remarkable musical skill, must remain secret, as his father has forbidden him to speak to swaggies, particularly one who has killed one of their sheep. Balance is restored when Paul plays his flute and his father realizes that this gift is well worth the sheep. *Australia's Book of the Year for Younger Readers Award. cmt*

**5.6** Fourie, Corlia. **Ganekwane and the Green Dragon: Four Stories from Africa**. Translated by Madeleine van Biljon. Illustrated by Christian Arthur Kingue Epanya. Albert Whitman, 1994. Originally published simultaneously in Afrikaans and English by Human & Rousseau in 1992. ISBN 0-8075-2744-0. 40 p. Transitional book. **Republic of South Africa.**

The tales in this entertaining, handsomely illustrated collection have both African and European origins. "Hlaulu and the Beast in the Forest" tells of a girl who overcomes her fear of a beast and discovers its roar is actually a howl of pain. "The Middle Sister and the Tree" tells of three sisters who rescue a small bird and are each granted a wish. "The Girl with the Laughing Voice" tells of a clever chief and his equally clever daughter. "Ganekwane and the Green Dragon" is about the power of story. Includes a glossary of Afrikaan terms and a pronunciation guide. *djg*

**5.7** Geras, Adèle. **My Grandmother's Stories: A Collection of Jewish Folk Tales**. Illustrated by Jael Jordan. Knopf, 1990. Originally published by Heinemann Young Books in 1990. ISBN 0-679-80910-4. 96p. (7-9). Transitional book. **Great Britain**.
When a young girl visits her grandmother, she hears these ten Jewish folktales, each called to mind by something in the apartment. For example, some silver buttons imprinted with the face of a king remind the grandmother of "The Faces of the Czar," in which a Russian farmer promises that he will not answer a question until he has seen the face of the Czar a hundred times—accomplished when he is given one hundred silver rubles, each with the face of the Czar imprinted on it. *jg*

**5.8** Hänel, Wolfram. **The Old Man and the Bear**. Translated by Rosemary Lanning. Illustrated by Jean-Pierre Corderoc'h. North-South, 1994. Originally published as *Der kleine Mann und der Bär* by Nord-Süd Verlag in 1994. ISBN 1-55858-253-3. 43 p. (6-8). Transitional book. **Switzerland**.
Initially rivals for the salmon swimming up the river, an old man and a bear learn to cooperate after they are swept downriver and land on a little island. They find that a varied diet is better than salmon every day. Bright illustrations help to make the text predictable. *cmt*

**5.9** Hendry, Diana. **The Not-Anywhere House**. Illustrated by Thor Wickstrom. Lothrop, 1991. Originally published by Julia MacRae in 1989. ISBN 0-688-10194-1. 48 p. (7-9). Transitional book. **Great Britain**.
Hannah hates that her family is moving from Dungee Farm Cottage with its beautiful talking willow outside her window. She doesn't like the new house in the city at all because it is so empty and cold. But as familiar,

cozy things begin to fill up the new house, Hannah decides that it looks like home after all. *CCBC Choices. jl*

**5.10** Hewitt, Garnet. **Ytek and the Arctic Orchid**. Illustrated by Heather Woodall.Vanguard, 1981. Originally published as *Ytek and the Arctic Orchid: An Inuit Legend* by Douglas & McIntyre in 1981. ISBN 0-8149-0836-5. 38p. (7-12). Transitional book. **Canada**.
This Inuit legend of the Arctic Barrens celebrates the inderdependence of Inuit and caribou and the mystical yet practical relationship the Inuit people have with the spirits of the earth. Ytek, a young shaman, sets out to discover why the caribou no longer migrate to the Inuit hunting grounds. His spiritual helper is a huge gyrfalcon who leads him to the place where the spirits of the caribou dwell and then helps him defeat the huge polar bear who is decimating the herds. Ytek returns to his people with the promise of spring. *Amelia Frances Howard-Gibbon Award. lg*

**5.11** Impey, Rose. **Desperate for a Dog**. Illustrated by Jolyene Knox. Dutton, 1989. Originally published by A & C Black, 1988. ISBN 0-525-44513-7. 62 p. (7-9). Transitional book. **Great Britain**.
The book is cleverly divided into "five rounds" (or chapters) as a metaphor for the battle two young sisters wage to convince their parents to let them have a dog. Persistent cajoling proves ineffective, but suddenly a neighbor, Mrs. Roper, must go to the hospital. The girls generously offer to mind her dog, Toby. When it's time for Toby to go back home, the house seems too empty and quiet, even for the parents. The girls' good deed has given them an opportunity to prove their responsibility, and their father rewards them with their own dog. Black and white line drawings with speech bubbles will entertain beginning readers. *djg, cb*

**5.12** Johansen, Hanna. **7x7 Tales of a Sevensleeper**. Translated by Christopher Franceschelli. Illustrated by Käthi Bhend. Dutton, 1989. Originally published as *Siebenschläfergeschichten* by Nagel & Kimche in 1985. ISBN 0-525-44491-2. 95 p. (7-9). Transitional book. **Switzerland**.
A sevensleeper is a kind of dormouse that lives in trees and eats nuts. When the author's son declared one morning that he was a sevensleeper too, she made up these stories for him, all revolving around the number seven. Hidden objects in the illustrations for these forty-nine stories reflect the sevensleeper's habit of hiding found objects. *CCBC Choices.*

*jl*

**5.13** Kidd, Diana. **Onion Tears**. Illustrated by Lucy Montgomery. Orchard, 1991. Originally published by William Collins in association with Anne Ingram Books in 1989. ISBN 0-531-05870-0. 62 p. (7-10). Transitional book. **Australia**.

When soldiers take away Nam-Huong's father, her mother sends her with Grandpa to escape by boat, the rest of the family remaining in Vietnam to wait for Father. Nam-Huong arrives in Australia, where she adjusts to life with a Vietnamese guardian. A second story is told in a series of letters Nam-Huong writes to a canary, a water buffalo, and other creatures from home. As the letters reveal the horror of Nam-Huong's past experiences, her numb silence begins to soften, until a culminating memory unleashes a flood of real tears, not just those she gets from chopping onions. *ss*

**5.14** King-Smith, Dick. **Sophie's Snail**. Illustrated by Claire Minter-Kemp. Delacorte, 1989. Originally published by Walker in 1988. ISBN 038-5298242. 65 p. (7-12). Transitional book. **Great Britain**.

Four-year-old Sophie amuses her family when she announces her intention to become a farmer and keeps "flocks" of snails and "herds" of centipedes. Her family never doubts that one day she will be a lady farmer for Sophie is a very determined girl. Further adventures: *Sophie's Tom* (1991); *Sophie Hits Six* (1993); *Sophie in the Saddle* (1994); *Sophie Is Seven* (1995); and *Sophie's Lucky* (1995). *djg*

**5.15** Klein, Robin. **Thing**. Illustrated by Alison Lester. Oxford, 1982. ISBN 0-19-554549-4. 32 p. (7-9). Transitional book. **Australia**.

Desperate for a pet, but living in a "No Pets Allowed" apartment, Emily settles on a pet rock and names it Thing. In the overheated apartment, the "rock" hatches into a tidy, well-behaved stegosaurus! All goes well until the landlord discovers the animal, banishes it to the yard, and threatens to have it stuffed and placed in a museum. That afternoon, however, Thing foils an attempted burglary and wins the landlord's approval and unending devotion. *Australia's Children's Book of the Year for Younger Readers Award. cmt*

**5.16** Korschunow, Irina. **Adam Draws Himself a Dragon**. Illustrated by Mary Rahn. Harper, 1986. (paperback: Harper Trophy. 1988) Originally published as *Hanno Malt Sich einen Drachen*. ISBN 0-060-23249-8 (paperback: 0-064-40229-0). 57 p. (6-8). Transitional book. **Switzerland**.

A young dragon comes to stay with Adam for awhile. They help one another overcome the problems that make their school days unhappy. *cmt*

**5.17** Korschunow, Irina. **Small Fur**. Translated by James Skofield. Illustrated by Reinhard Michl. Harper & Row, 1988. Originally published as *Kleiner Pelz* by Verlag Nagel & Kimche in 1984. ISBN 0-06-023247-1. 72 p. (7-9). Transitional book. **Switzerland**.

Small Fur is very sad when his friend Brown Fur moves away. Moreover, his Aunt Grouch has come for a long visit, and all she does is criticize him. Life improves when Little Fur goes through a magic gate and helps an elf with a missing wing, meets the legendary terrible Nock (who is just lonely), and gets to fly with the elf's borrowed wings. Curly Fur moves into Brown Fur's old house, and though the magic gate disappears, Small Fur is happy to have a new friend. *jl*

**5.18** Korschunow, Irina. **Small Fur Is Getting Bigger**. Translated by James Skofield. Illustrated by Reinhard Michl. Harper & Row, 1990. Originally published as *Kleiner Pelz Will Grösser Werden* by Verlag Nagel & Kimche AG in 1986. ISBN 0-06-023289-7. 70 p. (7-9). Transitional book. **Switzerland**.

Small Fur's Uncle Ned has very strict ideas about child rearing. After he tells his nephew how weak and lazy he is, Small Fur runs away. A gurgle-girl tries to pull Small Fur into the swamp, but Trulla, whom everyone says is a Fog Witch, thwarts the attempt. Grateful to Trulla but uncertain about whether she has magic powers or not, Small Fur returns home, feeling stronger and bigger. *jl*

**5.19** Kraan, Hanna. **Tales of the Wicked Witch**. Translated by Elisabeth Koolschijn. Illustrated by Annemarie van Haeringen. Front Street/ Lemniscaat, 1995. Originally published as *Verhalen Van de Boze Heks* by Lemniscaat in 1990. ISBN 1-886910-04-9. 107 p. (7-9). Transitional book. **Netherlands**.

In fourteen brief episodes a woodland witch struggles to uphold a witchlike image. Although the animals at times find her antics annoying, they also enjoy the excitement she causes. The animals realize that kindness is their best defense and deflect much of the witch's mischief by showing her that they love her. *cmt*

**5.20** Lassig, Jürgen. **Spiny**. Translated by J. Alison Kames. Illustrated by Uli Waas. North-South Books, 1995. Originally published as *Keine Spur von Spino-Dino* by Nord-Süd Verlag in 1995. ISBN 1-55858-401-3. 58 p. (7-9). Transitional book. **Switzerland**.
Spiny, a newly hatched spinosarus, cries out in hunger, sending his parents off in search of food. While they are gone, Spiny decides to explore and gets lost. Many different kinds of dinosaurs help to locate Spiny and save him from the terrible Tyrannosaurus Rex. Watercolor illustrations add an emotional dimension to this fantasy. Some difficult vocabulary, but children interested in the subject will not be deterred. *db*

**5.21** Little, Jean. **Hey World, Here I Am!** Illustrated by Sue Truesdell. Harper & Row, 1986. Originally published by Kids Can Press in 1986. ISBN 0-06-023989-1. 88 p. (7-9). Transitional book. **Canada**.
Kate Bloomfield, about eight, loves to write. Her poems and prose are collected in this slim volume. They cover a variety of topics from her feelings about being Jewish to mosquitoes—whatever Kate feels like writing about. *dd*

**5.22** Mahy, Margaret. **The Good Fortunes Gang**. Illustrated by Marian Young. Delacorte, 1993. Originally published in 1993. ISBN 0-385-31015-3. 100 p. (7-9). Transitional book. **New Zealand**.
In this first book of "The Cousins Quartet" the five ten-year-old cousins of the Fortune family are brought together for the first time when Pete moves with his family from Australia back to the family compound in New Zealand. Tessa, Tracey, and Jackson admit Pete into their club, the Fortunes Gang, but only after he has bravely met their challenges. Subsequent books deal with Lolly's finding acceptance into the club, Tessa's fund-raising adventure, and siblings Tracey and Jackson's learning to be independent of one another. These characters are very "clean" and their problems are not overwhelming. See also: *A Fortunate Name*; *A Fortune Branches Out*; *Tangled Fortunes*. *cmt*

**5.23** Mowat, Farley. **Owls in the Family**. Illustrated by Robert Frankenburg. Little, Brown, 1961. Originally published by McClelland & Stewart in 1961. LCCN 62-7169. 107 p. (7-12). Transitional book. **Canada**.

The author's childhood in Saskatoon in the great plains of Saskatchewan included an animal menagerie. When two great horned owls, named Wol and Weeps, are added to this collection, the neighborhood feels the difference. During the three years that the owls are a part of the Farley family, the author is continually surprised at their distinct personalities, intelligence, and adaptability. *cmt*

**5.24** Nabb, Magdalen. **Josie Smith**. Illustrated by Pirkko Vainio. McElderry, 1989. Originally published by William Collins & Sons in 1988. ISBN 0-689-50485-3. 72 p. (6-8). Transitional book. **Great Britain**.

Josie, about six, is well meaning and all too human. Her best efforts somehow go awry, as when she tries to refurbish her secondhand blackboard and gets paint all over everything. Josie's adventures while getting her mother a birthday present, running away from home, and adopting a cat give the reader a view of urban life in England. Pen and ink drawings help establish Josie's spunky character. *Smarties Book Award. cmt*

**5.25** Orr, Wendy. **Ark in the Park**. Illustrated by Kerry Millard. Angus & Robertson, 1994. ISBN 0-207-17633-7. 72p. (5-9). Transitional book. **Australia**.

Lonely Sophie lives with her busy, immigrant parents in an apartment that overlooks the world's biggest, most wonderful petstore. The owners of this amazing Noah's Ark are the elderly Mr. and Mrs. Noah, who have everything they ever wished for, except their one impossible wish— grandchildren. Sophie has her own impossible wishes, a pet and cousins, but on her seventh birthday she is granted her third wish, a visit to Noah's Ark. Sophie's meeting the kindly owners begins a beautiful friendship that enables all their "impossible wishes" to come true. *Australian Children's Book of the Year for Younger Readers Award. bt*

**5.26** Pearce, Philippa. **Lion at School and Other Stories**. Illustrated by Caroline Sharpe. Greenwillow, 1985. Originally published by Kestrel Penguin in 1985. ISBN 0-688-05996-1. 122 p. (4-6). Transitional book. **Great Britain**.

This collection of nine short stories combines fantasy, adventure, animals, and a bit of suspense. Examples include: a lion who promises to eat up a little girl unless she takes him to school with her; a little boy who runs away rather than face the mess he has made with the laundry; a mouse who is given a reprieve from a trap by an independent child; and a crooked little finger that magically gets Judy everything she wants. The other stories feature children in similarly amazing situations. Pen and ink drawings occasionally accent the stories. Perfect for read-aloud. *bb*

**5.27** Rodda, Emily. **The Best-Kept Secret.** Illustrated by Noela Young. Holt, 1990. Originally published by Angus & Robertson in 1988. ISBN 0-8050-0936-1. 119p. (7-9). Transitional book. **Australia.**

Jo, eleven, joins several other people from her village on a mysterious carousel ride that takes them seven years into the future, where they are allowed to spend one hour. Although the riders are unable to remember what they saw in future time, they gain a sense of hope, or not, as they deserve. A tantalizing explanation for the *déjà vu* phenomenon. *Australia's Children's Book of the Year for Younger Readers Award. cmt*

**5.28** Rodda, Emily. **Pigs Might Fly.** Illustrated by Noela Young. Puffin, 1988. Originally published by Angus & Robertson in 1986. ISBN 0-14-032634-0. 118 p. (7-9). Transitional book. **Australia.**

Rachel, seven, wishes that something interesting would happen to her but is not prepared for a visit to the "Inside," a world where an Unlikely Events Factor (UEF) in the air allows pigs to fly and causes people to do very odd things. While "Inside," Gloria's efforts to return home lead to the reunion of a long-lost child and her family and to the discovery that an interesting family friend has also been "Inside." Rachel makes it back to her world, along with a bottleful of UEF. *Australia's Children's Book of the Year for Younger Readers Award. cmt*

**5.29** Rodda, Emily. **Something Special.** Illustrated by Noela Young. Holt, 1989. Originally published by Angus & Robertson in 1984. ISBN 0-8050-1127-7. 74p. (7-9). Transitional book. **Australia.**

After helping her mother sort out secondhand clothes to sell at the school fair, Sam meets in a dream four of the original owners who reminisce about their "specials" or favorite articles of clothing. At the fair, Sam watches in wonder as each "special" seems to attract just the right buyer. Then she recognizes an elderly man as one of her dream characters and helps to reunite him with his favorite dressing gown. She's offered a glimpse of her own future when her mother gives her silver dancing shoes, formerly owned by a lovely young woman. *Australia's Children's Book of the Year for Younger Readers Award. cmt*

**5.30** Ruepp, Krista. **Midnight Rider**. Translated by J. Alison James. Illustrated by Ulrike Heyne. North-South Books, 1995. Originally published as *Mitternachtsreiter* by Nord-Süd Verlag in 1995. ISBN 1-1-55858-620-2. 58 p. (6-9). Transitional book. **Switzerland**.
Charlie's head has been filled with stories about a ghost, the Midnight Rider. When her own horse dies, she befriends Starbright, sour old Mr. Grimm's spirited horse. When Charlie sneaks out to ride Starbright one stormy night, she is mistaken for the ghost rider. She is thrown from the horse, but Mr. Grimm rescues her, and the two develop a warm friendship. Setting and mood are made real by the watercolor illustrations. *cp*

**5.31** Scheffler, Ursel. **Rinaldo, the Sly Fox**. Translated by J. Alison James. Illustrated by Iskender Gider. North-South Books, 1992. Originally published as *Der schlaue Fuchs Rinaldo* by Nord-Süd Verlag in 1992. ISBN 1-55858-622-9. 59 p. (6-9). Transitional book. **Switzerland**.
Rinaldo the Fox is wanted in Feathertown for stealing a goose and is pursued by Bruno, the Duck Detective. Leaving a string of crimes in his wake, sly Rinaldo evades the law for several weeks. Then, he is caught by Bruno in his own goose trap. Even hanging upside-down, he thinks of a brilliant plan of escape. Will it work? A cliffhanger ending leads to the next book in the series. Cheerful illustrations keep a light mood and make the text predictable. See other books in the series: *The Return of Rinaldo, the Sly Fox* (1993); *Rinaldo on the Run* (1995). *cmt*

**5.32** Scheidl, Gerda Marie. **Loretta and the Little Fairy**. Translated by J. Alison James. Illustrated by Christa Unsner-Fischer. North-South, 1993. Originally published as *Loretta und die kleine Fee* by Nord-Süd Verlag in 1993. ISBN 1-55858-185-5. 61 p. (7-9). Transitional book. **Switzerland**.
Loretta meets a young fairy, Xydaaqe Bowzd, in her backyard. The fairy has been sent to the human world to grow up. Loretta tries to help, but it is only when the fairy helps Loretta and her next-door neighbor to become friends that she is readmitted to the fairy world. Appropriately gauzy illustrations show that the little fairy is being watched over by her kin while she is in the human world. *cmt*

**5.33** Steele, Mary. **Arkwright**. Illustrated by the author. Hyland House, 1985. ISBN 0-908090-78-1. 96 p. (7-9). Transitional book. **Australia**.

In South America on his last voyage before retirement, Captain Chilblain meets Arkwright, a giant anteater with a longing to see the world. Arkwright sails with the captain to Australia where they eventually set up housekeeping in Candlebark, a remote coastal community with magnificent ocean views. The community quickly accepts the captain and his unusual companion, especially after Arkwright enlists the help of his Australian cousins, the echidnas, to rid the community of ant infestation without using harmful pollutants. *Australia's Book of the Year for Younger Readers Award. cmt*

**5.34** Uspensky, Eduard. **The Little Warranty People.** Translated by Nina Ignatowicz. Illustrated by Vladimir Shpitalnik. Knopf, 1994. Originally published by Murmansk Publishing Company in 1989. ISBN 0-679-82063-9. 133 p. (7-9). Transitional book. **Russia**.

Warranty people are the tiny folk who keep machines in working order as long as the warranty is in effect. When a group of warranty people decides to take a trip to the country together, they run afoul of a persistent little girl and a community of mice who take one of them prisoner. Their ingenuity, pluck, and efficient communication network enable the little friends to escape undetected and make their way back to their various factories and homes. *cmt*

**5.35** Uspensky, Eduard. **Uncle Fedya, His Dog, and His Cat**. Illustrated by Vladimir Shpitalnik. Translated by Michael Henry Heim. Knopf. 1993. Originally published by Murmansk Publishing Company in 1989. ISBN 0-679-82064-7. 136 p. (7-9). Transitional book. **Russia**.

Fedya, called *Uncle* Fedya because he was so serious, lived with his parents in the city until his mother refused to let him keep a marvelous talking cat. He and the cat ran away to the country, met up with a talking dog, took up residence in an abandoned house, found a buried treasure, and got along very well. With the help of the local postman, Uncle Fedya's parents located him and arrived just in time to help him cope with a nasty cold. Fedya's mother changed her mind about cats, and they agreed that Fedya should see his animal friends regularly. *cmt*

**5.36** Walsh, Jill Paton. **Birdy and the Ghosties**. Illustrated by Alan Marks. Farrar, 1989. Originally published in Great Britain by Macdonald

Children's Books, 1989. ISBN 0-374-30716-4. 46p. (7-9) Transitional book. **Great Britain.**

Bird Janet, Birdy for short, lives with Papa Jack and Mama Lucy in a cottage by the sea. Papa rows a ferry, and Birdy often accompanies him. On one fateful trip she "sees" some very unusual passengers in the boat. Perhaps it is this experience that helps her learn to trust her senses and prepares her for her continuing adventures in *Matthew and the Sea Singer*. Pale watercolor illustrations add to the magical atmosphere. *djg*

**5.37** Walsh, Jill Paton. **Matthew and the Sea Singer.** Illustrated by Alan Marks. Farrar, 1993. Originally published by Simon and Schuster, London in 1992. ISBN 0-374-34869-3. 46 p. (7-9). Transitional book. **Great Britain.**

Birdy uses her birthday shilling to buy a thin, raggedy boy from an orphan master. Matthew, it turns out, has a beautiful singing voice, and when he sings in the church, even the birds fall silent. One day Matthew disappears into the sea, and Birdy bargains with the seal queen: she will teach a seal-child to sing just as beautifully as Matthew, and in exchange the seal queen will return Matthew to land. She finds that teaching a barking seal-child to sing is no easy task. *ALA Notable Books for Children. jl, djg*

**5.38** Wheatley, Nadia and Rawlins, Donna. **My Place.** Illustrated by Donna Rawlins. Australia in Print, 1989. Originally published by Collins Dove in 1987. ISBN 0-7328-0010-2. Unpaginated. (7-12). Transitional book. **Australia.**

Written and illustrated as journal entries by various children who inhabited the same Australian community from 1788 to 1988, this book chronicles the events and changes brought to Australia by "civilization." Each double-page spread goes back one decade in time and includes a brief narrative of events by a child resident and a hand-drawn map of the community. Startling differences in aboriginals' and white settlers' attitudes toward the land make a poignant conclusion. *Australia's Children's Book of the Year for Younger Readers Award. cmt*

# REALISTIC FICTION

**6.1** Aamundsen, Nina Ring. **Two Short and One Long**. Translated by the author. Houghton Mifflin, 1990. Originally published as *To Korte og En Lang*. ISBN 0-395-52434-2. 103 p. (8-14). Novel. **Norway.**

Jonas, twelve, has always lived a settled, secure life in Oslo. His best friend, Einar (a terrific belcher; hence, the title), lives with his grandparents but spends most of his time at Jonas's. When a family of Afghanistian refugees moves into the neighborhood, Jonas befriends the son, Hewad, but others in the neighborhood display bigotry and prejudice against Hewad's family, and Einar becomes secretive and distant. After Einar reveals his fear of losing Jonas to Hewad, the three form a friendship that is much stronger than the devisiveness of their ignorant neighbors. *Honor Book: Mildred Batchelder Award. mew*

**6.2** Aiken, Joan. **The Wolves of Willoughby Chase**. Illustrated by Pat Marriott. Doubleday, 1963. Originally published by Jonathan Cape Limited in 1962. (paperback: Dell, 1987). LC 63-18034 (paperback ISBN: 0-440-49603-9). 168p. (9-11). Novel. **Great Britain.**

Rich Bonnie Green and her orphan cousin Sylvia are left in the care of the cruel Miss Slighcarp, Mrs. Brisket, and Mr. Grimshaw. These deliciously evil folks have set about to have the Green's fortune and their estate, Willoughby Chase, for their own. But with the help of faithful servants and Simon, the gooseboy, the girls outwit the wicked governess, escape from packs of hungry wolves and restore the estate to its rightful owners. Aiken brilliantly maintains the style of a Victorian melodrama in this satisfying, action-packed adventure. *cw*

**6.3** Alcock, Vivien. **The Cuckoo Sister.** Delacorte, 1985. Originally published by Methuen in 1985. ISBN 0-385-29467-0. 160 p. (10-14). Novel. **Great Britain.**
For years, eleven-year-old Kate and her parents have pondered the fate of her older sister Emma, kidnapped from her baby carriage as an infant. Then suddenly Rosie arrives on their doorstep, with a note from her "mother" confessing to the kidnapping and stating that Rosie is Emma. Could this rough, lower-class girl be the long-lost and much idealized Emma? Rosie, too, must struggle with her true identity and sudden abandonment to this family of strangers. A skillfully woven tale of unlikely associations and reconciliations. *ALA Notable Book; Junior Literary Guild Selection. djg*

**6.4** Aldridge, James. **The True Story of Lilli Stubeck.** Hyland House, 1984. ISBN 0-908090-71-4. 182p. (12-14). Novel. **Australia.**
Lilli Stubeck's deeply felt sense of self, her intelligence, and her family loyalty were quickly recognized after her disreputable family moved to the narrator's small community on the banks of the Murray River in southern New South Wales. When Miss Dalgleish, a rich, cultured spinster, took Lilli in and tried to remake her into a copy of herself, a quiet but intense, ten-year-long battle of strong wills ensued. This story of Lilli's struggle to be herself despite the pressures of mainstream society paints a detailed portrait of smalltown Australia of the 1930s. *Australia's Book of the Year for Older Readers Award. cmt*

**6.5** Aleksin, Anatolii. **A Late-Born Child.** Translated by Maria Polushkin. World, 1971. Originally published as *Pozdnii Rebenok*. 75 p. (10-12). Novel. **Russia**
Lenny was born late in the lives of his parents, and, consequently, they and his adult sister, Ludmilla, are very protective of him. Only Ivan, Ludmilla's fiancé, treats Lenny like an equal. Shortly before Ivan is to return from a six-month-long business trip, he contacts Lenny for help: he has fallen in love with someone else and wants Lenny's help in breaking the news to his sister. Lenny's maturity in dealing with this

situation shows everyone that he is no longer a child. *cmt*

**6.6** Anderson, Rachel. **Black Water**. Holt, 1995. Originally published by Oxford in 1994. (paperback: Paperstar, 1996). ISBN 0-8050-3847-7 (paperback: 0-698-11421-3). 168 p. (10-14). Novel. **Great Britain**.
Albert, growing up in nineteenth-century England, had lived a cloistered life. He was, in the term of that day, a "looney." More specifically, he suffered from epilepsy, but, if discovered, he could easily have landed in an asylum. A gifted artist, he hoped to pursue painting, despite his affliction. As his fits became more violent and various treatments proved useless, Albert fled south to France, where by chance he met Edward Lear, the poet and artist, himself an epileptic. Mr. Lear convinced Albert that travel and experience, not hiding, would develop his talent. *cmt*

**6.7** Anderson, Rachel. **The Bus People**. Holt, 1992. Originally published by Oxford in 1989. ISBN: 0-8050-2297-X (paperback: 0-8050-4250-4). 102 p. (10-14). Novel. **Great Britain**.
Eight vignettes explore the inner worlds of seven children with varying disabilities who ride the bus to their special school. Each vignette is written from the child's point of view, providing logical explanations for seemingly odd behavior and penetrating views of the wonderful connections and sad misunderstandings that often occur between the children and their caregivers. Bertram the busdriver, unschooled but full of common sense, intuitively looks for the best in each child and knows that these children have many of the same desires and motivations as other children. *ALA Best Book for Young Adults. cmt*

**6.8** Baillie, Allan. **Adrift**. Viking, 1992. Originally published by Blackie and Son in 1983. (paperback: Puffin, 1994). ISBN 0-670-84474-8. (paperback: 0-140-37010-2) 119 p. (10-12). Novel. **Australia**.
When Flynn, pretending to be a pirate, allows his pesky little sister Sally to join him on top of the old crate in the shallows, little does he expect that they would soon be drifting out to sea, unable to return to shore. Flynn's rudderless drifting parallels his own psychological drifting from his moorings caused by his family's recent move from a farm to the city and his consequent estrangement from his dad. After two harrowing days and nights at sea, Flynn manages to return to shore. As a result of his experience, he is better able to understand his father and the fact that he must adjust to their new life in the city. *Kathleen Fidler Award. jvl*

**6.9** Bawden, Nina. **Henry.** Illustrated by Joyce Powzyk. Lothrop, 1988. Originally published as *Keeping Henry* by Gollancz in 1988. ISBN 0-688-07894-X. 119 p. (10-12). Novel. **Great Britain.**

Children and their mother, forced out of London into the country by the blitzkrieg of World War II, lovingly raise Henry, a baby squirrel, after he falls out of his nest. They laugh at his antics and become attached to the lively little creature. All the while, they wait for their lives to return to normal and for their father to return home. Unsentimental and full of love and humor, the story is based on actual events from the author's childhood. *bb*

**6.10** Beake, Lesley. **Song of Be.** Holt, 1993. Originally published by Maskew Miller Longman in 1991. ISBN 0-8050-2905-2. 94 p. (12-14). Novel. **Republic of South Africa.**

Be, a Bushwoman of about fifteen, lives with her mother and grandfather on a European's farm at the edge of the Kalahari Desert in what is now Namibia. As Be grows into adulthood, she realizes how harshly her people have been treated by the whites and is told that better days for her people will soon come under a new, black government. As her old world crumbles, she despairs and tries to kill herself, but is found by Khu, a native activist who loves her, and is nursed back to health. *Namibia Children's Book Forum Prize. cmt*

**6.11** Beckman, Gunnel. **Mia Alone.** Translated by Joan Tate. Viking, 1975. Originally published as *Tre Veckor Over Tiden* by Bonniers Bokförlaget in 1973. ISBN 0-670-47394-4. 124 p. (12-YA). Novel. **Sweden.**

Mia, a high school student, is far past due for her monthly period and suspects that she is pregnant. For four grueling days while she waits for the results of a pregnancy test, she projects how having a child would affect her future and deliberates the pros and cons of having an abortion. By the time her period comes a month late, Mia's anguishing experience has forced her to see life as an adult and has helped her to understand her parents and her boyfriend better. *cmt*

**6.12** Bedard, Michael. **Redwork.** Avon, 1992 (paperback). Originally published by Lester & Orpen Denny's in 1990. ISBN 0-88619-276-5. 261p. (12-14). Novel. **Canada.**

With his mother hard at work, Cass has more responsibilities than most high-school boys. When they move into the upstairs flat in an old house, those responsibilities increase when he gets a job at a rundown movie theater to help pay their rent. In time, Cass comes to know his elderly landlord. This mysterious man, a wounded veteran of World War I, is secretly practicing alchemy in the garage behind the house. The lives of Cass and Mr. Magnus are mysteriously connected through memories and dreams. *Canadian Children's Book of the Year Award. lg*

**6.13** Bergman, Tamar. **The Boy from Over There**. Translated by Hillel Halkin. Houghton Mifflin, 1988. Originally published as *ha-Yeled mishamah* in 1984. ISBN 0-395-43077-1. 181 p. (12-14). Novel. **Israel**.
Avramik, a survivor of the Jewish Holocaust in Europe, was brought to a kibbutz in the Jordan Valley by his uncle in 1945. Deeply scarred by his experiences and the loss of his mother, the seven-year-old begins the slow process of assimilation and healing. As the Israeli War of Independence breaks out in 1948, Avramik realizes that he now belongs to this place and will help to defend the new state. *Best Children's Book, Center of Literature for Children and Youth, University of Haifa; Berenstein Prize for Best Children's Book of the Publishers' Association in Israel. cmt*

**6.14** Bohlmeijer, Arno. **Something Very Sorry**. Houghton Mifflin, 1996. Translated by the author. Originally published as *Ik Moetje iets Heel Jammers Vertellen* by Vangorr Publishers, Amsterdam, in 1994. ISBN 0-395-74679-5. 175 p. (9-12). Novel. **Netherlands**.
Nine-year-old Rosemyn and her family are in a car crash. Her mother is killed and her father and younger sister are seriously injured. Based on an actual incident in the author's life, this narration in the voice of his child reveals the emotional struggles Rosemyn has in coming to terms with the loss of her mother. Straightforward descriptions of some hospital procedures. *cmt*

**6.15** Bojunga-Nunes, Lygia. **My Friend the Painter**. Translated by Giovanni Pontiero. Illustrated by Christopher DeLorenzo. Harcourt, 1991. Originally published as *O Meu Amigo Pintor* by J. Olympio in 1987. (paperback: Harcourt, 1995). ISBN 0-15-256340-7. 85 p. (10-12). Novel. **Brazil**.
Claudio tries to understand why his neighbor and friend, a painter, committed suicide. In chapters designated by days of the week, he

remembers the mutual affection they shared, experiences disbelief and sadness, and realizes, only now that his friend is gone, how much the painter taught him about seeing the world and its colors. *Bojunga-Nunes: Hans Christian Andersen Medalist for Writing; CCBC Choices.* jk

**6.16** Boston, Lucy. **A Stranger at Green Knowe.** Voyager/HBJ, 1979. Originally published by Faber in 1961. ISBN 0-15-685657-3. 158p. (10-12). Novel. **Great Britain.**
Ping, a Chinese emigrant who has spent most of his life in refugee camps, sympathizes with Hanno, a magnificent gorilla at the London Zoo. Later, when Hanno escapes the zoo's confines, Ping encounters him in the wild at Green Knowe, where he is spending the summer with the charitable Mrs. Oldknow. A powerful tale of displacement and the yearning for a home. *Carnegie Medal.* al

**6.17** Brinsmead, Hesba F. **Pastures of the Blue Crane.** Puffin, 1978. Originally published by Oxford in 1964. ISBN 0-14-031014-2. 217 p. (12-14). Novel. **Australia.**
Amaryllis Merewether has spent 12 years in posh girls' schools, growing cold and unemotional from lack of family. Just before her graduation, her father dies and leaves her a small fortune, half interest in a farm in New South Wales, and news that she has a grandfather, Dusty. Ryl and Dusty, both at loose ends, spend a trial two months at the farm, and soon come to love the place and one another. Ryl's snobbery and racial prejudice fade as her respect for Perry, a biracial neighbor, grows and as she discovers her own family background. Contains some strong racial slurs. *Australia's Children's Book of the Year for Older Readers Award.* cmt

**6.18** Brooks, Martha. **Two Moons in August : A Novel.** Little, Brown, 1991. (paperback: Point, 1993) ISBN 0-316-10979-7. (paperback: 0-590-45923-6). 199 p. (12-14). Novel. **Canada.**
A year after Sidonie's mother dies, her family is still dysfunctional. Her father barely interacts with her and her older sister, Roberta, who is home for the summer. She no longer feels close to Roberta, though she finds a friend in Roberta's boyfriend. Then a new boy moves across the street and forces her to examine her relationships in a new light. She comes out of herself as she helps him as he struggles to deal with his

mother's recent divorce from an abusive husband. *bkn*

**6.19** Burnford, Sheila. **The Incredible Journey**. Bantam, 1962. Originally published by Little, Brown in 1962. ISBN 0-553-15126-6. 148p. (10-12). Novel. **Canada**.

When two dogs and a cat set off to make their way home across miles of trackless wilderness in northwestern Ontario, they encounter a series of life-threatening experiences. Fueled by their intense desire to return to the family they love and strengthened by their friendship and mutual regard, the three unlikely heroes find their way home. *Canadian Children's Book of the Year Award. lg*

**6.20** Bødker, Cecil. **The Leopard**. Translated by Gunnar Poulsen. Atheneum, 1975. Originally published as *Leoparden* by East African Publishing House, Nairobi, in 1972. ISBN 0-689-30444-7. 186 p. (10-12). Novel. **Ethiopia** (published in Kenya).

Tibeso, the cowherd for his mountain community in Ethiopia, is greatly concerned when a leopard begins to steal cattle in the area. But on his way to seek the advice of a wise man, Tibeso discovers that it is a blacksmith, not a leopard, who is the thief, and in so doing becomes the blacksmith's prey. Twice the boy is captured by the vicious smith, and twice he escapes in a flight that takes him far from his quiet home. When help finally arrives, Tibeso is more aware of how precious his family and community are to him. *Mildred Batchelder Award. cmt*

**6.21** Carpelan, Bo. **Dolphins in the City**. Translated by Sheila La Farge. Delacorte, 1976. Originally published as *Paradiset* by Albert Bonniers Förlag in 1973. ISBN 0-440-05073-1. 145 p. (12-14). Novel. **Sweden, Finland**.

Johan, fourteen, is concerned about how his mentally handicapped friend, Marvin, will fare, once he moves from his remote coastal island home to Helsinki. Over the course of a year, Johan realizes that Marvin has much to offer, especially his unique understanding of the world. This realization in turn helps Johan to appreciate an elderly friend's observation that without difficulty, we would not have any joy. *cmt*

**6.22** Case, Dianne. **Love, David**. Lodestar, 1991. Originally published by Maskew Miller Longman in 1986. ISBN 0-525-67350-4. 128 p. (12-YA). Novel. **Republic of South Africa**.

David, fourteen, and his half-sister Anna have a tough life in South Africa. David tries to alleviate their poverty by participating in illegal activities, but mainly succeeds in further upsetting his family. Anna's love for her brother and her dreams for a better life remain constant. *Young Africa Award. cmt*

**6.23** Case, Dianne. **92 Queens Road.** Farrar, 1995. Originally published in South Africa by Maskew Miller Longman in 1991. ISBN 0-374-35518-5. 164 p. (9-11). Novel. **Republic of South Africa.**
Six-year-old Kathy, a Colored girl in the apartheid society of South Africa in the 1960s, tells of life in her grandmother's home with her mother, a lodger, and an uncle and aunt. She learns what it means to be Colored when she is forced off a "white people's beach." Another aunt and uncle petition to be considered white and stop associating with the family. Other friends are forced.out of their homes by the government. In the end the aunt and uncle who live with them emigrate to Canada. This American edition includes an explanatory note by the author. *Young Africa Award. bkn*

**6.24** Casey, Maude. **Over the Water.** Holt, 1994. Originally published by The Women's Press Limited in 1987. (paperback: Puffin, 1996). ISBN 0-8050-3276-2. 241 p. (13 and up). Novel. **Great Britain.**
Mary and her family are Irish, but live in London, where she often feels like a foreigner. She has never understood her parents' loneliness, anger, and great devotion to Ireland. During this year's annual visit home, however, Mary, fourteen, learns more about her country's and family's struggles and begins to understand the sorrow and frustration the Irish feel in having to leave their country in order to earn a living. With the help of her aunt, she grows closer to her mother and sister and realizes her own pride in her heritage and great love for Ireland. *CCBC Choices. cmt, jk*

**6.25** Chauncey, Nan. **Devil's Hill.** Franklin Watts, 1960. Originally published by Oxford in 1958. ISBN 0-14011-062-3. 159 p. (10-12). Novel. **Australia.**
Three rather difficult, citified children are sent to spend a month with their relatives, the Lorenny family, in Tasmanian bush country. The Lorennys' no-nonsense ways, understanding, and kindness bring out the best in their visitors. The whole group treks overland in search of a lost

cow and discovers much about themselves. Good comparison between city life and farm life; glossary provided. *Australia's Children's Book of the Year for Older Readers Award. cmt*

**6.26** Clark, Mavis Thorpe. **The Min-Min.** Macmillan, 1969. Originally published by Landsdowne in 1966. (paperback: Collier, 1978). ISBN 0-02-042280-6. 216 p. (12-14). Novel. **Australia.**
Burdened with responsibilities far beyond her 13 years, Sylvie's life and future are as bleak as the endless Outback surrounding her shantytown home. Just as a new teacher inspires her to see beyond her squalid existence, her brother Reg, eleven, vandalizes the school, an offense almost certain to put him into a reformatory. Sylvie and Reg run away to seek help and advice from Mrs. Tucker, a kind friend who lives on a remote sheep station. A few days with the Tuckers help both children sort out their situations and set their sights on a brighter future. Glossary of Australian terms included. *Australia's Children's Book of the Year for Older Readers Award. cmt*

**6.27** Cresswell, Helen. **Ordinary Jack.** Macmillan, 1977. Originally published by Faber in 1977. ISBN 0-02-725540-9. 195 p. (10-14). **Great Britain.**
This first novel of the six-part Bagthorpe Saga introduces us to the eccentric members of the Bagthorpe family. They are all geniuses, except for ordinary eleven-year-old Jack and his ordinary dog, Zero. Jack is determined to distinguish himself, but his plans all backfire. His behavior becomes truly extraordinary when his Uncle Parker maps out a campaign to give him a new image as a prophet. Others in the series: *Absolute Zero* (1978); *Bagthorpes Unlimited* (1978); *Bagthorpes vs. the World* (1979); *Bagthorpes Abroad* (1984); and *Bagthorpes Haunted* (1985). *djg*

**6.28** Crew, Gary. **Angel's Gate.** Simon & Schuster, 1995. Originally published by William Heinemann Australia in 1993. ISBN 0-689-80166-1. 252p. (12-YA). Novel. **Australia.**
Kimmy's artistic talents are viewed with suspicion in the remote community where his father is doctor. After a derelict is murdered, two wild children are seen foraging in the region. The children are captured and brought to the doctor where, with Kimmy's help, they begin to recover from their sordid past and eventually identify the murderer. The rough

life of the outback and the huge, open spaces of Australia are well depicted. *Australia's Book of the Year for Older Readers Award. cmt*

**6.29** Cross, Gillian. **Chartbreaker**. Holiday House, 1987. Originally published as *Chartbreak* by Oxford in 1986. ISBN 0-8234-0647-4. 181 p. (12-14). Novel. **Great Britain**.
A terse news article announces the overnight success of the rock band Kelp. Janis May, seventeen and awkward, feeling unwanted at home and uncomfortable around her mother's new boyfriend, becomes infatuated with Kelp's lead singer, and runs away with him. The abrupt narration, as abrasive as the hard rock band and its music, is the perfect style for this story of two vulnerable teenagers coming to terms with who they are. Difficult issues are dealt with in a straightforward manner. *ALA Best Books for Young Adults. djg*

**6.30** Cross, Gillian. **The Great American Elephant Chase**. Holiday House, 1992. Originally published as *The Great Elephant Chase* by Oxford in 1992. ISBN 0-8234-1016-1. 193 p. (4-6). Novel. **Great Britain**.
After Cissie's father dies, the unscrupulous Mr. Jackson tries to appropriate the mighty elephant Khush, the star attraction of the family Medicine Show. Determined to save Khush, and keeping just one step ahead of their scheming pursuer, Cissie and the orphan boy Tad travel with Khush from Pennsylvania to the prairies of Nebraska. Set in the 1880s, this adventure story never lags and the ending contains a satisfying twist. *Smarties Grand Prize; Whitbread Award. cw*

**6.31** Cross, Gillian. **On the Edge**. Holiday House, 1985. Originally published by Oxford in 1984. (paperback: Dell, 1987). ISBN 0-8234-0559-1. 170 p. (12-14). Novel. **Great Britain**.
Tug wakes up one day in a strange house with a man and woman who insist that they are his parents. They are, in fact, terrorists who aim to abolish the family unit in England. They have kidnapped Tug because his mother is an investigative journalist who has been researching the terrorists. Tug does his best to maintain his identity, but finds himself increasingly uncertain about who he is. Meanwhile, Jinny, a girl who lives nearby, suspects that something odd is going on with the strange family that claims to be on holiday. When she recognizes Tug from pictures in the newspaper, she tries to find a way to save him before it is

too late. *jl*

**6.32** Cross, Gillian. **Wolf.** Holiday House, 1991. Originally published by Oxford in 1990. (paperback: Scholastic, 1993). ISBN 0-8234-0870-1 (paperback: 0-590-45608-3). 144p. (12-14). Novel. **Great Britain.**
Casey lives with her grandmother except for the times that she is hastily sent to stay with her mother, the irresponsible Goldie. On this visit, Casey finds Goldie living in an abandoned house with her boyfriend who gives thematic performances at local schools for a living. As Casey is drawn into assisting them with a performance on wolves, she becomes increasingly curious about her shadowy past and worried about her grandmother. A quick visit to check on her grandmother plunges Casey into a life-threatening situation and reveals the terrible truth about her father, a wolf of another sort. *Carnegie Medal. al*

**6.33** Dalokay, Vedat. **Sister Shako and Kolo the Goat.** Translated by Güner Ener. Lothrop, 1994. Originally published as *Kolo* by Cem Yayinevi in 1979. ISBN 0-688-13271-5. 96 p. (7-9). Novel. **Turkey.**
In these sometimes poetic memoirs of village life in eastern Turkey in the 1940s, the author provides insights into Turkish peasant culture, but also offers metaphors for life in general. The loving and wise Sister Shako is the soul of a rich, harmonious village community, and Kolo, her goat, symbolizes vitality, hope, and renewal. Shako's death and the flooding of the village as a result of a damming project, are sad, but they force the reader to reflect on what is important in life. *cmt*

**6.34** de Vries, Anke. **Bruises.** Translated by Stacey Knecht. Front Street/ Lemniscaat, 1995. Originally published by Lemniscaat as *Blauwe Plekken* in 1992. ISBN 1-886910-03-0. 168 p. (10-14). Novel. **Netherlands.**
Michael, athletic but reading disabled, and Judith, painfully withdrawn but intelligent, meet in school. They both have family secrets: Michael's overachiever father berates his every move; Judith is regularly and severely beaten by her mother. Both are scarred, but Michael is recovering with the help of his aunt and uncle. Despite obvious telltale signs, no one realizes Judith's problem until Michael sees her carefully concealed bruises and convinces Judith that she must take the first step to stop the abuse. Several violent scenes. *cmt*

**6.35** Dickinson, Peter. **AK**. Delacorte, 1992. Originally published by Victor Gollancz in 1990. ISBN 0-385-30608-3. 229 p. (12-14). Novel. **Great Britain**.

Paul, thirteen, is a boy soldier, fighting for freedom in his (fictional) African nation of Nagala. He has known little else but war. For him, conflict is an acceptable way of life, and his gun, an AK rifle, is a trusted companion. An older friend shows Paul that there is a better way of achieving one's goals than gunfire and bloodshed. Two endings set twenty years into the future project the results of a Nagala that has chosen peace or war. *Whitbread Literary Award (British) for Best Children's Novel. cmt*

**6.36** Dickinson, Peter. **A Bone from a Dry Sea**. Delacorte, 1993. Originally published by Gollancz in 1992. ISBN 0-385-30821-3. 200 p. (12-14). Novel. **Great Britain**.

Two alternating plots tell of Vinny, a modern-day girl visiting her father on a fossil dig in Africa, and Li, an early hominid living in the same general area four and a half million years ago. Vinny finds a bone that has a hole drilled through it. Li, a sea-ape possessed of intelligence far surpassing others of her kind, discovered how to drill such a hole. Li's story is based on the little-known theory that our ancestors were sea-apes, living in coastal waters. *cmt*

**6.37** Dijk, Lutz van. **Damned Strong Love: The True Story of Willi G. and Stefan K.** Translated by Elizabeth D. Crawford. Holt, 1995. Originally published as *Verdammt Starke Liebe* by Rowoldt Taschenbuch Verlag in 1991. ISBN 0-8050-3770-5. 134 p. (Mature 14 and older). Novel. **Germany**.

At fourteen, Stefan witnessed the invasion of his native Poland by the Nazis in 1939 and the immediate deportation of his father. At sixteen he realized that he was a homosexual. His brief but serious affair with Willi, an Austrian-born German soldier, ended when an incriminating letter from Stefan to Willi was intercepted by the Gestapo. Imprisoned for his "crime," Stefan endured torture, starvation, and slave labor until the liberation in 1945. Stefan never learned of Willi's fate. Based on Stefan K.'s own life story. *cmt*

**6.38** Doherty, Berlie. **Dear Nobody**. Orchard, 1992. Originally published by Hamish Hamilton in 1991. (paperback: Morrow, 1994). ISBN

0-531-05461-6 (paperback: 0-688-12764-9). 192p. (12-YA). Novel. **Great Britain**.
Helen and Chris, in love and in their last year at school, are shocked to discover that Helen is pregnant. Both young people face the situation seriously and mature rapidly as a result. As Chris faces parenthood and contends with Helen's thoughts about ending the pregnancy, he also renews his relationship with his own mother, who left the family when he was six. Helen writes poignant letters to her unborn child, "Dear Nobody," and it is through these letters that Helen's growth is monitored. *Carnegie Medal. al*

**6.39** Doherty, Berlie. **Granny Was a Buffer Girl**. Orchard, 1988. Originally published by Methuen in 1986. (paperback: Morrow, 1993). ISBN 0-531-05754-2 (paperback: 0-688-11863-1). 160p. (10-12). Novel. **Great Britain**.
On the eve of her departure to France, Jess attends a family reunion of four generations which helps her celebrate both love and loss as she contemplates the death of her brother Danny. Intertwined with the history of the rise and fall of the Sheffield mills are the memories of four generations of Jess's family. Skillful portrayals. *Carnegie Medal. al*

**6.40** Doherty, Berlie. **White Peak Farm**. Orchard, 1990. Originally published by Methuen in 1984. (paperback: Beech Tree, 1993). ISBN 0-531-05867-0. 128p. (12-14). Novel. **Great Britain**.
Jeannie Tanner, living on the family farm in the soft folding hills of Derbyshire where nothing seems to change, recounts family events over a period of four years. Her Gram prepares for her death, her sister Kathleen marries their father's worst enemy, and her artistic brother must choose between college and the farm. Jeannie's first-person narration is told with an economy of language in a polished and vivid style. Subtle insights into behavior and relationships are seamlessly interwoven into the narrative, and a sense of character and place is artfully evoked. *cw*

**6.41** Donnelly, Elfie. **So Long, Grandpa**. Translated by Anthea Bell. Crown, 1981. Originally published as *Servus, Opa, Sagte Ich Leise* by Cecilie Dressler Verlag in 1977. ISBN 0-517-54423-7. 92 p. (9-12). Novel. **Austria**.
Michael, nine, lives with his parents, sister, and grandfather. He and his

grandfather understand one another well, share secrets and stories, and are best friends. Michael learns that his grandfather has cancer, and they talk openly about death and even go to a funeral as the old man gradually weakens. After his grandfather's death, Michael realizes that no one is really dead as long as someone is still thinking of him, and Grandpa has left Michael rich in good memories. *cmt*

**6.42** Doyle, Brian. **Angel Square**. Bradbury, 1984. Originally published by Groundwood/Douglas & MacIntyre in 1984. ISBN 0-02-733210-1. 136 p. (10-12) Novel. **Canada**.
There is a permanent state of undeclared warfare among the students from the various denominational and public schools on Angel Square in Ottawa's Lowertown in 1945. In this fast-paced young detective novel, Tommy, also known as "The Shadow," along with a French Canadian friend and an Irish friend, search for answers when their friend Sammy's father is badly beaten in an anti-Semitic incident. *cb*

**6.43** Duder, Tessa. **Alex in Rome**. Houghton Mifflin, 1991. Originally published as *Alessandra: Alex in Rome* by Oxford in 1991. ISBN 0-395-62879-2. 166 p. (12-14). Novel. **New Zealand**.
Alex[andra] Archer and Tom Alexander tell their stories in alternating chapters, Alex in her diary and Tom in his journal. Alex, fifteen, arrives in Rome in 1960 for the Seventeenth Olympic Summer Games. Tom, twenty-three, is on vacation from his studies in Milan. He cheers Alex on as she wins a bronze medal, then shows her the sights of Rome. Though attracted to one another, they reluctantly part when Alex returns home. *Esther Glen Award. dd*

**6.44** Duder, Tessa. **In Lane Three, Alex Archer**. Houghton Mifflin, 1989. Originally published as *Alex* by Oxford in 1987. (paperback: Penguin,1989). ISBN 0-395-50927-0 (paperback: 0-553-29020-7 ). 176 p. (7-12). Novel. **New Zealand**.
In 1959, Alex, fifteen, works toward a national swimming championship and the chance to be New Zealand's representative at the 1960 Olympic Games. During the year, she faces personal trauma, disturbing social interactions, and a grueling training program. The characters play out the historically accurate attitudes and limitations that were imposed on women generally during the 1960s, affecting female participation in sports and challenging women to demand their rights as athletes. Alex-

andra demonstrates the brute strength, discipline, pain, and sacrifices necessary for overcoming those limitations and excelling as a swimmer. *Esther Glen Award*; *New Zealand Storybook of the Year Award.* See *Alex in Winter* and *Alex in Rome* for a continuation of Alex's story. *eb*

**6.45** Duder, Tessa. **Jellybean.** Viking Kestrel, 1986. Originally published in New Zealand by Oxford in 1985. (paperback: Viking, 1988) ISBN 0-670-81235-8. (paperback: 0-14-032114-4) 112 p. (9-11). Novel. **Australia.**
Geraldine, nicknamed Jellybean by her mother, is getting tired of all the time her single mother spends rehearsing and performing as a cellist. Then she meets someone who turns out to be an old friend of her mother's, and she discovers her own desire to become a conductor. Hidden in the orchestra pit during a performance of "The Nutcracker Suite," Geraldine observes a woman conductor. When her big chance comes unexpectedly at her school's annual orchestra concert, she surprises everyone with her skill. *bkn*

**6.46** Ellis, Sarah. **A Family Project**. McElderry, 1986. Originally published as *The Baby Project* by Douglas & McIntyre/Groundwood Books in 1986. ISBN 0-689-50444-6. 137 p. (10-14) Novel. **Canada**.
Eleven-year-old Jessica and her fellow family members—her grouchy, fourteen-year-old brother, her brother Rowan who has just moved out of the house, her Mum, an engineer, and her Dad, a cab driver—are excited when they learn that a new baby is on the way. This Canadian family eagerly prepares for the baby's arrival and happily adjusts after baby Lucie enters their home. The family is devastated when Lucie dies of crib death. This moving story follows the family through the grieving process. *cb*

**6.47** Ellis, Sarah. **Out of the Blue.** McElderry, 1995. Originally published by Groundwood in 1994. (paperback: Puffin, 1996). ISBN 0-689-80025-8. (paperback: 0-140-38066-3). 120 p. (9–12). Novel. **Canada.**
The day after her twelfth birthday, Megan Hungerford learns that she has a twenty-four-year-old half-sister, Natalie, whom their mother gave up for adoption. When Natalie visits, Megan struggles with feelings about the family "accident." With reassurance from her mother and support from her father, Megan grows to accept Natalie and to care for her younger tantrum-prone sister, Betsy. Vignettes of everyday family

life—mother's return to college, father's bedtime reading, sister's second-grade rivalry with a classmate—act as counterpoints to Megan's complicated concerns. *Vicky Metcalf Award* (Canada). *jsn*

**6.48** Fine, Anne. **Flour Babies and the Boys of Room 8.** Little, Brown, 1994. Originally published as **Flour Babies** by Hamish Hamilton in 1992. (paperback: Doubleday, 1994). ISBN 0-316-28319-3 (paperback: 0-440-21941-8). 178p. (10-12). Novel. **Great Britain.**
Unlike the other boys in Room 8, all classic underachievers, Simon Martin has become rather fond of his flour baby—an experimental assignment to teach the boys aspects of child development. The baby becomes a springboard for Simon's thoughts on the responsibilities of parenthood and his questions about his own father, who abandoned Simon at an early age. *Carnegie Medal. al*

**6.49** Fine, Anne. **My War with Goggle-Eyes.** Little, Brown, 1989. Originally published by Joy Street in 1989. ISBN 0-316-28314-2. 166p. (10-14). Novel. **Great Britain.**
When a classmate becomes upset at her mother's impending remarriage, Kitty recounts the tale of her own war with "Goggle-eyes," her mother's boyfriend. Kitty was shocked when her mother, a passionate feminist and antinuclear activist, took up with Gerald, a steady businessman who believed in nuclear weapons. In time, though, Gerald helped Kitty understand the politics of the antinuclear movement and gain valuable insights into her own family. *Carnegie Medal. al*

**6.50** Fowler, Thurley. **The Green Wind.** Originally published by Rigby in 1985. (paperback: Rigby, 1988). ISBN 0-7270-2031-5. 120p. (10-12). Novel. **Australia.**
In 1948, in a rural fruit growing area of Australia, a family struggles to overcome failed crops and their father's battle against the effects of his prisoner-of-war experiences. In her last year at elementary school, eleven-year-old Jennifer discovers much about herself and life in her efforts to find a true friend and to see her name in print for the first time. Humor and pathos are provided by the interactions between Jennifer and her younger brother, Alexander, as when his pet chicken is sacrificed to impress Jennifer's new friend at Sunday dinner. *Australian Children's Book of the Year for Older Readers Award. bt*

**6.51** Frank, Rudolf. **No Hero for the Kaiser.** Translated by Patricia Crampton. Illustrated by Klaus Steffens. Lothrop, 1986. Originally published as *Der Schädel des Negerhauptlings Makaua* by Müller und Kiepenheuer Verlag, Potsdam, 1931. ISBN 0-688-06093-5. 222 p. (12-14). Novel. **Germany.**

In 1914, after Jan Kubitsky's Polish village was destroyed in a skirmish between Russian and German armies, Jan, fourteen, was discovered by German soldiers and adopted. As World War I raged, he served heroically as a scout and, unwittingly, as a talisman for the 17th Battalion. In this awful year he learned of the utter stupidity, waste, corruption, and injustice of war. But when Jan realized that the German High Command planned to use him to raise money for the very war machine that he abhorred, he simply walked away and was never seen again. *Mildred Batchelder Award. cmt*

**6.52** French, Simon. **All We Know.** Angus & Robertson, UK, 1987. Originally published by Angus & Robertson, Australia in 1986. ISBN 0-207-15359-0. 255p. (12-14). Novel. **Australia.**

As Arkie, twelve, enters puberty, she begins to look more reflectively at herself, her family, and her associates. A chance gift of an excellent old camera helps Arkie record events, people, and relationships in this transitional year. In addition, she uses the lens of her own stable family to understand the lives of those around her. Australian idioms add interest. *Australia's Children's Book of the Year for Older Readers Award. cmt*

**6.53** Friedman, Carl. **Nightfather.** Translated by Arnold and Erica Pomerans. Persea, 1994. Originally published as *Tralievader* by Uitgeverij G.A. van Oorschot in 1991. (paperback: Persea, 1995). ISBN 0-89255-193-3. 130 p. (10-14). Novel. **Netherlands.**

A father's need to relive his time in a Nazi concentration camp affects the lives of his young daughter and her brothers. Each event in their lives evokes a wartime story from their father. The children live within the memory of the camp world as completely as within their own. Yet somehow the innocence of their childhood continues, parallel to the stories their father tells. The author is the son of a camp survivor. *jl, mew*

**6.54** Friis-Baastad, Babbis. **Don't Take Teddy.** Translated by Lise Sømme McKinnon. Originally published as *Ikke Ta Bamse* by Damm in

1964. Scribner's, 1967. 218p. (10-12). Novel. **Norway.**
Although thirteen-year-old Mikkel sometimes resents having to care for his older, mentally handicapped brother, Teddy, he loves him and cannot imagine life without him. Thinking that his parents are planning to send Teddy away to an institution, Mikkel leads his brother in a frantic, cross-country escape to a remote cabin in the mountains. Both boys catch pneumonia, but are soon discovered and returned home where Mikkel learns that the plan is to enroll Teddy in a nearby dayschool where he will receive the special instruction that he needs. *Mildred Batchelder Award.* cmt

**6.55** Gleitzman, Morris. **Belly Flop.** Pan Macmillan Australia, 1996. (paperback). ISBN 0-33-35684-4. 181 p. (10-12). Novel. **Australia.**
This humorous book paints a vivid picture of life in a one-street Australian town. We see the town through the eyes of Mitch, who, in vivid Aussie slang, calls on his guardian angel, Doug, between flights from the school bullies and dives from his rooftop onto piled up mattresses in his yard. Mitch's dad is the loan officer of the local bank. An eight-year drought is forcing him to foreclose on people's farms, and he is the most hated man in town. A week-long rain more than solves Mitch's problems. Most importantly, he learns to rely on his own efforts and on his true guardian angel, his dad. *jvl*

**6.56** Gordon, Sheila. **Waiting for the Rain: A Novel of South Africa.** Orchard, 1987. Originally published by Collins Educational in 1987. (paperback: Bantam, 1987). ISBN 0-531-05726-7 (paperback:0-553-27911-4). 214 p. (10-12). Novel. **Republic of South Africa.**
Tengo and Frikkie grow up in the Republic of South Africa on the same farm. They are childhood friends despite differences in their race and imposed social standing. As the boys grow, they find their relationship in crisis because of these differences and their beliefs. White Frikkie, nephew of the farm owner, joins the army but waits for the day that he can return to the farm. Black Tengo, son of the farm foreman, goes to the city, determined to get an education, and is drawn into the struggle against apartheid. Will their friendship survive? *dd, hr*

**6.57** Gripe, Maria. **Josephine.** Translated by Paul Britten Austin. Illustrated by Harald Gripe. Delacorte, 1970. Originally published as *Josefin* by Albert Bonniers Förlag in 1961. LCCN 79-111084. 133 p. (7-9).

Novel. **Sweden**.
Josephine, at six, is the late-born child of the village vicar and his wife. Her vivid imagination, curiosity, loneliness, and innocence often get her into scrapes. For several weeks Josephine mistakes the new gardener for Old Man God and thinks that he has come to fetch her to Heaven. She acts as naughty as possible to foil his plan, because she does not want to leave her family. She falls into bad company with gossipy Granny Lyra, but being bad is very hard work. Kind Papa-Father finally helps Josephine straighten everything out. First of the *Hugo and Josephine Trilogy*. See also *Hugo and Josephine* and *Hugo. Gripe: Hans Christian Andersen Medalist. cmt*

**6.58** Gripe, Maria. **The Night Daddy**. Translated by Gerry Bothmer. Illustrated by Harald Gripe. Delacorte, 1971. Originally published as *Natpappan* by Albert Bonniers Förlag in 1968. ISBN 0-440-06391-4. 151 p. (7-12). Novel. **Sweden**.
Julia at first objects to the babysitter that her single, working mother hires. Eventually, however, she becomes attached to her "Night Daddy" and his owl, Smuggler. They enjoy sharing their ideas, and begin writing stories together. After they set Smuggler free, they write a story about their relationship, which helps them to cope with the loss of the owl, to make their friendship permanent, and to prove to Julia's classmates that the "night daddy" exists. The author makes good use of alternating voices. *jl, cmt*

**6.59** Härtling, Peter. **Crutches**. Translated by Elizabeth D. Crawford. Lothrop, 1988. Originally published as *Krücke* by Beltz Verlag in 1986. ISBN 0-688-07991-1. 163 p. (9-12). Novel. **Germany**.
In post-World War II Austria, twelve-year-old Thomas, starving, filthy, and homeless, searches in vain for his mother. He is befriended by a one-legged man on crutches, and together they wander in search of some piece of their former lives on which to build a future. The ending is bittersweet, as Crutches succeeds in reuniting Thomas and his mother, but then must leave his young friend. *Mildred Batchelder Award, 1989; ALA Notable Children's Book. mew*

**6.60** Härtling, Peter. **Old John**. Translated by Elizabeth D. Crawford. Lothrop, 1990. Originally published as *Alter John* by Beltz Verlag in 1981. ISBN 0-688-08734-3. 120 p. (10-12). Novel. **Germany**.

At seventy-five, Old John agreed to move in with his daughter, son-in-law, and two grandchildren, Laura and Jacob. Everyone had to adjust, but iconoclastic Old John soon became a favorite with his grandchildren and most of the villagers. Inevitably, his health failed, he weakened in mind and body, and he died at home; but his family was much richer for their memories of him. *cmt*

**6.61** Hathorn, Libby. **Thunderwith**. Little, Brown, 1991. Originally published by William Heinemann Australia in 1989. ISBN 0-316-35034-6. 214 p. (12-14). Novel. **Australia.**

When Lara's mother dies of cancer, Lara is reunited with her long-lost father who takes her to live on his remote, coastal rainforest farm in New South Wales. In addition to coping with the loss of her mother, Lara must deal with her stepmother's rejection, a power-hungry neighbor-boy's bullying, and backbreaking work. With the help of an aboriginal storyteller and a wonderful dog, Thunderwith, that appears on the farm as if by magic, Lara finds the courage and resolve she needs to survive and to find a family. *Honor Award for Australia's Children's Book of the Year for Older Readers Award. cmt*

**6.62** Haugen, Tormod. **Keeping Secrets**. Translated by David R. Jacobs. Illustrated by Donna Diamond. HarperCollins, 1994. Originally published as *Zeppelin* by Gyldendal in 1976. ISBN 0-06-020881-3. 127 p. (10-14). Novel. **Norway.**

Nina, 10, and her parents arrive at their summer home and find that an intruder has been living there. Already questioning her parents' infallibility, Nina keeps the truth to herself when she discovers that the intruder is a neighborhood boy who has run away from his quarreling parents. Knowing what she does, Nina sees the fear, uncertainty, and errors made by the adults. Roles are switched as she and the boy are in power and the adults are powerless. As a result of this episode, the children and their parents take a step toward understanding one another better. *Haugen: Hans Christian Andersen Medalist for Writing. cmt*

**6.63** Haugen, Tormod. **The Night Birds**. Translated by Sheila LaFarge. Delacorte, 1982. Originally published as *Nattfuglene* by Gyldendal in 1975. ISBN 0-440-06451-1. 135 p. (9-12). Novel. **Norway.**

Jake, a second-grader, is worried about his father's emotional problems. His fear of losing his father takes the form of imaginary monster birds that lurk in his closet to prey on him at night. Gullible and vulnerable, Jake is manipulated by most of the neighborhood children, but gradually he learns to distinguish fact from fantasy and gains the strength to cope with his problems. *Norwegian Children's Book Prize; German Juvenile Book Award. cmt*

**6.64** Hiçyilmaz, Gaye. **Against the Storm.** Little, Brown, 1992. Originally published by Penguin in 1990. ISBN 0-316-36078-3. 200p. (12-14) Novel. **Great Britain.**
Seeking a better life, twelve-year-old Mehmet and his family move from their rural Turkish village to Ankara. There they find themselves worse off than before, forced to live at the mercy of uncaring relatives in a squalid and dehumanizing slum. The story ends on a hopeful note when Mehmet decides to return alone to his village where he will try to restore the water system. The characters, the setting, and the social injustices of contemporary Turkey are convincingly depicted by the author who lived in Turkey for many years. *cw*

**6.65** Howker, Janni. **Isaac Campion.** Greenwillow, 1986. Originally published by Julia MacRae in 1986. ISBN 0-688-06658-5. 88p. (10-12). Novel. **Great Britain.**
Isaac, now an old man, recalls the months following the death of his older brother and his father's favorite, Dan, in 1901. Isaac, embroiled in his father's petty squabbles and lingering hatreds, describes life on his family's small English horsefarm. He is more attuned to his uncles' values than to his father's. When a ship, thought to be lost, arrives with a shipment of mares from Ireland, saving his father from financial ruin, Isaac immigrates to America with his Uncle Harry. *jg*

**6.66** Klein, Robin. **Came Back to Show You I Could Fly.** Viking, 1989. ISBN: 0-670-82901-3. 189p. (13-YA). Novel. **Australia.**
Facing a bleak future as a timid loser, Seymour, eleven, can't believe his luck when glitzy, beautiful Angie from across the alley befriends him. He loves their secret forays into the city, but suspects that Angie, too, has big problems. She does. Angie is a drug addict, and she's pregnant. Their friendship helps these two confront their problems and begin to overcome them. Some harsh language. *Australia's Children's Book of the Year for Older Readers Award. cmt*

**6.67** Klein, Robin. **Hating Alison Ashley.** Penguin, 1984. ISBN 0-14-031672-8. 182p. 10-12. Novel. **Australia.**

Erica Yurken, "Yuk", feels superior to her classmates at her notoriously rowdy school until Alison Ashley enrolls and impresses everyone with her talent, brains, and good looks. Yuk's disorganized but loving home-life appeals to overly disciplined Alison, but jealous Yuk can see only the worst in the newcomer. At school camp Alison helps Yuk discover that her talent is for writing, not acting, and Yuk realizes how much she loves her family and how much she would gain from Alison's friend-ship. Broad humor and exaggerated characterizations add interest. *cmt*

**6.68** Klein, Robin. **Laurie Loved Me Best.** Viking, 1988. ISBN 0-670-82211-6. 203 p. (12-14). Novel. **Australia.**

Andre and Julia, fourteen-year-old "misfits" at exclusive Rossiter School, are best friends, yet each mistakenly believes that the other has a "perfect" home-life. Artistic, scatter-brained Andre lives with a perfec-tionist mom and an emotionally withdrawn dad and longs to have a relaxed and chummy mother like Julia's. But to organized and sensible Julia, her mother's communal life style is completely alienating. Both, however, come to terms with their own families and each other after they meet charming seventeen-year-old Laurie, who nearly wrecks their friendship by making each believe that he loves her best. *jvl*

**6.69** Korman, Gordon. **Losing Joe's Place.** Scholastic, 1990. ISBN 0-590-42768-7. 233 p. (12-14). Novel. **Canada.**

Joe Cardone rents his apartment in downtown Toronto to his brother Jason and his two buddies, Ferguson and Don. One mishap after another occurs to the three boys before the summer is over. *dd*

**6.70** Kullman, Harry. **The Battle Horse.** Translated by George Blecher and Lone Thygesen-Blecher. Bradbury, 1981. Originally published as *Strids-hästen* in 1977. ISBN 0-02-751240-1. 183 p. (10-12). Novel. **Sweden.**

In a Stockholm neighborhood in the 1930s the children hold jousting matches in which the rich kids are the knights and their "horses" are the kids from working class homes. Roland, enamored of the rich kids despite his working class status, becomes involved in a scheme to defeat the mysterious Black Knight. The scheme works, but its disastrous consequences force Roland to see that he must join the working class struggle for social equity and justice. *Mildred Batchelder Award. cmt*

**6.71** Laird, Elizabeth. **Kiss the Dust**. Dutton, 1992. Originally published by William Heinemann Limited in 1991. (paperback: Puffin, 1994). ISBN 0-525-44893-4. 282 p. (10-12). Novel. **Great Britain**.
Tara is twelve in 1984 when she and her family flee Sulaimaniya to escape the Iraqi secret police. They join other Kurds in the mountains, cross into Iran, and finally manage to immigrate to London. Tara grows from naive child to responsible adolescent as she withstands hardships in refugee camps, cares for her mother during an illness, and adapts to new cultures and customs. *jg*

**6.72** Likhanov, Albert. **Shadows Across the Sun**. Translated by Richard Lourie. Harper & Row, 1983. Originally published as *Solnechnoe Zatmenie* by Moldaya Gvardia in 1979. ISBN 0-06-023868-2. 150 p. (10-12). Novel. **Russia**.
Lena is confined to a wheelchair and watches the world through her window. Fedya looks after his pigeons and feels angry and embarrassed by his father's drinking. These teenagers meet and fall in love. Despite their youth and the demolition of their old neighborhood which threatens to separate them, Lena and Fedya find a way to add something to each other's life. *jl*

**6.73** Lindgren, Astrid. **Rasmus and the Vagabond**. Translated by Gerry Bothmer. Illustrated by Eric Palmquist. Viking, 1960. Originally published as *Rasmus på Luffen*. (paperback: Puffin, 1987; ISBN 0-140-32304-X). 192 p. (7-9). Novel. **Sweden**.
Rasmus, an orphan, runs away from the orphanage in hopes of finding a home and parents. He meets Oscar, a tramp, and they help capture two thieves. During this time Rasmus comes to love Oscar, and, to his surprise, Oscar comes to love him. An even greater surprise is finding out that Oscar is not a full-time tramp, but a farmer with a wife, a home, and a kitten. Rasmus finally has a home of his own. Excellent for read-aloud. *cmt*

**6.74** Lingard, Joan. **Between Two Worlds**. Lodestar Books, 1991. Originally published by Hamish Hamilton in 1991. ISBN 0-525-67-360-1. 186 p. (12-14). Novel. **Canada**.
A Latvian family, the Petersons, arrive in Toronto, Canada, in 1948 as

refugees. Lukas, Kristina, their eighteen-year-old twins Astra and Hugo, and twelve-year-old Tomas are ready to start a new life under the sponsorship of the Frasers. Many mishaps occur before the family saves enough money to buy a small piece of land for themselves. The author and her husband, whose family provided the inspiration for this story, now live in Scotland. *dd*

**6.75** Little, Jean. **Different Dragons**. Illustrated by Laura Fernandez. Viking Kestrel, 1986. ISBN 0-670-80836-9. 123 p. (10-12). Novel. **Canada**.

Ben is afraid of dogs, thunderstorms, and many other things. His parents leave him with Aunt Rose for a weekend, and she introduces him to a Labrador retriever named Gulliver Gallivant. When he discovers that Hana, the girl next door, and the dog also have fears, he manages to kill this particular dragon. *dd*

**6.76** Little, Jean. **Lost and Found**. Illustrated by Leoung O'Young. Viking Kestrel, 1985. ISBN 0-670-80835-0. 82 p. (7-9). Novel. **Canada**.

Lucy Bell and her family have just moved to Riverside, and Lucy has no friends. She finds a friendly dog and wants to keep him. But Nan, the girl next door, likes to play detective; and together they find the owner of the dog at the animal shelter. There Lucy finds a new dog. *dd*

**6.77** Little, Jean. **Mama's Going to Buy You a Mockingbird**. Viking, 1985. Originally published by Penguin Books Canada in 1984. (Paperback: Puffin, 1985). ISBN 0-14-031737-6. 208p. (10-14). Novel. **Canada**.

The summer before sixth grade isn't what Jeremy expected; his father is in the hospital and his mother preoccupied with her husband. Going back to school isn't any better, especially after his father dies. As Jeremy struggles to work through his anger and grief, he learns to reach out to his restructured family, and realizes that his father's legacy will live in him forever. Excellent for helping adults and children understand the feelings of children when a parent dies. *Canadian Children's Book of the Year Award; Ruth Schwartz Children's Book Award. lg, dd*

**6.78** Llorente, Pilar Molina. **The Apprentice**. Translated by Robin Longshaw. Illustrated by Juan Ramón Alonso. Farrar, 1993. Originally published as *El Aprendiz* by Ediciones Riap, S. A., in 1989. ISBN 0-

374-30389-4. 101 p. (8-14). Novel. **Spain**.

Arduino, a tailor's son, dreams of becoming a painter, but in fifteenth-century Italy occupation shifts are difficult. Reluctantly, Arduino's father apprentices him to a renowned painting master for three years. Arduino's joy quickly sours as he and his fellow apprentices are subjected to cruel living conditions and both physical and verbal abuse. He is even more troubled to discover that his master is holding Donato, a gifted apprentice, prisoner. Together, the two escape this tyranny by proving to a wealthy client that Donato is the true genius and that the master is a fraud. *Mildred Batchelder Award; ALA Notable Book; Best Book for Young Adults. mew*

**6.79** Lottridge, Celia Barker. **Ticket to Curlew**. Illustrated by Wendy Wolsak-Frith. Groundwood/Douglas & McIntyre, 1992. ISBN 0-88899-163-0. (10-12). Novel. **Canada**.

When almost-12-year-old Sam and his father arrive in Curlew, Alberta, in 1915, there is little other than grass and sky. At first Sam is lonely and a bit frightened by the vastness of his new home, especially when he remembers the familiar corners of his Iowa farm. Nevertheless, he soon grows to love the prairie, and after his mother, brother, and sister join them, Sam makes a new friend, enjoys school, and gets a horse that he loves. Along with the horse comes the freedom to explore his new home. *Canadian Children's Book of the Year Award.* lg

**6.80** Maartens, Maretha. **Paper Bird: A Novel of South Africa**. Translated by Madeleine Van Biljon. Clarion, 1991. Originally published as *Die Inkvoël* by Tafelberg Publishers Limited in 1987. ISBN 0-395-56490-5. 146 p. (12-14). Novel. **Republic of South Africa**.

Adam lives in dire poverty with his widowed mother and siblings in the black township of Phameng. The sole breadwinner for his family, he sells newspapers on the streets of the nearby city of Bloemfontein. Despite trigger-happy riot police and marauding gangs preying on those who work in the city, Adam makes his way to work, despite being desperately ill, so as to provide for his mother's newborn twins. Black Africans' sense of desperation is well described. Glossary of Afrikaans terms included. *cmt*

**6.81** Magorian, Michelle. **Not a Swan**. HarperCollins, 1992. Originally published by Methuen in 1991. ISBN 0-06-024214-0. 408 p. (12-YA).

Novel. **Great Britain**.

Seventeen-year-old Rose is evacuated from London to a seaside village during World War II. No sooner do she and her two older sisters arrive than they discover that their chaperone has been drafted, leaving them to fend for themselves. All three sisters discover something about their own strength and abilities, but it is Rose in particular who comes to recognize and find pleasure in the woman she has become. *jl*

**6.82** Mahy, Margaret. **The Catalogue of the Universe**. Margaret K. McElderry, 1986. (paperback: Puffin, 1994). ISBN 0-689-50391-1. (paperback: 0-140-36600-8). 185 p. (14-YA). Novel. **New Zealand**.

Poor in material things, eighteen-year-old Angela May is rich in the confidence that her mother's love, her own stunning beauty, and the enduring friendship of homely but brilliant Tycho give her. This confidence is temporarily shaken when she meets her father for the first time and discovers that, as far as he is concerned, she is not a "love child" but an "accident." She learns to live with the new reality, to value her mother all the more, and to truly love Tycho. Tycho's fascination with the stars helps Angela to think beyond the confines of her own world. *jvl*

**6.83** Mahy, Margaret. **Memory**. McElderry, 1988. Originally published in Great Britain by Dent in 1987. ISBN 0-689-50446-2. 278 p. (14-YA). Novel. **New Zealand**.

Nineteen-year-old Jonny Dart has spent the past five years tormented by the disturbing memory of his sister Janine's death. He begins a search for the only other witness to her death, hoping to find the truth. Instead, he finds Sophie, a gentle woman suffering from Alzheimer's Disease and is drawn into her troubled world. It is through his initially begrudging efforts to help Sophie cope with her failing memory, that Jonny is able to come to terms with his own memory of his sister. A cathartic story. *ALA Best Young Adult Books; Society of School Libraries International Book Award. djg*

**6.84** Mahy, Margaret. **The Underrunners**. Viking, 1992. Originally published by Hamish Hamilton in 1992. ISBN 0-670-84179-X. 169 p. (10-14). Novel. **New Zealand**.

Tristam Catt, twelve, most often lives in a dream world, but he alone is familiar with the underrunners, washed-out tunnels that lace his New Zealand peninsula. Thirteen-year-old Winola is a runaway from a children's home who is being pursued by a would-be kidnapper. Tris hides her in the underrunners. Helping Winola, Tris must confront the terrible secret from which his father has tried to protect him, and Winola, in turn, helps Tris. Underrunners twist beneath the surface of this intriguing novel both literally and figuratively, leaving the reader to puzzle out the complex relationships. *Esther Glen Award. djg, eb*

**6.85** Major, Kevin. **Eating Between the Lines**. Illustrated by Marion Stuck. Doubleday Canada, 1991. ISBN 0-385-25293-5. 136p. (12-14). Novel. **Canada**.

Teenaged Jackson lives with his finicky father and restless mother and worries, rightly, that they are drifting apart. Discovering that a pizza medal combined with a good book gives him time-travel powers, he battles the Cyclops with Odysseus and gives a brilliant oral report in class, is imprisoned as Jim in *Huck Finn* and subsequently makes a compelling speech opposing censorship of the novel, becomes Romeo to romance the girl of his dreams; and takes his parents on a trip back in time to recapture the happiest day of their lives. Zany and funny, Jackson is one of a kind. *Canadian Children's Book of the Year Award. lg*

**6.86** Marsden, John. **Letters from the Inside**. Houghton Mifflin, 1994. Originally published by Pan Macmillan in 1991. ISBN 0-395-68985-6. 146 p. (12-14). Novel. **Australia**.

Mandy, about fifteen, responds to Tracey's magazine ad for a penpal. Their letters reveal the details of their lives, as well as their secrets, hopes, and fears. In time, each discovers that the other's life is not exactly as she has portrayed it. An original concept with a jolting ending. *clb*

**6.87** Marsden, John. **So Much to Tell You....** Little Brown, 1987. Originally published by Walter McVitty Books in 1987. ISBN 0-316-54877-4. 117 p. (12-14). Novel. **Australia**.

Through a diary assigned to her by her English teacher, fourteen-year-old Marina gradually reveals the tragedy that has caused her to withdraw into total silence. Her life in a girls' boarding school where she has been sent to recuperate provides the backdrop for candid sketches of her classmates and reflective comments about her life. Suspenseful. *Australian Children's Book of the Year for Older Readers Award, 1988. clb*

**6.88** McCaughrean, Geraldine. **Pack of Lies**. Oxford, 1989. Originally published by Oxford in 1988. ISBN 0-19-271612-3. 168p. (10-12). Novel. **Great Britain**.

When Ailsa brings home a strange man, M.C.C. Berkshire, from the library, she and her mother are not sure that they can afford to feed him, much less trust him. In spite of his "pack of lies"—stories he tells their antique shop customers to lure them into buying various items—a bond forms between Ailsa, her mother, and the man. *Carnegie Medal. al*

**6.89** McKay, Hilary. **The Exiles**. Margaret McElderry Books, 1992. Originally published by Victor Gollancz in 1991. ISBN 0-689-50555-8. 217 p. (10-14). Novel. **Great Britain**.

Ruth, Naomi, Rachel, and Phoebe, sisters ranging in age from 13 to 6, generally set their own course in life. When they are sent to their grandmother's to spend the summer, she aims to "cure" them of their addiction to books and to get them outdoors. As they pursue their reckless adventures, the girls gradually fall in love with the seaside village and their crusty grandmother. Humorous. Sequel: *The Exiles at Home.* *cmt*

**6.90** Mebs, Gudrun. **Sunday's Child**. Translated by Sarah Gibson. Dial, 1986. Originally published as *Sonntagskind* by Verlag Sauerländer in 1983. (paperback: Dell, 1989). ISBN 0-8037-0192-6. 136 p. (10-12). Novel. **Switzerland**.

Jenny, an orphan, wants desperately to have a Sunday foster family to take her out for the day and do special things, like the other children in the orphanage. So she is thrilled when someone picks her to be a Sunday child. Despite a rocky start with a Sunday mommy not at all like she imagined, things turn out better than Jenny ever dreamed possible. *jl*

**6.91** Merino, José María. **The Gold of Dreams**. Translated by Helen Lane. Farrar, 1991. Originally published as *El Oro de los Sueños* by Alfaguara Press in 1986. ISBN 0-374-32692-4. 217 p. (12-14). Novel. **Spain**.

Miguel, 15, son of a Spanish soldier of fortune and a Mexican mother, lives near Mexico City in the early sixteenth century and longs for the life of a conquistador. He is invited by his godfather to join an expedition to southern Mexico in search of gold. During the grueling months that follow, his dreams are replaced by the harsh realities of greed and the cruelty and suffering it causes. Miguel finds gold, but, more importantly, he finds his father, whom he believed to be dead. His father remains in the jungle, and Miguel returns home a wiser person. *cmt*

**6.92** Moloney, James. **Swashbuckler**. University of Queensland, 1995 (distributed in U.S. by International Specialized Book Services). ISBN 0-7022-2825-7. 83p. (7-11). Novel. **Australia**.

At his new school, Peter befriends Anton, a strange boy who rescues him from school bullies, brandishing a wooden sword and speaking an "outlandish concoction of words" of the swashbuckling heroes of the past. Anton has immersed himself in a fantasy world of heroic quests and brave deeds to protect himself from the fear and anger he feels towards his dying father. Peter must enter Anton's world of demons and dragons to help his friend make peace with his father. As a result, Peter is able to resolve his bitter feelings towards his own father, whose gambling addiction had torn his family apart. *Australian Children's Book of the Year for Younger Readers Award. bt*

**6.93** Morgenstern, Susie Hoch. **It's Not Fair**. Translated by Susie Hoch Morgenstern. Illustrated by Kathie Abrams. Farrar, 1983. Originally published as *C'est Pas Juste, ou Les Déboires d'une Petite Fille Entreprenante* by Éditions de l'Amitié—G.T. Rageot in 1982. ISBN 0-374-33649-0. 101 p. (10-12). Novel. **France**.

Stacey is keen on getting rich, so she dreams up one scheme after another to earn money. In this first-person narrative she tells of selling snacks on the playground, selling poetry to her classmates, and producing her own newspaper, among other variously successful ventures. In the end she decides to write a novel about her efforts to get rich quick. *jl*

**6.94** Naidoo, Beverley. **Chain of Fire**. Illustrated by Eric Velasquez. HarperCollins, 1990. Originally published in England by William Collins in 1989. ISBN 0-397-32426-X. 242 p. (12-14). Novel. **Great Britain**.

In this sequel to *Journey to Jo'burg*, Naledi and her brother Tiro join in the escalating fight of black South Africans against apartheid. After the government decrees that everyone in their village must relocate to a desolate enclave, the schoolchildren hold a protest demonstration that is met with violence by police. Naledi finds strength in her convictions through her association with Taolo and his parents, anti-apartheid activists. Although her friends are jailed, killed, or driven into hiding and her village is lost, Naledi realizes that she is now part of the struggle that will eventually lead her people to freedom. *cmt*

**6.95** Naidoo, Beverley. **Journey to Jo'burg: A South African Story.** Illustrated by Eric Velasquez. Lippincott, 1986. Originally published in England by Longman House in 1985. ISBN 0-397-32168-6. 80 p. (10-14). Novel. **Great Britain.**
Naledi (13) and her brother Tiro (9) live with their grandmother and little sister in a remote village in South Africa. Their mother must work far away in Johannesburg. When their sister falls ill, Naledi and Tiro make the journey to Jo'burg to find their mother and bring her back to save the baby. The children's experiences on their journey reveal the injustices, dangers, extreme poverty, and insults that black South Africans endured under apartheid. As a result of this experience, Naledi understands that revolt, not quiet endurance, is the only path to freedom for her people. *cmt*

**6.96** Naidoo, Beverley. **No Turning Back: A Novel of South Africa.** HarperCollins, 1997. Originally published by Penguin Group in 1995. ISBN 0-06-027505-7. 185 p. (10-14). Novel. **Great Britain.**
Twelve-year-old Sipho runs away from his black township to Johannesburg to escape his stepfather's beatings and joins a group of street children. His story of living on the street, being terrorized by white police, and finally finding help in a shelter school reveals the struggles of South Africa to overcome its long-held traditions of racism and apartheid and its efforts to achieve racial harmony. Glossary of Zulu and Afrikaans terms included. *Smarties Book Prize shortlist. cmt*

**6.97** Newth, Mette. **The Abduction.** Translated by Tiina Nunnally and Steve Murray. Farrar, 1989. Originally published as *Bortførelsen* by Tiden Norsk Forlag, Oslo, in 1987. ISBN 0-374-30008-9. 238 p. (Mature 13-YA). Novel. **Norway.**
Osuqo, a Greenland Inuit, and Christine, a Norwegian, both about thirteen, tell this sad and often horrifying tale of ignorance, cruelty, and human degradation in seventeenth-century Norway. Osuqo and Poq, her fiancé, kidnapped in Greenland by Norwegian traders, endure months of humiliation, ill treatment, and torture at the hands of their captors. Christine, herself doomed to permanent servitude, at first considers the

foreigners to be animals, but realizes that these remarkably stoic people are as human as she is and that she and they share a similar fate, unless she helps them to escape. *School Library Journal Best Books List. cmt*

**6.98** Nilsson, Ulf. **If You Didn't Have Me.** Translated by Lone Thygesen Blecher and George Blecher. Illustrated by Eva Eriksson. Margaret K. McElderry, 1987. Originally published as *Om Ni Inte Hade Mig* in 1985. ISBN 0-689-50406-3. 113 p. (7-9). Novel. **Sweden.**
Left with his baby brother at his grandmother's farm for the summer while his parents are building their house, a little boy bravely makes the best of the situation while missing his parents. There is much to be learned about life and death on a farm. Occasionally lonely in this busy time at the farm, he is often reassured, helped out of scrapes, guided, and consoled by his grandma and her hired hand, Edwin. Direct language (e.g., description of Grandma's false teeth, hog butchering) adds cultural flavor. *Mildred Batchelder Award. cmt*

**6.99** Orlev, Uri. **Lydia, Queen of Palestine.** Translated by Hillel Halkin. Houghton Mifflin, 1993. Originally published as *Lidyah, malkat Erets Yisra'el* by Keter Publishing House in 1991. (paperback: Puffin, 1995). ISBN 0-14-037089-7. 168 p. (10-14). Novel. **Israel.**
Lydia, irrepressible and funny, has a flair for acting, languages, and getting her own way. In 1943 this ten-year-old must travel alone to a kibbutz in Palestine to escape the Nazis. At the same time, she is determined to find a way to bring her estranged parents back together. She adjusts well to her new life, even learning to accept her parents' divorce and their new spouses. Story contains insights into the communal life of a kibbutz. *cmt*

**6.100** Pausewang, Gudrun. **Fall-Out.** Translated by Patricia Crampton. Viking, 1994. Originally published as *Die Wolke* by Ravensburger Buchverlag Otto Maier in 1987. ISBN 0-670-86104-9. 171 p. (12-YA). **Germany.**
A nuclear leak occurs at the Grafenrheinfeld power station near Schweinfurth, Germany, and panic sets in. The country's disaster plans collapse, and everything in the area is poisoned indefinitely. Fourteen-year-old Janna is the only one in her family to survive. Janna, left totally bald by radiation sickness, wants this disaster acknowledged, but many just want to forget that it happened or could happen again. She chooses

to show her bald head as a statement of protest, and to live with her Aunt Almut, a fellow protester against nuclear power. *German Children's and Young Adult Literature Award. mew, dd*

**6.101** Pearson, Kit. **A Handful of Time.** Puffin, 1988. Originally published by Penguin, 1987. ISBN 0-14-032268-X. 186p. (10-12). Novel. **Canada.**
Twelve-year-old Patricia does not want to be sent to Alberta to spend the summer at a lake with an aunt, uncle, and cousins that she's never met. She'd rather stay home in Toronto, but her parents are divorcing. In Alberta, she finds an old watch under the floorboards in an old cottage, and her desire to escape is granted. She travels through time to the summer that her own perfect mother was an imperfect and unhappy 12-year-old at the lake. Finding out about her mother as a girl helps her realize her love for her as a woman. *Canadian Children's Book of the Year Award. lg*

**6.102** Phipson, Joan. **The Family Conspiracy.** Harcourt, Brace, 1962. Originally published by Angus & Robertson, 1962. ISBN 0-15227-112-0. 224 p. (10-12). Novel. **Australia.**
When they learn that their mother must have an operation, the six Barker children decide in secret to raise the money to pay the medical bill. The children's jobs and adventures in raising the money, as well as the family's everyday concerns, paint a portrait of life in the Outback, with emphasis upon Mrs. Barker's hard life. *Australia's Children's Book of the Year for Older Readers Award. cmt*

**6.103** Phipson, Joan. **When the City Stopped.** Atheneum, 1978. ISBN 0-68950-121-8. 181p. (10-12). Novel. **Australia.**
Utilities and labor strikes shut down the city of Sydney, leaving Nick and Binkie on their own. They decide to go to their aunt in the country, soliciting the help of their cleaning lady and her crippled husband. As the children escape the city, they are made aware of how thin the veneer of civilization is and how easily it can be stripped away to reveal the ugly, primitive side of human nature. *cmt*

**6.104** Procházková, Iva. **The Season of Secret Wishes.** Translated by Elizabeth D. Crawford. Lothrop, 1989. Originally published as *Die Zeit der Geheimen Wünsche* (from a Czech manuscript) by Beltz Verlag,

Weinheim, in 1988. ISBN 0-688-08735-3. 213 p. (12-14). Novel. **Czechoslovakia.**
Kapka, eleven, and her parents move into a new neighborhood in present-day Prague. At her suggestion, Kapka's artist father stages a successful, but unauthorized, showing of his sculptures, and, as a result, has a run-in with repressive government authorities. Nonetheless, Kapka has hope for a bright future, thanks to her good friends and supportive family. *cmt*

**6.105** Pullman, Philip. **The Broken Bridge.** Knopf, 1992. Originally published by Macmillan Children's Books in 1990. ISBN 0-679-81972-X. 256p. (12-14). Novel. **Great Britain.**
Sixteen-year-old Ginny finds it hard to fit into her small town in Wales. As an only child and the daughter of a Haitian artist mother whom she never knew, she is different. Her quiet life suddenly changes when she learns that she has a half brother who will be coming to live with her and her father. Neither child has known the truth about their family, and it is only their compelling desire to know the truth that helps them overcome their confusion and anger. *djg*

**6.106** Pullman, Philip. **The Ruby in the Smoke.** Knopf, 1985. Originally published by Oxford in 1985. ISBN 0-394-88826-X. 230 p. (13-YA). Novel. **Great Britain.**
Victorian London provides an appropriately atmospheric background for a story in which sixteen-year-old Sally Lockhart becomes involved in a deadly search for a mysterious ruby. Sequels: *The Shadow in the North; The Tiger in the Well. International Reading Association Children's Book Award (for first two titles in the series). be*

**6.107** Ransome, Arthur. **Pigeon Post.** Lippincott, 1937. Originally published by Cape in 1936. (paperback: Godine, 1992). ISBN 0-87923-864-X (paperback). 372p. (10-14). Novel. **Great Britain.**
The four Walker children spend their summers in England's Lake District, where they create and act out elaborate, fantastical adventures. In this, the sixth volume of the *Swallows and Amazons* series, the children's adventures include a brush fire and repeated encounters with the mysterious "squashy hat." *Carnegie Medal. al*

**6.108** Reuter, Bjarne. **The Boys from St. Petrie.** Translated by Anthea

Bell. Dutton, 1994. Originally published as *Drengene fra Sankt Petri* by Gyldendal in 1991. ISBN 0-525-45121-8. 215 p. (12-14). Novel. **Denmark.**

As a lark, six upper-class teenagers play pranks on the Nazi occupation forces in their quiet Danish town in 1942. Then they find a German gun, and Otto, a fervent freedom fighter from the working class, joins the group. As the gravity of the occupation becomes clear to the boys, their pranks give way to serious acts of sabotage, culminating in an effort to blow up a Nazi munitions train. Their mission is accomplished, some of the boys are killed, others are captured, but Otto remains at large. Based on actual incidents that galvanized Denmark's Resistance efforts. *Mildred Batchelder Award; ALA Notable Book; Best Book for Young Adults.* mew, cmt

**6.109** Reuter, Bjarne. **Buster's World.** Translated by Anthea Bell. Dutton, 1989. Originally published as *Busters Verden* by Branner og Korch in 1980. ISBN 0-525-44475-0. 154 p. (9-14). Novel. **Denmark.**

Buster, ten, copes with his disastrous homelife, his poverty, and the taunts of other children by performing magic tricks, acting like a hyena or gorilla, and causing trouble at school. Against great odds, Buster retains his capacity to love, his positive outlook, and his wonderful imagination. *Mildred Batchelder Award; ALA Notable Book.* Sequel: *The Sheik of Hope Street.* mew, cmt

**6.110** Semel, Nava. **Becoming Gershona.** Translated by Seymour Simckes. Viking, 1990. (paperback: Puffin, 1992). Originally published as *Gershona Shona* by Am Oved in 1988. ISBN 0-670-83105-0. 128 p. (10-14). Novel. **Israel.**

Gershona, twelve, is two years older than the state of Israel. Like the other immigrant families in their Tel Aviv housing development, all touched in some way by the Holocaust, her family is intent on building a future and putting the past behind. Thus Gershona notices things—a tattered photograph, a whispered conversation—and senses that everyone is keeping secrets. As Gershona grows in understanding, the secrets are revealed to her. *National Jewish Book Award.* ss

**6.111** Shelley, Noreen. **Family at The Lookout.** Oxford, 1972. ISBN 0-19272-067-8. 153p. (10-12). Novel. **Australia.**

When Mr. Wetherall inherits The Lookout, a huge house in the Blue

Mountains, his son Mark, twelve, looks forward to living there. But the former housekeeper's suspicious ways and his neighbor's ethnic prejudices against Mark's non-English friend Joss bother Mark. The threat of a bush fire resolves the problems, however, forcing the housekeeper to return stolen property and the neighbor to admit that Joss, who works tirelessly to save The Lookout, is a fine person. *Australia's Children's Book of the Year for Older Readers Award. cmt*

**6.112** Silver, Norman. **No Tigers in Africa**. Dutton, 1992. Originally published by Faber & Faber in 1990. (paperback: Faber & Faber, 1992). ISBN 0-525-44733-4 (paperback: 0-571-14297-4). 138 p. (13 and up). Novel. **Republic of South Africa.**

Selwyn Lewis, a white teenager newly arrived in England, denies his racism. Still, he is haunted by guilt, because he feels that he may have caused the death of a black teenager back in South Africa. *hr*

**6.113** Southall, Ivan. **Ash Road**. Viking, 1966. Originally published by Angus & Robertson in 1966. (paperback: Greenwillow, 1978). ISBN 0-14-030314-6 (paperback: 0-68880-135-8). 187 p. (10-14). Novel. **Australia.**

A twenty-four-hour nightmare is caused when three teenaged campers carelessly start a bushfire in the foothills around Tinley, Australia. Trying to escape the fire and the blame for having started it, the boys come to Tinley and see what havoc they have wrought, as children whose parents have gone to fight the fire narrowly avoid death. The courage and cowardice that lies in everyone, as well as the power of cooperation, are explored during this wild narrative of emergency. *Australia's Children's Book of the Year for Older Readers Award. cmt*

**6.114** Southall, Ivan. **Hills End**. Viking, 1962. Originally published by Angus & Robertson in 1962. (paperback: Puffin, 1965). ISBN 0-14-030245-X. 222 p. (10-12). Novel. **Australia.**

Seven children and their teacher are left behind in the remote village of Hills End while the rest of the townspeople travel to an annual picnic. A freakish cyclone destroys the village and floods the river, marooning the children. Adversity brings out the best in these young people, and they begin to respect one another as never before. Humor lightens even the scariest situations. *cmt*

**6.115** Southall, Ivan. **Josh**. Macmillan, 1971. Originally published by Angus & Robertson in 1971. ISBN 0-027-86280-1. 179 p. (12-14). Novel. **Australia.**
Fourteen-year-old Josh Plowman from Melbourne visits his great-aunt Clara at Ryan's Creek, the sleepy town founded by Great Grandfather Plowman. A sensitive boy, more interested in writing poetry than in playing cricket, Josh is half curious, half apprehensive about his redoubtable relative. What he does not expect is the hostility and prejudice of the young people in the town who see him as just another spoiled and selfish Plowman come to sponge off his aunt. An internal, psychological novel, this book vividly describes life in a rural Australian town. *IBBY Honour List; Carnegie Medal. jvl*

**6.116** Southall, Ivan. **To the Wild Sky**. Penguin, 1967. Originally published by Angus & Robertson, 1967. (paperback: Puffin, 1971). ISBN 0-14-030483-5. 220 p. (10-14). Novel. **Australia.**
Flying off for a weekend at his ranch in New South Wales, Gerald and his five schoolmates are suddenly in peril when the pilot dies of a heart attack. Flying above the clouds for eight hours, Gerald manages to crash land on a parched, deserted island. In their struggles to survive, the children must confront their prejudices, secrets, weaknesses and strengths. Slowly they realize that only cooperation with one another can save them until help arrives. *Australia's Children's Book of the Year for Older Readers Award. cmt*

**6.117** Spence, Eleanor. **The Green Laurel**. Roy Publishers, 1963. Originally published by Oxford in 1963. 181p. (10-14). Novel. **Australia.**
For most of her childhood Lesley has followed the carnival circuit with her family. During their four-month hiatus north of Sydney, Lesley, now eleven, confronts her desire for a permanent home. Then her father is taken ill and the family must move to a housing settlement for immigrants while he convalesces. Lesley takes heart when invited to join the "Outcasts", a group of children whose goal is to leave the settlement as soon as possible. But her life takes root only when she helps develop a library at the settlement and begins to help others. *Australia's Children's Book of the Year for Older Readers Award. cmt*

**6.118** Spence, Eleanor. **The October Child**. Oxford, 1976. Originally published as *The Devil Hole*. ISBN 0-340-60548-0. 151p. (10-14). Novel. **Australia.**

The Mariners welcome baby Carl into their lives. For awhile, his exceptional physical beauty disguises Carl's profound mental disability; but within three years, the once-happy family is on the brink of collapse. Told from the point of view of brother Douglas Mariner, ten when Carl is born, this story closely inspects the effects, both good and bad, on a family that result from coping with a mentally disabled child. *Australia's Children's Book of the Year for Older Readers Award.* cmt

**6.119** Swindells, Robert. **Stone Cold**. Hamish Hamilton, 1993. ISBN 0-2411-3300-9. 132p. (14-YA). Novel. **Great Britain.**

Teenaged Link struggles to survive after fleeing his home and violent stepfather. Shelter is a severely disturbed ex-army NCO who murders homeless people. As their stories converge, an alarming portrait of homelessness unfolds. *Carnegie Medal.* al

**6.120** Taylor, William. **Agnes the Sheep**. Scholastic, 1990. Originally published by Ashton Scholastic in 1990. ISBN 0-590-43365-2. 132 p. (10-12). Novel. **New Zealand.**

For a class project, Joe and Belinda interview Mrs. Carpenter, an elderly and eccentric pioneer of the community. Mrs. Carpenter's tape-recorded accounts of her encounters with the young Adolf Hitler and whiskey smugglers during prohibition in the U.S. gave the class a new perspective on world history. In exchange, Joe and Belinda promised to take care of Agnes, Mrs. Carpenter's pet sheep, when she passed away. A faithful pet, Agnes became completely intractable in a rollicking series of buttings when Joe and Belinda "nicked" her off to a new home, to save her from ending up as mutton stew. *Esther Glen Award.* eb

**6.121** Thiele, Colin. **The Fire in the Stone**. Harper & Row, 1974. Originally published by Rigby in 1973. (paperback: Puffin, 1981). ISBN 0-14-031360-5. 228 p. (10-14). Novel. **Australia.**

Deserted by his parents, Ernie, fourteen, lives a lonely, rough life in the opal mining fields of South Australia. His fortunes take a wild swing when he hits a jackpot of opal only to have it stolen within one day. Ernie and two friends conspire to find the stolen gems, trap the thief, and collect the reward. When a booby trap kills Willie, Ernie's Aboriginal friend, and foils the boys' plan, a disgusted Ernie leaves for Adelaide.

*cmt*

**6.122** Thiele, Colin. **Jodie's Journey.** Harper and Row, 1990. Originally published by McVitty in 1988. ISBN 0-06-026132-3. 114 p. (10-14). Novel. **Australia.**
Jodie at 12 is looking forward to many years of races and awards for her beloved horse Monarch, but her dreams are cut short when she discovers that she has rheumatoid arthritis, a condition that will soon confine her to a wheelchair. Jodie battles against discouragement caused by constant, excruciating pain, and the lack of understanding by her teachers and classmates about her condition. It is a difficult mental "journey." The author combines clear medical descriptions with suspenseful scenes, such as when a sudden bush-fire engulfs Jodie's house, where she is alone for the day. *jvl*

**6.123** Thiele, Colin. **Shadow Shark.** Harper & Row, 1985. Originally published by Walter McVitty in 1985. ISBN 0-06-026178-1. 214 p. (10-12). Novel. **Australia.**
Having spent his first twelve years in Melbourne, Joe feels ill prepared for the rigors of life in a fishing village on Cockle Bay off the Antarctic Ocean. When he, his cousin Meg, and his uncle go fishing with a famous deep-sea fisherman for Scarface, a notorious shark, Joe must find untapped inner resources. Their boat explodes, and the children are stranded on an island for days tending Meg's injured father and trying to get help. *jvl*

**6.124** Thorvall, Kerstin. **And Leffe Was Instead of a Dad.** Translated by Kees de Kiefte. Bradbury, 1974. Originally published as *I Stallet for en Pappa.* ISBN 0-878-88103-4. 131 p. (8-10). Novel. **Sweden.**
Nine-year-old Magnus does not remember his father and is glad when his mother's friend Leffe comes to live with them. (FirstSearch) *cmt*

**6.125** Tomlinson, Theresa. **The Forestwife.** Orchard, 1995. First published by Julia MacRae Books in 1993. ISBN 0-531-09450-2. 166 p. (10-14). Novel. **Great Britain.**
Mary was raised by her nurse, Agnes, in the home of her cruel uncle during the reign of Richard I at the end of the twelfth century in England. To escape an arranged marriage, Mary fled with Agnes to the forest wilderness near Sheffield, where they changed Mary's name to

Marion and cared for the sick and needy. While kings and lords fought for power, these women dealt with the pitiful results: famine and starvation. When Agnes's son, Robert, became disenchanted with King Richard, he swore allegiance to Marion, the Forestwife. A retelling of the legend of Robin Hood. *cmt*

**6.126** Townsend, Sue. **The Secret Diary of Adrian Mole, Aged 13¾.** Avon, 1982. Originally published by Methuen in 1982. ISBN 0-380-86876-8. 185 p. (12-14). Novel. **Great Britain.**

Adrian's engaging and often hilarious journal entries reflect on everyday events in his home, school, and neighborhood over a fifteen-month period. In a larger sense, they capture the essence of adolescence— idealism, contradiction, self-absorption, and passion. Adrian comments frankly on his parents' infidelities and his own hormone-induced urges. *cmt*

**6.127** van Iterson, Siny R. **The Smugglers of Buenaventura.** Translated by Hilda Van Stockum. Morrow, 1974. (10-14). Novel. **Netherlands** (set in Colombia).

Roberto, living in coastal, western Colombia in the 1960s, is concerned only with his own petty desires and problems until he is accidentally involved in a weapons smuggling operation. He is swiftly made aware of life's larger, crueler realities when he is betrayed and left to die in the jungle. Rescued by Ordulio, Roberto begins to learn the meaning of true friendship and loyalty. Many references to life in the rainforests of Colombia. *cmt*

**6.128** van Iterson, Siny R. **Pulga.** Translated by Alexander and Alison Gode. Morrow, 1971. Originally published as *De Adjudant van de Vrachtwagen* by Uitgeverij Leopold in 1971. LC 77-143462. 240 p. (12-14). Novel. **Netherlands** (set in Colombia).

Pulga (*flea* in Spanish), fifteen, a street urchin in Bogotá, Colombia, has little to live for and no one to care if he lives or dies. Recruited as a helper by a truck driver, Pulga makes an eventful trip over the mountains to the coast and back, and proves his mettle more than once in this outlaw-infested region. Back in the city, Pulga is once again on his own, but now he has some hope of finding a place for himself. *Mildred Batchelder Award. cmt*

**6.129** Westall, Robert. **The Machine-Gunners.** Greenwillow, 1976. Originally published by Macmillan in 1975. (paperback: Random House, 1990). ISBN 0-688-84055-8 (paperback: 0-679-80130-8). 186p. (11-14). Novel. **Great Britain.**
During World War II after an air raid, Chas McGill and his friends discover a dead German pilot and his machine gun. The boys hide the machine gun and build a secret emplacement for it. Rumors of imminent Nazi invasion induce the boys to use the gun against German hit-and-run bombers—with tragic results. *Carnegie Medal. al*

**6.130** Westall, Robert. **The Scarecrows.** Greenwillow, 1981. Originally published by Chatto and Windus in 1981. ISBN 0-688-00612-4. 185p. (12-14). Novel. **Great Britain.**
Menacing scarecrows suddenly appear outside thirteen-year-old Simon's window. Each morning, these apparitions are more and more threatening. Simon realizes that he must discover their identity and set things right before the scarecrows consume him and his family. Simultaneously, Simon has to reconcile the memory of his deceased soldier father with the reality of his new stepfather, an artist. *Carnegie Medal. al*

**6.131** Wieler, Diana. **Bad Boy.** Delacorte, 1992. Originally published by Groundwood in 1989. ISBN 0-385-30415-3. 184 p. (14-YA). Novel. **Canada.**
A. J. Brandiosa has much to cope with during his senior year in high school. He becomes the bad boy of his hockey team, learns that his best friend is gay, and attempts to deal with his own sexuality. *IBBY Honour List, Canada. cmt*

**6.132** Williams, Michael. **Crocodile Burning.** Dutton, 1992. Originally published by Oxford in 1992. ISBN 0-525-67401-2. (paperback: 0-195-70908-X). 208 p. (12-YA). Novel. **Republic of South Africa.**
For Sowetan teenager Seraki Nzule, getting a role in a township musical is a way to express his rage at the social conditions in his South African township and a chance to escape from the shambles of school, the poverty, the thugs, and his fear for his brother in jail. Then the musical moves to Broadway, and Seraki finds himself in New York. *hr*

**6.133** Wilson, Jacqueline. **Double Act.** Delacorte, 1998. Originally published by Doubleday in 1995. ISBN 0-38-532312-3. 188 p. (9-11).

**Great Britain.**
Ruby and Garnet, ten-year-old twins, try to deal with the changes in their lives when their father starts dating, and they face the possibility of being separated. (FirstSearch) *Smarties Prize. cmt*

**6.134** Wrightson, Patricia. **Night Outside.** Illustrated by Beth Peck. Atheneum/Margaret K. McElderry, 1985. Originally published in 1979. ISBN 0-689-50363-6. 67 p. (10-12). Novel. **Australia.**
Anne, nine, and her brother James, seven, live confined lives in their Sydney apartment. When their parents quarrel one night and their father throws James's budgie out the window, the children go out onto the streets to find the bird. Not only do they find their pet, but they also meet four people who live on the fringes of society. Meeting them enlarges Anne's perception of the world around her. *cmt*

**6.135** Wrightson, Patricia. **A Racecourse for Andy.** Harcourt, 1968. Originally published under the title *I Own the Racecourse* by Hutchinson in 1968. ISBN 0-14-036834-5. 155 p. (8-12). Novel. **Australia.**
Andy, though mentally disabled, has always been liked for his sunny disposition. When a bum offers to "sell" Andy the local racecourse for three dollars, Andy works hard to earn the money, gives it to the bum, and concludes that the racecourse is really his. The racecourse crew go along with the ruse until Andy decides to "fix up" the property. An understanding foreman solves the problem by buying the racecourse back from Andy for ten dollars. *cmt*

**6.136** Yumoto, Kazumi. **The Friends.** Translated by Cathy Hirano. Farrar, 1996. Originally published as *Natsu No Niwa* by Fukutake Publishing Co. in 1992. ISBN 0-374-32460-3. 170 p. (10-14). Novel. **Japan.**
Twelve-year-old Kiyama and two friends become intrigued with death and begin to spy on a solitary old man who lives in a decrepit house in their neighborhood. According to rumor, the old man is about to die and the boys want to witness this step in life. Under their watchful eyes, however, the man's health improves, and the boys develop a bond with him as they help him clean and restore his house. When the old man dies, the boys experience grief; but, as a result of their friendship, they also have a better understanding of the stages of life. *Mildred Batchelder Award; ALA Notable Book. sl*

**6.137** Zheleznikov, Vladimir. **Scarecrow**. Translated by Antonia W. Bouis. Lippincott, 1990. Originally published as *Chuchelo* by Molodaya Gvardia in 1983. ISBN 0-397-32316-6. 148 p. (10-12). Novel. **Russia.** Lena, an awkward thirteen-year-old, arrives in a small town to live with her grandfather, an artist. The children in school make fun of her, because she is so skinny. Only Dimka befriends her, but pays a terrible price for doing so. Grandfather saves Lena by donating his paintings to the town to start a museum and then taking his granddaughter away with him. *dd*

# HISTORICAL FICTION

**7.1** Almagor, Gila. **Under the Domim Tree**. Translated by Hillel Schenkel. Simon & Schuster, 1995. Originally published as *Etz Ha-domim Tafus* by Am Oved in 1992. ISBN 0-671-89020-4. 176 p. (12-14). Novel. **Israel.**

The Israeli youth village in which Aviya,Yola, and Mira live in 1953 is a place of transition for children whose parents are either missing or unable to care for them in the aftermath of the Holocaust. As they come to terms with their grief and the uncertainty of their futures, the children establish their own rituals and codes of conduct, which include allowing one another privacy in the only available place—under the domim tree atop a nearby hill. These survivors must deal with death, depression, and dashed hopes as they make their journey to adulthood. *sl, ss*

**7.2** Baklanov, Grigory. **Forever Nineteen**. Translated by Antonina W. Bouis. Lippincott, 1989. Originally published as *Naveki—deviatnadtsatiletnie* by Grigory Baklanov in 1979. ISBN 0-397-32296-8. 168 p. (12-YA). Novel. **Russia.**

Volodya Tretyakov is a nineteen-year-old lieutenant serving on the Russian front against the Germans during World War II. The harshness, urgency, gore, and senselessness of war are played out in Tretyakov's short lifetime. Based upon the author's own wartime experiences. *CCBC Choices. jl*

**7.3** Bergman, Tamar. **Along the Tracks**. Translated by Michael Swirsky. Houghton, 1991. Originally published as *Le-Orekh Ha-Mesilah* by Schoken Publishing House in 1988. ISBN 0-395-55328-8. 245 p. (10-14). Novel. **Israel**.

When Yankele, a Jew, was six, the Nazis invaded Poland, and his family fled to Russia for safety. There, he was separated from his family. For years he wandered across the vast Kazakhstan region of the Soviet Union by stealing rides aboard freight trains, barely surviving. Miraculously, Yankele's family was reunited after the war and emigrated to Israel. Epilogue states that Yankele and the events in this story are real. *Ze'ev Prize of the Ministry of Education* (Israel). *cw, cmt*

**7.4** Berry, James. **Ajeemah and His Son**. HarperCollins, 1992. Originally published by Hamish Hamilton in the collection, *The Future-Telling Lady* in 1991. (paperback: Harper Trophy, 1994). ISBN 0-06-021043-5 (Paperback: 0-06-440523-0). 83 p. (10-14). Novel. **Great Britain**.

In 1807 Africa, as Ajeemah and his 18-year-old son, Atu, were walking to the next village to finalize Atu's marriage agreement, they were captured by slavers. Taken to Jamaica, they were sold to owners of neighboring sugar plantations, but never saw one another again. Atu, convinced that he would never be able to return to Africa, ended his own life. Ajeemah, though faithful to the memory of his family in Africa, eventually found love again, bought his freedom, and made a new life for himself. *Boston Globe-Horn Book Award. cmt*

**7.5** Conlon-McKenna, Marita. **Under the Hawthorn Tree**. Holiday House, 1990. Originally published by O'Brien Press in 1990 (paperback: Puffin, 1992). ISBN 0-14-036031-X. 124 p. (10-14). Novel. **Ireland**.

At twelve, Eily was the eldest and had to care for her brother and sister when her parents disappeared during the dreadful Potato Famine in Ireland in the 1840s. Not wanting to be sent to a workhouse and separated, they made their way overland to great-aunts they had only heard of in family stories. Their harrowing, three-week journey reveals the utter misery and destitution that prevailed in this country when a million people were lost to starvation in five years. *International Reading Association Children's Book Award. cmt*

**7.6** Doyle, Brian. **Easy Avenue**. Groundwood/Douglas & McIntyre,

1988. (paperback: Firefly Books). ISBN 0-88899-065-0. 118p. (10-14). Novel. **Canada**.

Hulbert (Hubbo) O'Driscoll, orphaned at an early age, lives in an "emergency shelter" with his adoptive mother who is the cleaning lady at the high school where he is a freshman. After Hubbo saves the life of a rich man he caddies for, he is offered a job as companion for a rich, elderly woman and given a monthly sum from a mysterious donor. Hubbo struggles with issues of honor, acceptance, and class consciousness as he adjusts to high school life in post-World War II Ottawa. *Canadian Children's Book of the Year Award. lg*

**7.7** Fährmann, Willi. **The Long Journey of Lukas B.** Translated by Anthea Bell. Bradbury, 1985. Originally published as *Der Lange Weg des Lukas B.* by Arena-Verlag Georg Popp in 1980. ISBN 0-02-734330-8. 280 p. (12-14). Novel. **Germany**.

Fourteen-year-old Lukas, living in Prussia in the 1870s, longs to find his father Karl, who left home because he wanted to be a painter against his father's wishes. Lukas accompanies his master carpenter grandfather and his carpentry gang to America to earn money to repay Karl's debts. Along the way, Lukas learns more about his father, and eventually, about himself. Interesting observations of social customs of the day. *German Children's Book Prize; Austrian State Prize for Children's Literature. jl, cmt*

**7.8** Gehrts, Barbara. **Don't Say A Word**. Translated by Elizabeth D. Crawford. McElderry, 1986. Originally published as *Nie Wieder ein Wort Davon* in 1975. ISBN 0-689-50412-8. 169 p. (10-14). Novel. **Germany**.

Growing up in Berlin during World War II, Anna grows increasingly aware of the dangerous direction in which her country is moving. Her father, a high-ranking staff officer in the Luftwaffe, is unalterably opposed to the Hitler regime and secretly works to assist the Jews. When Anna and her older brother Hannes discover their father's covert activities, they understand that they must never say a word. Even when the Gestapo arrests their father they remain silent, lest further harm come to their family and friends. Based on the author's childhood experiences in Nazi Germany. *djg*

**7.9** Härtling, Peter. **Crutches**. Translated by Elizabeth D. Crawford.

Lothrop, 1988. *See Realistic Fiction.*

**7.10** Hartman, Evert. **War Without Friends**. Crown, 1982. Originally published as *Oorlog Zonder Vrienden* in 1982. ISBN 0-517-54754-6. 218 p. (12-14). Novel. **Netherlands**.

In a small Dutch town during World War II, fourteen-year-old Arnold, a member of the Hitler Youth, feels increasingly isolated and trapped between his father's fervent support of the Nazi Party and his classmates' hostile opposition to all the Nazis stand for. (FirstSearch) *cmt*

**7.11** Hendry, Frances. **Quest for a Kelpie**. Holiday House, 1988. Originally published by Canongate Publishing Ltd. in 1986. ISBN 0-82434-0680-6. 154 p. (12-14). Novel. **Scotland**.

Jeannie Main, fisherman's daughter, plays a pivotal role in Prince Charles's Scottish Rebellion against King George II in 1745. Aided by a band of gypsies that she once helped, Jeannie sometimes believes that she has magic on her side, but lives through the horrors of war and plague, filth, and the casual brutality of the times to realize that her intellect, hard work, honesty, and decisions are the real protagonists in her life. Told as a memoir, the story is rich in Scottish dialect. The extensive glossary is essential, and the author's note about Scottish history, 1689-1745, is helpful. *cmt*

**7.12** Heuck, Sigrid. **The Hideout**. Translated by Rika Lesser. Illustrated by Jindra Câpek. Dutton, 1988. Originally published as *Maisfrieden* by K. Thienemanns Verlag in 1986. ISBN 0-525-44343-6. 183 p. (10-12). Novel. **Germany**.

A little girl named Rebecca is found among the ruins of a building bombed during World War II. She remembers nothing but her first name. She is sent to an orphanage, but en route an air raid stops the train and sends her running into a corn field. There she meets a boy named Sami who has hidden in the field for weeks. Sami invites Rebecca to join him in his fantasy world, far away from war. Story is based upon the author's own childhood memories. *jl*

**7.13** Hudson, Jan. **Dawn Rider**. Philomel, 1990. ISBN 0-399-22178-6. 173 p. (10-12). Novel. **Canada**.

Kit Fox, a sixteen-year-old Blackfoot woman living on the western prairie of Canada in 1750, wants to ride the first horse that her people,

the Bloods, have acquired. She gets her wish, because her friend Found
Arrow is the horse's guard. When the Snakes attack, she rides the horse
to the Cree camp to get guns to protect her people. An intimate picture
of the daily life of eighteenth-century Blackfoot people. *dd*

**7.14** Hudson, Jan. **Sweetgrass**. Philomel, 1989. Originally published by
Tree Frog, 1984. (Paperback: Scholastic, 1991). ISBN 0-399-21721-5.
159p. (12-14). Novel. **Canada.**
Sweetgrass, at fifteen, is the only one of her friends not married or
betrothed. When the smallpox epidemic of 1837-1838 decimates her
tribe, Sweetgrass heroically nurses her mother and brother to recovery
and is finally considered a woman by her father. The book ends as she
moves toward her destiny as wife, mother, and a strong member of her
Blackfoot Indian tribe. *Canadian Library Association Book of the Year
for Children; Canada Council Children's Literature Prize. lg*

**7.15** Hunter, Mollie. **The Stronghold**. Harper & Row, 1974. Originally
published by Hamilton in 1974. ISBN 0-06-022653-6. 259p. (12-14).
Novel. **Great Britain.**
Wounded in a Roman raid when he was young, Coll, a Scot, is determined to design and build a defense against the Romans. His efforts
result in the "broch", or stone stronghold. In order to save the woman he
loves from being sacrificed, Coll has to convince Druid priests that the
Stronghold is his people's only salvation against the raiding Romans.
*Carnegie Medal. al*

**7.16** Jicai, Feng. **Let One Hundred Flowers Bloom**. Translated by
Christopher Smith. Viking, 1995. Copublished by Penguin Books
worldwide in 1995. ISBN 0-670-85805-6. 106 p. (12-YA). Novel.
**China.**
Hua Xiayu, an artist, tells the painful story of his physical and mental
persecution and years of exile at the hands of Mao Tse Tung's Red
Guard during China's Cultural Revolution from the mid-1960s to 1976.
His resilience and ability to find some good in the worst situations are
presented as characteristic of the Chinese people. Short glossary of
Chinese words and political terms. *cmt*

**7.17** Körner, Wolfgang. **The Green Frontier**. Morrow, 1977. Originally
published as *Der Weg Nach Druben*. ISBN 0-688-22124-6. 190 p. (10-

12). Novel. **Germany.**

Before the building of the Berlin Wall, an East German schoolboy reluctantly accompanies his family in their flight to the West. (First-Search) *cmt*

**7.18** Lasenby, Jack. **The Mangrove Summer.** Oxford, 1988. ISBN 0-19-558194-6. 177 p. (10-12). Novel. **New Zealand.**

Jill, George, and Jimmy learn in December, 1941, that their father is a prisoner of war in Germany. As the Japanese approach Singapore, the family removes to their remote coastal cottage to stay with cousins. When the adults leave temporarily, Jill is convinced that the Japanese will soon arrive and takes the children into the wilderness to escape. They learn how to survive in the wilderness as they flee pursuers who turn out to be a rescue party. Glossary of New Zealand terms included. *Esther Glen Award. dd*

**7.19** Linevski, Aleksandr. **An Old Tale Carved Out of Stone.** Translated by Maria Polushkin. Crown, 1973. Originally published as *Listy kamennoi knigi.* LCCN 72-92386. 230 p. (12-14). Novel. **Russia.**

Liok's childhood ends abruptly during his fourteenth year when his clan's *shaman,* or wiseman, dies, and Liok is forced to replace him. Life in coastal Siberia at the end of the Stone Age is ruled by weather, superstition, and complex traditions. Liok soon realizes that much of what the *shaman* does is a sham, and regrets having to lie to his people. Unschooled in the ways of the *shaman,* he violates several taboos and is forced to flee southward where he joins a more advanced clan. After many months, Liok, now truly a wise man, risks returning to his clan to share with them the valuable skills that he has learned. *Mildred Batchelder Award, 1975. cmt*

**7.20** Magorian, Michelle. **Goodnight, Mr. Tom.** Harper and Row, 1981. Originally published by Kestrel in 1981. ISBN 0-06-024078-4. 318p. (12-14). Novel. **Great Britain**

Frail, nine-year-old Willie Beech is evacuated from London during the World War II bombings and is billeted with Mr. Tom Oakley. Willie, an abused child, seems like a frightened rabbit. Tom, a reclusive old man, widowed for many years, seems an unlikely guardian. But patiently and gently, Mr. Tom soothes Willie's wounds, body and, eventually, soul, and in the process finds release from the pain of the loss of his own wife and child. *International Reading Association Children's Book Award; West Australian Young Readers' Book Award; ALA Best Books for Young Adults; Guardian Award for Children's Literature* (Great Britain). *djg*

**7.21** Morpurgo, Michael. **The Wreck of the Zanzibar.** Illustrated by Francois Place. Viking, 1995. Originally published by Methuen in 1994. ISBN 0-670-86360-2. 68 p. (12-14). Illustrated novella. **Great Britain.** The year of 1907 has not been good for fourteen-year-old Laura and her family. Living on one of the stormy Scilly Islands off the British coast, the Perrymans can eke out a living only by salvaging cargo that is washed up from wrecked ships. As Laura records in her diary her family misfortunes and her dream of participating in a shipwreck rescue that will save the family from ruin, little does she suspect that her dream will come true. *Whitbread Award. cmt*

**7.22** Orlev, Uri. **The Island on Bird Street.** Translated by Hillel Halkin. Houghton Mifflin, 1984. Originally published as *Ha-l-bi-Rehov Ha-Tsip-orim* by Keter Publishing, Jerusalem, in 1981 (paperback: Sandpiper, 1991). ISBN 0-395-33887-5. 162 p. (10-12). Novel. **Israel.** Eleven-year-old Alex lived with his parents in the Jewish ghetto in Warsaw during World War II. First, his mother "disappeared" while visiting friends, and then his father was abruptly taken by the German army. Following his father's frantic last-minute instructions, Alex went into hiding in a bombed-out house at the edge of the ghetto, surviving for ten months by his wits and ingenuity. Despite his perilous circumstances and constant exposure to the cruelty around him, Alex retained his pluck, compassion, and hope until help arrived. *Mildred Batchelder Award; ALA Notable Book; Booklist Editor's Choice; Association of Jewish Libraries Best Book Award; Horn Book's Fanfare; Jane Addams Peace Award; Orlev: Hans Christian Andersen Medalist for Writing. cmt*

**7.23** Orlev, Uri. **The Lady with the Hat.** Translated by Hillel Halkin. Houghton Mifflin, 1995. Originally published by Keter Publishing, Jerusalem, in 1990. ISBN 0-395-69957-6. 185 p. (12-14). Novel. **Israel.** Seventeen-year-old Yulek searches in vain for family survivors in Poland in 1947. He is determined to immigrate to Israel, but must do so illegally, due to strict immigration laws enforced by the Allied Forces.

As he trains at a refugee camp in Italy for life on a kibbutz, little does he know that an aunt, living in England, has seen his picture and is searching for him. Fate keeps the two apart until they meet briefly, but happily, just as Yulek successfully makes his way to a new life in Palestine. *Mildred Batchelder Award; ALA Notable Book. mew, cmt*

**7.24** Orlev, Uri. **The Man from the Other Side.** Translated by Hillel Halkin. Houghton Mifflin, 1991. Originally published as *Ish Min Hatsad Ha-aher* by The Domino Press in 1989. ISBN 0-305-53808-4. 186 p. (12-14). Novel. **Israel.**

In Warsaw, Poland, Marek, fourteen, reluctantly helps his stepfather smuggle food and supplies through sewer tunnels to the Jewish Ghetto during World War II. His mother discovers that he has blackmailed an escapee from the ghetto and tells Marek that his father was Jewish. His reluctance turned to zeal, he participates in a dangerous mission to smuggle Jews out of the ghetto and participates in an important Jewish uprising. *Mildred Batchelder Award; ALA Notable Book. cmt, mew*

**7.25** Pausewang, Gudrun. **The Final Journey.** Translated by Patricia Crampton. Viking, 1996. Originally published as *Reise im August* by Ravensburger Buchverlag Otto Maier GmbH in 1992. ISBN 0-670-86456-0. 155 p. (14-YA). Novel. **Germany.**

Alice, an eleven-year-old girl on the brink of womanhood, endures a horrific several-day journey to Auschwitz in a closed cattle-car. Sheltered by her family from most facts of life, including the Nazi atrocities, she learns much from her fifty fellow travelers, young and old, as they react to unthinkable misery. Even as they enter the "showers" at Auschwitz, Alice and others do not suspect the ultimate purpose of their journey. *Bulletin of the Center for Children's Books Blue Ribbon. mew, cmt*

**7.26** Pearson, Kit. **The Sky Is Falling.** Viking 1990. Originally published by Penguin Ltd. in 1989. (paperback: Puffin, 1995). ISBN 0-670-82849-1. 256 p. (10-12). Novel. **Canada.**

At ten-and-a-half Norah feels grown-up enough to help fight the Battle of Britain, but her parents send her and her six-year-old brother to Ontario where they will be safe. Norah's feeling of betrayal at being sent away makes it difficult for her to adjust to her new life, and the woman she is sent to seems to want only her little brother, anyway. When Norah runs away with her brother, she learns just how much they both mean to their new family and friends. By Christmastime, she is beginning to adjust to her new life. Sequels: *Looking at the Moon; The Lights Are on Again. Canadian Children's Book of the Year Award. lg, be*

**7.27** Pelgrom, Els. **The Winter When Time Was Frozen.** Translated by Maryka and Raphael Rudnik. Morrow, 1980. Originally published as *De Kinderen van het Achtste Woud* by Uitgeverij Kosmos, Amsterdam, 1977. ISBN 0-688-33347-1. 253 p. (10-12). Novel. **Netherlands.**
During the last months of World War II, Noortje, twelve, and her father are forced by the Germans to evacuate their home in the city and to seek sanctuary on the Klaphek farm. In this surreal juxtaposition of war and routine, Noortje quickly matures as she helps to hide a Jewish family, helps to deliver a baby, becomes aware of the underground movement, and cares for a handicapped child. The Klapheks' great courage and empathy inspire her. *Mildred Batchelder Award. cmt*

**7.28** Richter, Hans Peter. **Friedrich.** Translated by Edite Kroll. Holt, 1970. Originally published as *Damals War Es Friedrich* by Sebaldus-Verlag G.m.b.H. Nürnberg in 1961. (Paperback, Puffin, 1987). ISBN 0-14-032205-1. 149p. 12-14. Novel. **Germany.**
Friedrich Schneider and the narrator were born within a week of one another in 1925 Germany, and then grew up as best friends. Life went well for the able, hardworking Schneiders until 1933, when Hitler came to power; but then their world began to fall apart, for the Schneiders were Jewish. Told from the point of view of Friedrich's friend, this very personal account of the gradual degradation and destruction of a family will enable young readers to grasp the terrible injustice and senseless brutality of the Jewish pogrom. A chronology of German political events from 1933-45 is included. *Mildred Batchelder Award. cmt*

**7.29** Schami, Rafik. **A Hand Full of Stars.** Translated by Rika Lesser. Dutton, 1990. Originally published as *Eine Hand voller Sterne* by Beltz Verlag in 1987. (paperback: Puffin, 1992). ISBN 0-14-036073-5. 195p. (12-14). Novel. **Germany.**
At age fourteen Hanne decides to become a journalist and begins to keep a journal of his life in politically turbulent, modern-day Damascus, Syria. His spirited, humorous, yet thoughtful journal entries paint

vivid pictures of his family, neighbors, and friends and their struggles with the poverty and chaos caused by four despotic governments in as many years. Guided by his wise old friend, Uncle Salim, and his mentor, newspaperman Habib, the boy discovers a way to strike back at the injustice surrounding him and, at the same time, to realize his dream. *Mildred Batchelder Award; ALA Notable Book; ALA Best Book for Young Adults. cmt*

**7.30** Seed, Jenny. **The Great Thirst**. Bradbury, 1973. Originally published by Hamish Hamilton/Tafelburg in 1971. ISBN 0-878-88058-5. 191 p. (10-12). Novel. **Republic of South Africa.**

In South-West Africa in the 1830s Garib's father is killed by a warrior from a neighboring tribe. Garib, seven, vows to avenge his father's death, but, years later, when he faces his father's killer as an adult, he cannot kill. Having lost everything in the tribal conflict, Garib decides to return to his family, free at last of his burden of revenge. *dd*

**7.31** Seed, Jenny. **The Voice of the Great Elephant**. Pantheon, 1968. Originally published by Hamish Hamilton in 1968. 178 p. (10-12). Novel. **Great Britain, Republic of South Africa.**

In the early 1800s in Zulu territory in Africa, Vika is selected to live in the house of Shaka, the famed Zulu chieftain (the Great Elephant), as an apprentice. At first he watches as Shaka, his idol, subdues the neighboring tribes in battle, but is repulsed as the battle turns into massacre. Finally Vika and his father stand up to Shaka, return home, and decide to migrate to the mountains. In so doing, they contribute to the downfall of the Zulu chief. *dd*

**7.32** Sevela, Ephraim. **We Were Not Like Other People**. Translated by Antonina W. Bouis. Harper & Row, 1989. ISBN 0-06-025507-2. 216 p. (12-14). Novel. **Russia.**

A Jewish boy, separated from his parents by the Stalinist purge and World War II, makes his way over six years from Siberia to Germany. Learning fast how to be a survivor, he barely gains a new family and community before he loses them. His relationships with a once-hated teacher, a Siberian farm family, a Russian colonel, and a private in the Soviet army are all too temporary. *CCBC Choices. jl, djg*

**7.33** Sutcliff, Rosemary. **Flame-Colored Taffeta**. Farrar, 1986. Originally published as *Flame-Coloured Taffeta* by Oxford in 1986. 130 p. Novel. **Great Britain.**

In the mid-1700s on the coast of Sussex in southern England, smuggling goods from Europe to avoid tariffs and sympathy for Bonnie Prince Charlie, exiled pretender to the throne of King George II, were facts of life. When twelve-year-old Damaris and her best friend Peter hide a mysterious, wounded stranger in their forest hideout, they play a part in both matters. Damaris's trust in the stranger is rewarded when, five years later, she receives from him a petticoat of flame-colored taffeta—a symbol of her independent, fiery spirit—on the eve of her wedding. Interesting portrait of eighteenth-century rural English life. *cmt*

**7.34** Sutcliff, Rosemary. **The Lantern Bearers**. Peter Smith, 1995. Originally published by Oxford in 1959. (paperback: Farrar, 1994). ISBN 0-8446-6837-0 (paperback: 0-374-44302-5). 252p. (14-YA). Novel. **Great Britain.**

Aquila, a young Roman officer, chooses to remain in Britain when his comrades sail for home, only to have all that he loves destroyed by Saxon invaders. His struggles, both in and out of battle, finally allow him to make amends with his sister, who has married a Saxon man. A stirring saga set in the chaotic period of British history prior to the Dark Ages. *Carnegie Medal. al*

**7.35** Sutcliff, Rosemary. **The Shining Company**. Farrar, 1990. Originally published by The Bodley Head in 1990. ISBN 0-374-46616-5. 296 p. (12-14). Novel. **Great Britain.**

The world of 600 A.D. Britain is brought to life in this epic story of courage and brotherhood as ancient tribes battle for supremacy. The story is based on The Gododdin, the earliest surviving North British poem. *be*

**7.36** Taylor, Cora. **Summer of the Mad Monk**. Greystone/Douglas & McIntyre, 1994. ISBN 1-55054-174-9. 145p. (10-14). Novel. **Canada.**

In 1932 twelve-year-old Pip and his family are suffering from the Depression and the dust storms that are destroying their farm in southern Alberta. Poor in material goods, Pip is rich in family and imagination. His imagination is fueled by the books he borrows from an elderly neighbor, and when he reads about Rasputin, he is certain that the Russian blacksmith in town is the mad monk himself. His certainty grows when he discovers that the blacksmith is hiding a wounded young man. Pip uses his courage and his imagination to help the two as they try to avoid discovery by the Soviet agents seeking them. *Canadian Children's Book of the Year Award. lg*

**7.37** Thiele, Colin. **The Valley Between.** Rigby, 1981. ISBN 0-72701-782-9. 168p. (12-14). Novel. **Australia.**
Set in the German agricultural community of Gonunda in South Australia in the 1920s, these mostly humorous episodes feature Benno, a 13-year-old farmer-to-be, and two rival neighborhood farmers. Details of post-World War II life, such as hand-knit woolen bathing suits, beef slaughtering procedures, and Model T Fords are woven into each chapter. The importance of family and community is emphasized, but the narrow-mindedness and greed endemic to humans is acknowledged as well. Glossary of Australian and German terms provided. *Australia's Children's Book of the Year for Older Readers Award. cmt*

**7.38** Vos, Ida. **Dancing on the Bridge of Avignon**. Translated by Terese Edelstein and Inez Smidt. Houghton Mifflin, 1995. Originally published as *Dansen op de Brug van Avignon* by Uitgeverij Leopold in 1989. ISBN 0-395-72039-7. 183 p. (10-14). **Netherlands.**
Ten-year-old Rosa and her family watch as their neighbors are taken to concentration camps in Holland in 1942. To cope with her fear, Rosa spends more and more time dreaming of prewar days and escape to Avignon in the south of France. A new violin teacher offers a temporary diversion, but then he, too, is taken away. Then, Rosa's family is deported to Poland. Luckily, Rosa reminds a German officer of his daughter who is also a violinist, and she is allowed to escape. Includes an informative epilogue. Also by the same author: *Hide and Seek* (1990) and *Anna Is Still Here* (1993). *mw, djg*

**7.39** Walsh, Jill Paton. **Grace**. Farrar, 1992. Originally published by Viking Kestrel in 1991. ISBN 0-374-32758-0. 256p. (12-14). Novel. **Great Britain**.
When a storm hits the Northumbrian coast of England in 1838, it drives the frigate *Forfarshire* aground. Grace Darling's brother is away on the mainland, and so she must assist her father in the rescue. Word of Grace's courage and bravery spreads throughout England, and she is catapulted into fame. The attention and intrusion upon her quiet life is

difficult enough for Grace to bear, but when rumors spread accusing her of attempting the rescue for the reward, she becomes deeply troubled. A poignant and tragic story based on true accounts. *djg*

**7.40** Zei, Alki. **Petros' War.** Translated by Edward Fenton. Dutton, 1972. Originally published as *Ho Megalos Peripatos tou Petrou* by Editions "Kedros" in 1971. ISBN 0-525-36962-7. 236 p. (10-12). Novel. **Greece.**
Petros' once-happy life in Athens, Greece, has been shattered by World War II. Invasion, loss of freedom, famine, and depression quickly mature this child and convince him to join the Resistance. After his friends are murdered, Petros is ready to continue their fight. *Mildred Batchelder Award. cmt*

**7.41** Zei, Alki. **The Sound of the Dragon's Feet.** Translated by Edward Fenton. Dutton, 1979. Originally published as *Konta Stis Ragies.* ISBN 0-525-39712-4. 113 p. (10-12). Novel. **Greece.**
Life in prerevolutionary Russia might well have remained hidden from sheltered ten-year-old Sasha, had not her tutor, Mooney Moonevitch, opened her eyes to the terror and injustice suffered daily by people living all around her. Anxious to know the reasons for such phenomenal wrong, Sasha forced her father and her tutor to face the injustices of the monarchy and thus acted as a catalyst for the revolution. *Mildred Batchelder Award. cmt*

**7.42** Zei, Alki. **Wildcat Under Glass.** Translated by Edward Fenton. Holt, 1968. Originally published as *To Kaplani tis Vitrinas* by Editions "Themelio" in 1963. ISBN 03-068010-7. 177 p. (10-12). Novel. **Greece.**
A Fascist dictator takes over the government of Greece in 1936. The loss of freedom and the strain of opposing loyalties are felt everywhere in the country, even on the island where Melia and her family live. Melia is forced to ponder her own loyalties when her sister joins the fascist youth movement and her cousin becomes an antifascist freedom fighter. For Melia, the stuffed wildcat in a glass case in their parlor becomes a symbol for the resistance when she discovers that it is the hiding place for her cousin's messages. *Mildred Batchelder Award. cmt*

# FANTASY

**8.1** Adams, Richard. **Watership Down**. Macmillan, 1974. Originally published by Rex Collings in 1972. (Paperback, Avon, 1976). ISBN 0-02-700030-3 (paperback: 0-380-00293-0). 429p. (12-14). Novel. **Great Britain**.
Hazel, a young rabbit, envisions the destruction of his Berkshire warren, and with his companions, Fiver and Bigwig, begins a quest for a new home site. Though the rabbits cover only a few square miles, their journey is nonetheless an epic, with detailed characterization, intricate descriptions of rabbit life, and many literary references and allusions that have made this story a perennial favorite with children and adults. *Carnegie Medal. al*

**8.2** Ahlberg, Alan. **Woof!** Illustrated by Fritz Wegner. Viking Kestrel, 1986. ISBN 0-670-80832-6. 154 p. (9-12). Novel. **Great Britain**.
One ordinary summer evening, ten-year-old Eric Banks is turned into a Norfolk terrier. Extraordinary and humorous events follow. *IBBY Honour List. cmt*

**8.3** Alcock, Vivien. **The Monster Garden**. Delacorte, 1988. Originally published by Methuen in 1988. (paperback: Dell, 1990). ISBN 0-440-50053-2. 134 p. (10-12). Novel. **Great Britain**.

Although Frankie is interested in science, her genetic engineer father only takes her brothers' academic interests seriously. Experimenting alone, she manages to grow a monster out of some goo from the lab. Quickly growing attached to Monnie, her monster, Frankie enlists some friends in keeping her secret and taking care of her creation. *ALA Notable Books for Children; CCBC Choice. jl*

**8.4** Alcock, Vivien. **The Mysterious Mr. Ross**. Delacorte, 1987. Originally published by Methuen in 1987. (paperback: Dell, 1990). ISBN 0-385-29581-2. 161 p. (10-12). Novel. **Great Britain**.
Twelve-year-old Felicity, awkward on land, but graceful in the sea, rescues a mysterious young man from drowning. He ingratiates himself with Felicity's family and community, making it difficult for her to discover who or what he really is. *CCBC Choices. jl*

**8.5** Breslin, Theresa. **Whispers in the Graveyard**. Heinemann, 1994. Originally published by Methuen in 1994. ISBN 0-4161-9052-9. 127 p. (12-14). Novel. **Great Britain**.
Solomon, who has a learning disability, lives in Scotland with his alcoholic and abusive father. He often escapes from his troubles to a hiding place in an old churchyard. But construction around the graveyard riles an evil spirit, and Solomon has yet another battle on his hands. Fortunately, he comes to this confrontation well prepared. *Carnegie Medal. cmt*

**8.6** Carmody, Isobelle. **The Gathering**. Dial, 1994. Originally published by Penguin Books Australia Ltd. in 1993. ISBN 0-8037-1716-4. 279p. (12-14). Novel. **Australia**.
From the moment he arrives in Cheshunt, Nathaniel is filled with foreboding. Evil seems to saturate the place. Then he is "selected" to join four oddballs at his high school who plan to rescue the town from an evil force embodied in the school principal, Mr. Karle. Guided by an ethereal spirit, the five young people gather symbols of good while trying to avoid Mr. Karle's insidious and often violent attempts to thwart their efforts. Nathaniel's growing affection for his cohort, Nissa, and the slowly unraveling mystery of his deceased father add interest. *Co-Winner: Australia's Children's Book of the Year for Older Readers Award. cmt*

**8.7** Chauncey, Nan. **Tangara.** Penguin, 1987. Originally published by Oxford in 1960. ISBN 0-19277-094-2. 180p. (12-14). Novel. **Australia.**
On a hike to a remote and mysterious gully, Lexie, nine, meets Merrina, a Tasmanian aboriginal whose race was thought to be extinct. Lexie befriends Merrina who introduces her to her tribe and customs. But one day two white men appear, and Lexie envisions a terrible massacre. Months later Lexie tells Kent, her brother, about the episode and then seems to forget everything. Five years later Kent disappears and Merrina, in a dream, leads Lexie to the gully and her injured brother. Kent explains that the massacre really happened 70 years ago. *Australia's Book of the Year for Older Readers Award. cmt*

**8.8** Christopher, John. **The White Mountains.** Macmillan, 1967. Originally published by Hamish Hamilton in 1967. (paperback: Macmillan, 1988). ISBN 0-02-718360-2. 184p. (11-13). Novel. **Great Britain.**
The world has been overtaken by powerful machine-creatures, the Tripods, who control humans by implanting metal caps in the heads of young people at age 13. Will, Henry, and Beanpole (Jean Paul) manage to elude their capping ceremonies and flee to the White Mountains (the Swiss Alps) where there is rumored to be a colony of freedom fighters. This engrossing and original science-fiction story is continued in *The City of Gold and Lead* (ISBN 0-02-718380-7, 1968). The trilogy triumphantly concludes with *The Pool of Fire* (ISBN 0-02-718350-5, 1968). *cw. Editor's note: A prequel,* How the Tripods Came, *is of lesser quality.*

**8.9** Crew, Gary. **Strange Objects.** Simon & Schuster, 1993. Originally published by Reed International in 1990. ISBN 0-671-79759-X. 216 p. (12-14). Novel. **Australia.**
Mystery surrounds Steven Messenger's discovery of three-hundred-year-old relics in a coastal cave in Western Australia. While authorities piece together the tragic story behind the relics—an iron pot, a mummified human hand, and a sailor's journal—the sixteen-year-old Messenger experiences frightening dreams, visions, and hallucinations seemingly brought on by the missing relic, a ring that the boy cannot part with. Messenger's disappearance and other inexplicable occurrences leave much to ponder. *Australia's Children's Book of the Year for Older Readers Award. cmt*

**8.10** Cross, Gillian. **New World**. Holiday House, 1995. Originally published by Oxford in 1994. (paperback: Viking Penguin, 1996). ISBN 0-8234-1166-4. 171 p. (12-14). Novel. **Great Britain**.

Miriam and Stewart have been selected, supposedly at random, to test a new virtual reality computer game, "New World." They are to tell no one about the experience. Miriam finds the game frightening, yet thrilling and addictive, but soon feels certain that someone unknown is also playing the game. When her secret childhood nightmare appears in the game, Miriam's fear becomes real. *CCBC Choices. jl*

**8.11** Cross, Gillian. **Roscoe's Leap**. Holiday, 1987. Originally published by Oxford in 1987. ISBN 0-8234-0669-5. 160 p. (12-14). Novel. **Great Britain**.

In this suspense-filled part-mystery, part-supernatural tale, a twelve-year-old boy searches for the meaning of a collection of old wind-up toys in the decrepit home of a long-dead eccentric millionaire. *be*

**8.12** Dickinson, Peter. **The Devil's Children**. Little, Brown, 1970. Originally published by Gollancz in 1970. (paperback: Dell, 1988). ISBN 0-440-20082-2. 187 p. (12-14). Novel. **Great Britain**.

Book One of The Changes Trilogy begins five weeks after a strange power is unleashed that throws the people of Great Britain into a fearful, Middle Ages mentality, causing them to reject the world of machines and revert to an agrarian lifestyle. Since Nicky Gore has been separated from her parents, she takes up with a group of Sikhs as they search for a place to settle. Nicky acts as a liaison between the Sikhs and people who have been affected by the madness, and as such, she understands that the cruel prejudices against the Sikhs are completely unfounded. Her mettle in a battle against marauding robbers wins the Sikhs' admiration, but they decide that she must escape England and find her family before she loses her capacity to love. Book Two, *Heartsease*, set four years into the Changes, follows the efforts of two young people to save a "witch", or outsider, from the mob hysteria of the villagers. Book Three, *The Weathermonger*, set five years into the Changes as the mysterious enchantment is weakening, follows Geoffrey as he seeks to discover the cause of the Changes. *cmt*

**8.13** Dickinson, Peter. **Eva**. Delacorte, 1989. Originally published by Victor Gollancz Ltd. in 1988. ISBN 0-385-29702-5. 219. (Mature 13-

YA). Novel. **Great Britain.**
In this future world, though medical science has advanced, quality of life has declined with overpopulation and loss of wilderness. When Eva's body is destroyed in a car accident, her parents, in an effort to save her, decide to have her brain implanted in the body of a chimpanzee. Over the years, Eva grows more and more sympathetic to the nonhuman perspective and is able to guide the last colony of chimpanzees in a return to their natural state as the human world continues to deteriorate. *Boston Globe/Horn Book Honor Book; ALA Notable Book; ALA Best Book for Young Adults; SLJ Best Books of the Year. cmt*

**8.14** Dickinson, Peter. **Healer**. Delacorte. 1985. Originally published by Gollancz in 1983. ISBN 0-385-29372-0. 184pp. (12-14). Novel. **Great Britain.**
Ten-year-old Pinky has the power to heal. She is being exploited by her stepfather to draw desperately sick people to his otherwise bogus health compound, Foundation of Harmony. Remembering the shy little girl he had befriended years before, sixteen-year-old Barry, encouraged by Pinky's grandfather, attempts to rescue the unhappy child from the prisonlike compound. Complex and fully realized characters and suspense-filled plot. *bb*

**8.15** Ende, Michael. **The Neverending Story**. Translated by Ralph Manheim. Doubleday, 1983. Originally published as *Die Unendliche Geschichte* by K. Thiennemanns Verlag in 1979. (paperback: Puffin, 1985). ISBN 0-14-031793-7. 445 p. (12-14). Novel. **Germany.**
Bastian, "a fat little boy of ten or twelve," was miserable. His mother had died, he was teased at school, and he was ignored at home by a father lost in grief. But having a wonderful imagination and loving to read, Bastian found his way to Fantastica, a marvelous world nourished by the human imagination but now threatened by extinction for lack of human visitors. Aided by the friends he made there, Bastian, in a succession of monumental adventures, saved the realm and became the person he wanted to be, namely himself, but fully aware of his potential and capacity to love. *Janusz Korczak Literary Prize. cmt*

**8.16** Furlong, Monica. **Juniper**. Knopf, 1991. Originally published by Gollancz in 1990. (paperback: Knopf, 1992). ISBN 0-394-83220-5 (paperback: 0-679-83369-2). 198 p. (12-14). Novel. **Great Britain.**

Pampered and spoiled, young princess Juniper is horrified when she learns that she must leave her father's castle and live for a year and a day in the outland with her strange godmother. Once there, Juniper mulishly begins to learn the skills necessary to combat her evil aunt and protect her father's kingdom, but then begins to love her strange and very wise teacher. A captivating fantasy adventure filled with three-dimensional characters and a strong sense of place. Prequel to *Wise Child. bb*

**8.17** Gaarder, Jostein. **The Solitaire Mystery**. Translated by Sarah Jane Hails. Illustrated by Hilde Kramer. Farrar, 1996. Originally published as *Kabalmysteriet* by Aschehong & Co. in 1990. ISBN 1-897-58009-6. 292 p. (12-YA). Novel. **Norway**.
This intricately-plotted mystery features a story within a story. Hans Thomas, about twelve, and his father journey from Arendal, Norway, to Athens, Greece, in search of Hans Thomas's mother who ran away when he was four. Along the way Hans Thomas finds a small book hidden in a sticky bun. This book tells a story that begins in 1842 on a strange island in the Atlantic. Each of the 53 chapters is named for a playing card, and the chapters are organized by the four card suits. The two stories intertwine in this tale of self-discovery. *clb*

**8.18** Garner, Alan. **The Owl Service**. Walck, 1968. Originally published by Collins in 1967. ISBN 0-8098-3073-6. 202p. (14-YA). **Great Britain**.
Based on the tragic Welsh legend of Blodeuwedd who destroyed her husband when she turned into an owl, this story tells of three present-day adolescents whose lives are haunted by this story from the Mabinogion. The legend comes to life when the patterns on an old set of china dishes ("the owl service") are rearranged to reveal the shape of an owl. Unexplainable accidents heighten the many tensions already existing between the characters. A complex plot. *Carnegie Medal. al*

**8.19** Gee, Maurice. **Motherstone**. Oxford, 1985. ISBN 0-19-558030-X. 184 p. (10-12). Novel. **New Zealand**.
At the conclusion of *The Priests of Ferris*, Susan Ferris and Nicholas Quinn prepare to leave the world of O to return to Earth. But Orso, a renegade priest, has other plans for them. Susan is captured, but Nicholas escapes and gets help from Kenno. After much struggle against the forces of evil, Susan also escapes and the two children again prepare to

return to Earth. *Esther Glen Award. dd*

**8.20** Gripe, Maria. **Agnes Cecilia.** Translated by Rika Lesser. Harper & Row, 1990. Originally published by Albert Bonniers Junior Förlag in 1981. ISBN 0-06-022281-6. 282 p. (13-YA). Novel. **Sweden.**
Since being orphaned as a child, Nora, now sixteen, has always been sensitive to the idea of abandonment and has felt uncertain of her place. When she moves with her guardians to a new house, she begins to have visitations from the spirit of a former tenant. Then a mysterious telephone call leads her to a beautiful, old doll named Agnes Cecelia. Her efforts to unravel the mystery of this doll lead Nora to discover a present-day Agnes Cecelia, her distant cousin, and to resolve to break the cycle of abandonment in her family history. *cmt*

**8.21** Gripe, Maria. **The Glassblower's Children.** Translated by Sheila La Farge. Illustrated by Harald Gripe. Delacorte, 1973. Originally published as *Glasblåsarns Barn* by Albert Bonniers Förlag in 1964. ISBN 0-426-11228-8 (pbk.). 170 p. (7-9). Novel. **Sweden.**
A village glassblower, his wife, and two small children, Klara and Klas, live in such poverty that the wife wishes a better life for her children. A lord, hoping to please his bored wife, kidnaps the children and takes them to his distant castle where they are terrorized by mountainous, malicious Nana, the governess. Distraught, the glassblower's wife seeks the help of good Flutter Weathermild, the village witch, who happens to be Nana's sister. In a confrontation of good and evil, Flutter wins the children back and returns them to their parents. *cmt*

**8.22** Hendry, Frances. **Quest for a Maid.** Farrar, 1990. Originally published by Canongate in 1988. ISBN 0-374-36162-2. 273p. (10-12). Novel. **Great Britain.**
Meg, the daughter of a Norwegian shipbuilder living in Scotland in the late 1200s, grows from a courageous child of nine to an adventurous young woman of fifteen. She is particularly troubled by her love for and fear of her older sister, Inge, a woman who uses her special powers to cause the death of Alexander III, King of Scotland. Meg eventually helps the young Maid of Norway, sent to marry Edward I of England, escape from the unpleasant life planned for her. An intriguing blend of historical fact, fiction, and fantasy. *jg*

**8.23** Houston, James. **The White Archer: An Eskimo Legend.** Harcourt, 1967. (paperback: 0-15-696224-1). ISBN 0-8446-6671-8. 95p. (10-12). Novel. **Canada.**

When Kungo's family extends hospitality to three Eskimo hunters who have wronged the neighboring Indians, they are attacked and killed by those seeking revenge. Kungo escapes with his life, but carries with him an immense burden of hate and fear. He makes his way to an island where an old man, his wife, and their servant live. When Kungo demonstrates that he has the ability to be a great archer, the old man takes him as his pupil, and Kungo learns the way of the white archer. Instead of using his skill for revenge, Kungo, on a dangerous journey, learns how to forgive. *Canadian Children's Book of the Year Award. lg*

**8.24** Howarth, Lesley. **MapHead.** Candlewick, 1994. Originally published by Walker in 1994. ISBN 1-564-02416-4. 153 p. (12-14). Novel. **Great Britain.**

Twelve-year-old MapHead visits Earth with his father to find and meet his human mother before assuming his adult status. While they search, MapHead goes to school. His efforts to fit in and to learn English result in much humor as well as some sobering moments. *Guardian Children's Fiction Award* (British). *cmt*

**8.25** Howarth, Lesley. **Weather Eye.** Candlewick, 1995. Originally published by Walker in 1995. ISBN 1-56-402616-7. 224 p. (12-14). **Great Britain.**

In England in 1999, thirteen-year-old Telly organizes her fellow climate observation club members to calm the planet's turbulent weather. (FirstSearch). *Smarties Prize. cmt*

**8.26** Hughes, Monica. **The Dream Catcher.** Atheneum, 1986. 0-689-31331- 4.171 p. (10-12). Novel. **Canada.**

Ruth does not fit in the peaceful life of Ark Three, a domed city created after the Age of Confusion. She has special talents which are finally recognized on New Year's Day in 2147 when she is fifteen. She leads a group of twenty outside to discover Ark One and to save the people enslaved there by a computer. *dd*

**8.27** Hughes, Monica. **The Golden Aquarians.** Simon & Schuster, 1995. Originally published by HarperCollins Publishers Ltd., Canada, in

1995. ISBN 0-671-50543-2. 182 p. (10-14). Novel. **Canada**.
In 2092, Walt Elliot, thirteen, is summoned to planet Aqua by his stern and disapproving father. Col. Elliot intends to "make something" of his sensitive son the way he does the planets he is famous for transforming for human colonization. Walt discovers that Aqua is inhabited by highly intelligent, amphibious beings, and tries to convince his father to abandon his plans to "terraform," or destroy, the environment. Only when the Aquarians destroy the Space Station does the colonel see the truth and begin to recognize his son's excellent qualities. *cmt*

**8.28** Hughes, Monica. **Invitation to The Game**. Simon & Schuster, 1990. Originally published by HarperCollins Publishers Ltd., Canada, in 1990. (paperback: Aladdin, 1993). ISBN 0-671-86692-3. 183 p. (12-14). Novel. **Canada**.
When Lisse and nine friends graduate, at age 16, in 2154, they face an overcrowded, robotized world where humans stagnate as unemployed outcasts. After coping successfully with the challenges of this world, the group receives a mysterious government invitation to participate in The Game. From boredom, they accept. For over a year they make brief visits through hypnosis to an alien, but strangely fresh and beautiful, place looking for "clues," as directed. When one such trip does not end, they realize that they have been searching for clues to survival on another planet, now their new, and permanent, home. *cmt*

**8.29** Jacques, Brian. **Redwall**. Philomel, 1986. Originally published by Hutchinson in 1986. ISBN 0-399-21424-0. 351 p. Novel. **Great Britain**.
Robust humor and swashbuckling adventure abound as the stalwart animals of Redwall Abbey struggle agains the forces of evil. To his credit, the author maintains high appeal for children and credibility throughout this multibook series. Some other titles in the series: *Mossflower; Mattimeo; Mariel of Redwall; Salamandastron, the Bellmaker. be*

**8.30** Jansson, Tove. **Finn Family Moomintroll**. Translated by Elizabeth Portch. Farrar, 1990. Originally published as *Trollkarlens hatt* (Original English publication in 1950 by Benn). ISBN 0-374-42307-5. 170 p. (5-12). Novel. **Finland**.
The moomins are lovable (make-believe) creatures who live in the bogs and moorlands of Finland. One day they find a Hobgoblin's hat, and this

leads them to many adventures. Good for read-aloud to younger audiences. *cmt*

**8.31** Jones, Diana Wynne. **Castle in the Air.** Greenwillow Books, 1991. Originally published by Methuen in 1990. ISBN 0-688-09686-7. 199 p. (10-14). Novel. **Great Britain.**
Abdullah is not a very successful carpet seller. The prophecy made at his birth foretold this, but also said that "he will be raised above all others." One day, he buys a magic carpet that allows the second part of the prophecy to come true. The carpet transports Abdullah to the princess of his dreams. When she is kidnapped by an evil djinn, Abdullah, with the help of a genie, is able to defeat the djinn and evil wizards and to rescue his beautiful princess, Flower in the Night. A sequel to *Howl's Moving Castle* (Greenwillow, 1986). *djg*

**8.32** Jones, Diana Wynne. **The Lives of Christopher Chant.** Greenwillow, 1988. Simultaneously published by Methuen in 1988. (paperback: Random House, 1990). ISBN 0-688-07806-0. 230 p. (10-12). Novel. **Great Britain.**
Magic is such a staple of his existence that young Christopher does not associate it with the "dreams" which take him to other worlds and allow him to bring back special gifts. When his ability to visit these parallel worlds is discovered, Christopher is exploited by his unscrupulous uncle. What starts out as fun turns into something ultimately cruel and evil, threatening the very existence of those who maintain the balance of the worlds. A thoughtful fantasy containing humor, adventure, suspense and interesting characters. Prequel to *Charmed Life*. *bb*

**8.33** Kästner, Erich. **Emil and the Detectives.** Translated by May Massee. Illustrated by Walter Trier. Originally published as *Emil und die Detektive* in 1929. 224 p. (7-9). Novel. **Germany.**
Emil Tischbein and his widowed mother are poor but happy and hardworking. On his way to visit his grandmother in Berlin, Emil falls asleep on the train and is robbed by a suspicious-looking man. The quick-witted boy follows the man and soon engages neighborhood children in a scheme to force the thief to return the money. The scheme works, the money is retrieved, the thief is identified as a notorious bank robber, and Emil is celebrated as a hero in Berlin and given a large reward. *cmt*

**8.34** Kästner, Erich. **The Little Man.** Translated by James Kirkup. Illustrated by Rick Schreiter. Knopf, 1966. Originally published as *Der Kleine Mann* by Atrium Verlag, Zürich, in 1963. 184 p. (7-9). Novel. **Germany.**
Maxie Pichelsteiner, a two-inch-tall orphan, is the ward of kindly Professor Hokus von Pokus, a circus magician. With the professor's support, Maxie becomes an artiste, joins the professor's act, and is an overnight sensation. When he is kidnapped, Maxie orchestrates his own rescue. Sequel: *The Little Man and the Big Thief. Mildred Batchelder Award. cmt*

**8.35** King-Smith, Dick. **Babe, the Gallant Pig.** Illustrated by Mary Rayner. Crown, 1985. Originally published as *The Sheep-Pig* by Gollancz in 1983. ISBN 0-517-55556-5. 118 p. (7-9). Novel. **Great Britain.**
Taciturn Farmer Hogget won Babe, a piglet, at a fair and put him in a stall next to a maternal sheep dog and a sickly ewe. From these two neighbors, Babe, an extremely bright pig, acquired the ambition and knowledge to herd sheep. As the amazed Farmer Hogget watched Babe's adroit barnyard herding maneuvers, he determined to train the pig secretly and enter him in the prestigious National Sheepherding Trials. There, Babe's uniquely polite style is unbeatable. No Christmas ham, this porker. Book far surpasses the popular film version. Other popular animal fantasies by this author: *Pigs Might Fly* (1982); *Harry's Mad* (1987); *Martin's Mice* (1989); *Three Terrible Trins* (1994). *cmt*

**8.36** King-Smith, Dick. **The Fox Busters.** Illustrated by Jon Miller. Delacorte, 1978. Originally published by Gollancz in 1978. ISBN 0-440-50064-8. 117 p. (10-12). Novel. **Great Britain.**
This story presents a new twist on the old contest between the fox and the chickens. Fox Earth Farm is the setting for this fantastic tale of three pullets who have developed extraordinary powers and use them to great advantage. *djg*

**8.37** King-Smith, Dick. **The School Mouse.** Illustrated by Cynthia Fisher. Hyperion, 1995. Originally published by Penguin in 1994. ISBN 0-7868-0036-4. 124 p. (7-10). Novel. **Great Britain.**
Flora and her mouse family have always lived in the school house, but Flora is the first mouse ever to learn to read. No one in her family can see the use of it, until Flora's skill prevents the family from eating a box

of poison. Being an educated mouse has its difficulties, as Flora finds out when she sets about the task of enlightening her family. Black and white illustrations complement the tongue-in-cheek text. *djg*

**8.38** Lawrence, Louise. **Children of the Dust.** Harper & Row, 1985. Originally published by The Bodley Head in 1985. ISBN 0-06-023738-4. 183 p. (12 and up). Novel. **Great Britain.**
A nuclear bomb has left Catherine stranded with her mother and younger brother. As they struggle to survive the aftermath of the bomb, hardship gives way to grief. Catherine survives and lives to see the children of the next generation, born with mutations. Other notable works of fantasy by Lawrence include: *Andrea* (1991); *Calling B for Butterfly* (1982); *Cat Call* (1980); *Dram Road* (1983); *The Earthwatch* (1981); *Keeper of the Universe* (1992); *Moonwind* (1986); *The Patchwork People*, originally published as *The Dispossessed* (1994); *Star Lord* (1978); *The Warriors of Taan* (1988); and *The Wyndcliffe* (1975). *djg*

**8.39** Lewis, C.S. **The Last Battle.** Illustrated by Pauline Baynes. Harper-Collins, 1994. Originally published by The Bodley Head in 1956. (paperback: HarperTrophy, 1994). ISBN 0-06-023493-8 (paperback: 0-06-447108-X). 176p. (10-12). Novel. **Great Britain.**
When a great evil comes to the land of Narnia, Jill and Eustace help fight the last battle, and the mighty lion Aslan leads the people of Narnia to a glorious new paradise. Seventh and last of the *Chronicles of Narnia* series. *Carnegie Medal. al*

**8.40** Lindgren, Astrid. **The Brothers Lionheart.** Translated by Joan Tate. Illustrated by J. K. Lambert. Viking, 1975. Originally published as *Bröderna Lejonhjärta* by Rabén Sjögren in 1973. (paperback: Puffin, 1985). ISBN 0-14-03.19557. 183 p. (7-12). Novel. **Sweden.**
Karl, a ten-year-old cripple, idolized his thirteen-year-old brother, Jonathon. And so, when Jonathon gave his life to save his brother in a housefire, it is little wonder that, two months later, Karl, too, died. As Jonathon had promised, the two brothers meet in Nangiyala, a paradise of campfires and sagas; and there they intend to live in eternal bliss, Karl no longer being a cripple. But soon the brothers are swept up in an effort to overthrow the odious tyrant, Tergil. In defeating their foe, Karl acquires the bravery he needs to save Jonathon and bring them both to Nangilima, a land where all the sagas are happy. *Janusz Korczak Liter-*

*ary Prize. cmt*

**8.41** Lindgren, Astrid. **Pippi Longstocking**. Translated by Florence Lamborn. Illustrated by Louis S. Glanzman. Viking, 1950. Originally published as *Pippi Längstrump* in 1950. ISBN 0-670-55745-5. 160 p. (7-9). Novel. **Sweden**.

Pippi, without parents, has taken up residence in her ramshackle family home, Villa Villekulla, next door to Tommy and Annika. Pippi is in the enviable position to do just what she wants to do, and *only* that, since she is as rich as a troll and stronger than anyone. The well-behaved Tommy and Annika are often shocked, but more often delighted, with Pippi's antics, since they always end well. A modern classic. See also: *Pippi Goes On Board*; *Pippi in the South Seas*; *Pippi on the Run. Lindgren: Hans Christian Andersen Award. cmt*

**8.42** Lindgren, Astrid. **Ronia, The Robber's Daughter**. Translated by Patricia Crompton. Viking, 1983. Originally published as *Ronja Rövardotter* by Rabén & Sjögren Bokforlag in 1981. ISBN 0-670-60640-5. 176 p. (10-12). Novel. **Sweden**.

Long ago, two rival robber clans plied their rough trade in the deep, northern forests. Although neither could remember the cause of this enmity, both leaders assumed that their children, Ronia and Birk, would grow up to continue the robbery and the feud. Instead, the children meet, become friends, and pledge themselves as sister and brother. Afraid of losing their children forever, the clan chiefs come to realize the senselessness of their feud and join forces. Ronia and Birk pledge to end the robbery when the clan leadership passes to them. *Mildred Batchelder Award. cmt*

**8.43** Lively, Penelope. **The Ghost of Thomas Kempe**. Illustrated by Anthony Maitland. Dutton, 1973. Originally published by Heinemann in 1973. (paperback: Puffin, 1995). ISBN 0-525-30495-9 (paperback: 0-14-037794-8). 192p. (7-11). Novel. **Great Britain**.

When James and his family refurbish their old cottage, a spirit is released and odd things begin to happen. The spirit is that of seventeenth-century sorcerer Thomas Kempe, who tries to commandeer James into being his assistant in sorcery. As the ghost's actions—all wrongly blamed on James—become more destructive, James enlists the help of an amateur exorcist in hopes of clearing his own name. *Carnegie Medal.*

*al*

**8.44** Lunn, Janet. **Shadow in Hawthorne Bay.** Scribners/Macmillan, 1986. Originally published by Lester & Opren Dennys, 1986. ISBN 0-684-18843-0. 180 p. (12-14). Novel. **Canada.**

When she "hears" her beloved cousin calling to her from his new home in the Canadian wilderness, 15-year-old Mary journeys alone from Scotland to an island in Lake Ontario. Once there, she discovers that Duncan has died and his family has left. Although she alienates the other settlers with her psychic powers, she eventually recognizes and embraces her destiny. *Canada Children's Book Award. lg*

**8.45** Lunn, Janet. **The Root Cellar.** Scribner's, 1983. Originally published by Dennys in 1981. (paperback: Puffin, 1985). ISBN 0-684-17855-9. 229p. (10-12). Novel. **Canada.**

When her grandmother and guardian dies, twelve-year-old Rose goes to live with her aunt, uncle, and cousins in a ramshackle house on Hawthorne Bay, Lake Ontario. The transition is difficult for Rose, and so when she discovers a way to travel through time to the Civil War era when her aunt's house was beautiful, she welcomes the opportunity. A journey into the war-torn States to save a distant relative, however, helps her find her place in her new family. *Canadian Children's Book of the Year Award. lg*

**8.46** Mahy, Margaret. **The Blood and Thunder Adventure on Hurricane Peak.** Illustrated by Wendy Smith. Margaret K. McElderry, 1989. Originally published by J. M. Dent & Sons, 1989. (paperback: Yearling Books, 1991). ISBN 0-689-50488-8. (paperback: 0-440-40422-3). 132 p. (7-9). Novel. **New Zealand.**

The Unexpected School on Hurricane Ridge, run by the magician Heathcliff Warlock and Zanzibar the cat, seems like the perfect kind of school to Huxley and his little sister Zaza, themselves the author and illustrator of many blood-and-thunder adventure stories. An out-and-out villain, his henchmen, and a ginger-haired maiden who is an inventor and definitely not in distress, complete this humorous melodramatic fantasy. Huxley and Zaza affirm that science and magic, or analytical and imaginative thinking, are both essential for solving problems and for coping with life. *jvl*

**8.47** Mahy, Margaret. **The Changeover: A Supernatural Romance**. Scholastic, 1984. Originally published by Scholastic in 1974. ISBN 0-590-33798-X. *264 p.* (13 and up). Novel. **New Zealand.**
When a stranger puts an indelible mark on the hand of Laura Chant's little brother, the child's life seems to start draining away. Laura seeks the help of Sorenson Carlisle, an acquaintance she suspects of being a witch. Laura confronts her own supernatural powers as she assumes adult responsibilities and develops mastery over natural and supernatural forces that shape the interplay between life and death. This book is frank about teenage emotions and facts of life, about adults who have affairs, get divorces, and sleep with new friends. It also affirms the strength of family and the power of love. *Esther Glen Award; Carnegie Medal. eb, al*

**8.48** Mahy, Margaret. **Dangerous Spaces**. Viking, 1991. (paperback: Puffin, 1993). ISBN 0-670-83734-2. (paperback: 014-036-3629). 154 p. (10-12). Novel. **New Zealand.**
Eleven-year-old Anthea is considered too romantic by her sturdier cousin Flora, with whose warm and haphazard family Anthea has come to live after losing her parents in a boating accident. Needing a special space of her own, Anthea embarks on a dangerous journey through the dream world of Veridian with the boy ghost of her long-dead great uncle. As Anthea learns that there is a place for her in her new family, she manages, with the help of sensible Flora, to break free of the hold of Veridian, which symbolizes death. *jvl*

**8.49** Mahy, Margaret. **The Haunting**. Simon and Schuster, 1982. Originally published by Dent in 1982. (paperback: Dell/Yearling, 1991). ISBN 0-689-50243-5 (paperback: 0-440-40408-8). 144p. (10-12). Novel. **New Zealand.**
Eight-year-old Barney discovers his extrasensory powers when he begins to receive frightening images and messages which claim, "Barney is dead." After his great-uncle (also named Barney) dies, he finds that his family has some strange secrets, one of which is the one-per-generation magician. To his great relief, this turns out to be his sister. With this knowledge, Barney begins to find his place among his family. *Carnegie Medal. al*

**8.50** Mahy, Margaret. **The Tricksters**. McElderry, 1986. Originally published by Dent in 1986. ISBN 0-689-50400-4. 266 p. (14-YA). Novel. **New Zealand**.

While gathered for the Christmas holiday, a large New Zealand family and their guests find their lives suddenly invaded by three fascinating but rather sinister brothers. By New Year's, nothing is the same. (CIP Summary) *ALA Young Adult Best Books. djg*

**8.51** Marsden, John. **Tomorrow, When the War Began**. Houghton Mifflin, 1995. Originally published by Pan Macmillan in 1993. ISBN 0-395-70673-4. 286 p. (Mature 13 and up). Novel. **Australia**.

Seven Australian teenage boys and girls return from a week's camping trip in the bush to discover that their country has been invaded by foreign troops, their families taken as prisoners, and the world as they have known it totally changed. As they hide out in the bush, Ellie is selected by the group to record these extraordinary events, and the adventure is told through her eyes. Some sexual allusions. *clb*

**8.52** Melling, O.R. **The Singing Stone**. Viking, 1987. ISBN 0-670-80817-2. 206 p. (12-14). Novel. **Canada**.

An 18-year-old orphan, Kay, is encouraged through a mysterious package of books to study Celtic legends. As a result, she visits Ireland, where she hopes to find answers to her identity. There she travels back in time to an ancient civilization and becomes involved in a quest to restore the four treasures of a mighty tribe of island people. Fighting against powerful Druids, she helps a designated queen to fulfill her own destiny and learns many lessons of human conduct. Contains suspense, romance, and adventure. *mb*

**8.53** Nilsson, Eleanor. **The House Guest**. Penguin, 1991. (paperback: Puffin, 1993). ISBN 0-14-034601-5. 159p. (10-14). Novel. **Australia**.

Bored and unsupervised, 12-year-old Gunno joins a home burglary gang, which considers itself honorable professionals, dealing kindly with its "clients" by merely "creaming off a bit of their spare cash." Things change when Gunno becomes strangely drawn to an old, secluded house and is compelled to return again and again as he slowly unravels the mystery of Hugh, the missing son. A sense of foreboding builds to a gripping climax, with interwoven supernatural elements, as Gunno meets Hugh in a backward timeshift and desperately tries to avert the cave-in that claimed Hugh's life years ago. *Australia's Children's Book of the*

*Year for Older Readers Award. bt*

**8.54** Nodelman, Perry. **The Same Place but Different**. Simon & Schuster, 1995. ISBN 0-671-89839-6. 181 p. (9–11). Novel. **Canada**.
John Nesbit learns that the changes in his Winnipeg neighborhood and in his baby sister, Andrea, are caused by Strangers—ancient, dangerous fairies. Venturing into the queen's castle, John brings Andrea safely home and routs the Changeling who had taken her place. Nodelman juxtaposes the ordinary (Safeway shopping, schoolyard bully) with the fantastic (doglike Sky Yelpers, flying horse-taxis). The first-person narrative includes humor and youthful slang. A two-page historical note at story's end gives background information on folklore alluded to in the story. *jsn*

**8.55** Norton, Mary. **The Borrowers**. Illustrated by Joe Krush. Harcourt, 1952. Originally published by Dent in 1952. (paperback: Odyssey, 1989). ISBN 0-15-209987-5 (0-15-209990-5). 180p. (8-10). Novel. **Great Britain**.
The Clock family—small people that live in a miniature apartment under the grandfather clock in a human house—exists by "borrowing" from the house's occupants. This precarious but comfortable existence comes to an abrupt end when young Arrietty Clock meets the boy of the house, and the Borrowers have to flee for their lives. Norton's convincing small-scale world captivates young readers who can follow the Clock family adventures in four sequels: *The Borrowers Afield*, *The Borrowers Afloat*; *The Borrowers Aloft*; and *The Borrowers Avenged*. *Carnegie Medal. al, cmt*

**8.56** Nöstlinger, Christine. **The Cucumber King**. Translated by Anthea Bell. Bergh, 1985. Originally published as *Wir Pfeifen auf den Gurkenkönig* by Beltz Verlag in 1972. ISBN 0-930267-01-X. 154 p. (10-12). Novel. **Germany**.
Wolfi and his family are more than a little surprised one day when the Cucumber King shows up in their kitchen claiming that his subjects, the Kumi-Oris, have overthrown him. After meeting the peaceful Kumi-Ori people who live in the cellar, Wolfi realizes that the Cucumber King is a manipulative, scheming vegetable who just wants Wolfi's father to exterminate his former subjects. Wolfi, with the help of other family members, helps to bring peace and a just rule to the Kumi-Oris. *Nöst-*

*linger: Hans Christian Andersen Medalist for Writing. jl*

**8.57** Nöstlinger, Christine. **Konrad.** Translated by Anthea Bell. Illustrated by Carol Nicklaus. Franklin Watts, 1977 (paperback: Avon, 1983). Originally published as *Konrad* by Verlag Friedrich Oetinger in 1975. ISBN 0-531-01341-3 (paperback: 0-380-62018-9). 135 p. (7-12). Novel. **Austria.**
Konrad, a factory-made-to-order seven-year-old boy, is delivered by mistake to eccentric but loveable Mrs. Bartolotti. The nearly perfect Konrad is a bit bewildering for Mrs. Bartolotti, not to mention his schoolmates, but they all love him. On discovering its error, the factory attempts to retrieve Konrad, but a new friend gives him a successful crash course in being "normal"—a little naughty, that is—and so unsuitable for the company's purposes. Humorous commentary on family life. *Mildred Batchelder Award; Nöstlinger: Hans Christian Andersen Medalist for Writing. mew*

**8.58** Park, Ruth. **Playing Beatie Bow.** Atheneum, 1983. Originally published by Nelson, 1980. ISBN 0-689-30889-2. 196 p. (10-14). Novel. **Australia.**
Disgruntled and confused by her parents' broken marriage, Abby suddenly finds herself transported a hundred years into the past. In Victorian Sydney of the 1880s Abby lives for months with the Bow family, having many adventures and falling in love with Judah Bow. When she returns to her own time, no one has noticed her absence, but she is a much-matured person, now capable of understanding her parents' continued love for one another. Four years later, Abby meets Robert Bow, great-great grandnephew to Judah, and resumes her romance. *Australia's Book of the Year for Older Readers Award. cmt*

**8.59** Pearce, Phillipa. **Tom's Midnight Garden.** Lippincott, 1992. Originally published by Oxford in 1958. (paperback: HarperTrophy, 1992). ISBN 0-397-30477-3 (0-06-440445-5). 240p. (10-14). Novel. **Great Britain.**
Tom is angry and bored when he is sent to his aunt and uncle's apartment after his brother catches the measles during summer vacation. One night the old grandfather clock in the hall strikes thirteen, and to Tom's amazement, the parking lot outside becomes a nineteenth-century garden. There, Tom meets Hatty, a child from another time. From then on,

Tom is anything but bored. The mystery of the garden is finally made clear when Tom meets another occupant of the house, an elderly lady who has been dreaming of her childhood. *Carnegie Medal. al, cmt*

**8.60** Preussler, Otfried. **The Satanic Mill**. Translated by Anthea Bell. Collier/Macmillan, 1991. Originally published as *Krabat* by Arena Verlag in 1971. ISBN 0-02-044775-2 (paperback). 250 p. (12-14). Novel. **Germany**.

In seventeenth-century Germany, fourteen-year-old Krabat is compelled to travel to an isolated mill and there become the apprentice of an evil Master of the Black Arts. Over three years Krabat becomes the Master's star pupil, but learns of the evil done by the Master and longs to regain his freedom. Only the love of a young girl from a nearby village saves Krabat and destroys the Master and his mill. *cmt*

**8.61** Price, Susan. **The Ghost Drum**. Farrar, 1987. Originally published by Faber in 1987. (paperback: Farrar, 1989). ISBN 0-374-32538-3 (0-374-42547-7). 176p. (9-12). Novel. **Great Britain**.

Chingis, a slave girl brought up by a Russian witch, rescues an imprisoned Czar's son, and the two join forces to combat the Czar's evil sister. With the help of a magic hut that runs on chicken legs, Chingis can travel to many worlds, and she uses her ghost drum to understand messages from the spirits. *Carnegie Medal. al*

**8.62** Pullman, Philip. **The Golden Compass**. Knopf, 1996. Originally published as *His Dark Materials: Book I, Northern Lights* by Scholastic in 1995. ISBN 0-679-87924-2. 399 p. (13-YA). Novel. **Great Britain**.

Lyra Belacqua is a street-wise tomboy of uncertain lineage and limited goals living as a ward of the scholars of Jordan College in an England where high technology and baroque wizardry intersect. An overheard conversation and a visit by her Uncle Asriel propel Lyra into an epic adventure in which she and her companion spirit discover and destroy a despicable crime ring involving kidnapped children and hideous scientific experiments. Classic high fantasy. First part of a projected trilogy. *Carnegie Medal. cmt*

**8.63** Rodda, Emily. **Finders Keepers**. Greenwillow, 1991. Originally published by Omnibus Books in 1990. (paperback: Beech Tree, 1993). ISBN 0-68810-516-5. 184p. (10-12). Novel. **Australia**.

Patrick wants a computer more than anything and fools around with display models in the mall whenever he can. One day, a message flashes on the computer screen telling Patrick that he has won a chance to play "Finders Keepers" and win big prizes. Seeing a chance to win a computer, Patrick accepts and is transported to a television game show in a parallel world. There he is challenged to find objects from "their" side that have slipped through cracks in the barrier to "our" side. In his role as "Finder" Patrick not only finds the objects, but also learns much about human motivations. The story's rapid pace and completely sewn-up, happy ending will appeal to readers. *Australia's Children's Book of the Year for Younger Readers Award. cmt*

**8.64** Rodda, Emily. **Rowan of Rin**. Omnibus/Ashton Scholastic, 1993. ISBN 1-86291-182-7. 138p. (7-12). Novel. **Australia**.
The villagers of Rin view young Rowan as a timid weakling, until he is needed to guide a search party up the forbidden mountain to investigate the sudden drying-up of their life-sustaining stream. At first reluctant to become the bearer of the bewitched map of the mountain given to him by the prophet Sheba, Rowan proves to be the only one of the group able to master the trials of terror and solve the final riddle. When Rowan discovers the secret of the dragon who lives atop the mountain, he is able to restore the stream's flow, and thus save his village. A gripping fantasy. *Australia's Children's Book of the Year for Younger Readers Award. bt*

**8.65** Rubinstein, Gillian. **Beyond the Labyrinth**. Orchard, 1990. Originally published by Hyland House in 1988. ISBN 0-531-05899-9. 245p. (14-YA). Novel. **Australia**.
Brenton has always felt at odds with the world, but at fourteen his alienation is so deep that he has begun basing all of his decisions on a throw of dice. In this way he decides to accept Victoria, the daughter of family friends, when she arrives for an extended visit. Their encounter with a being from an advanced civilization causes them to reflect on both positive and negative aspects of modern culture. The author provides two endings, one of which is to be chosen by the reader by a throw of dice. Some harsh language. *Australia's Children's Book of the Year for Older Readers Award. cmt*

**8.66** Rubinstein, Gillian. **Foxspell**. Simon & Schuster, 1996. Originally published by Hyland House in 1994. ISBN 0-689-80602-7. 219p. (12-

14). Novel. **Australia.**

Tod's grandmother tries to hold together his dysfunctional family when his father deserts them and his mother becomes preoccupied with her career. To escape from the messy complexities of his world, including pressure to join a local gang of hoodlums, Tod, twelve, observes the foxes that stalk the quarries. After burying a fox shot by the gang, Tod becomes mystically drawn into the animal-spirit world. When his body takes on the form of a fox, he experiences firsthand the thrill of the hunt and the kill. Rubinstein handles the transitions from reality to fantasy convincingly, leaving the reader breathless in a dramatic, open-ended conclusion. *Australia's Children's Book of the Year for Older Readers Award.* bt

**8.67** Rubinstein, Gillian. **Galax-Arena.** Simon and Schuster, 1995. Originally published by Hyland House in 1992. (paperback: Aladdin, 1997). ISBN 0-689-80136-X. (paperback: 0-689-81235-3). 138 p. (12-14). Novel. **Australia.**

Unlike her athletic siblings, Joella, 13, is too clumsy to make it in the unforgiving world of Galax-Arena where you either perform increasingly daring feats until you make a fatal slip or become a pet or an experiment for the "space creatures," the Vaxa. When Joella discovers that their captors are not space creatures but humans and that Galax-Arena is on earth, few of the captive children choose to escape, preferring the danger and glory of the Arena to their former lives as the dispossessed of the world. Issues of class, power, group dynamics, and human exploitation are explored. *Australia's Children's Book of the Year for Older Readers, Honor Book.* jvl

**8.68** Taylor, Cora. **Julie.** Prairie, 1985. ISBN 0-88833-172-X. 101p. (10-12). Novel. **Canada.**

Julie had always been different. When she was little, she told stories about the buffalo who used to roam her prairie farm before she even knew what "buffalo" meant. Often, she entertained her family with her "stories." Over the years, however, she learned to keep her stories to herself as they began to make others uncomfortable. When she realized that she was psychic, she could not decide whether it was a gift or a great burden. She learned to use her powers, however, when she saved her father's life after a tractor accident. lg

**8.69** Walsh, Jill Paton. **Torch**. Farrar, 1988. Originally published by Viking Kestrel in 1987. ISBN 0-374-37684-0. 176p. (10-12). Novel. **Great Britain**.

Cal and Dio, in keeping with village tradition, seek approval of their impending marriage from the old sage. They find him on his death bed. He relates the story of the torch which lies in his cottage. It is a relic from "Ago," the last of its kind, which legend predicts someone will eventually come seeking. Although these young people do not understand the torch's significance, they nevertheless light it and set out to discover its true meaning and its home. *mja*

**8.70** Waugh, Sylvia. **The Mennyms**. Greenwillow, 1994. Originally published by Julia MacRae Books in 1993. ISBN 0-688-13070-4. 213 p. (10-12). Novel. **Great Britain**.

For the past forty years, the Mennyms, a family of life-sized dolls, have been living a quiet, "pretend" existence in a large, secluded house in London. They successfully masquerade as human by avoiding direct contact with people. But when their landlord announces that he is coming for a visit, the household is thrown into panic. A delightfully unexpected ending results, not in disaster, but in changes for this lovable, quirky family. See other, equally entertaining volumes in this projected quintet: *Mennyms in the Wilderness*, 1995; *Mennyms Under Siege*, 1996; *Mennyms Alone*, 1997. *cmt*

**8.71** Westall, Robert. **Stones of Muncaster Cathedral**. Farrar, 1993. Originally published by Viking in 1991. (paperback: Farrar, 1994). ISBN 0-3743-7263-2. 97p. (10-14). Novel. **Great Britain**.

Joe Clarke cannot believe his luck when he gets the job of repairing the steeple on Muncaster Cathedral. It is only when he and his partner begin working on the southwest tower that they discover the horrific circumstances under which it was built. Now, someone or something is seeking retribution from Joe and the town. *mja*

**8.72** Westall, Robert. **Stormsearch**. Farrar, 1992. Originally published by Blackie and Son in 1990. ISBN 0-374-37272-1. 124p. (10-12). Novel. **Great Britain**.

Tim and his sister Tracey spend summers with their aunt and uncle at Mount House on the English seacoast. There Tim discovers an antique model ship that leads him on a search into the past, involving not only his immediate family, but his ancestors as well. The search reveals an episode of unfulfilled love and its consequences. *mja*

**8.73** Wrightson, Patricia. **Balyet.** Macmillan/McElderry, 1989. Originally published by Hutchinson in 1989. ISBN 0-689-50468-3. 130 p. (12-14). Novel. **Australia.**
Jo, fourteen, connives to accompany Mrs. Willet, an Aborigine, to the remote Australian hills. Mrs. Willet warns Jo of the dangerous, thousand-year-old Aborigine wraith, Balyet (echo), who lures young people into the hills, craving their company, but killing them with her touch. At first obstinate and skeptical, Jo learns to respect Mrs. Willet's wisdom and gains compassion for the pitiful Balyet. Based on an Aboriginal legend. *Wrightson: Hans Christian Andersen Medal for Writing.* *cmt*

**8.74** Wrightson, Patricia. **A Little Fear.** Atheneum, 1984. Originally published by Hutchinson in 1983. ISBN 0-689-50291-5. 111 p. (10-14). Novel. **Australia.**
Mrs. Tucker, newly installed by her insensitive daughter in a rest home that she hates, slyly moves to a remote cottage, hoping to regain her independence and self-respect. But an ancient gnome has taken up residence in the chicken house and makes mischief in an effort to drive away the unwanted company. For days the gnome's antics have Mrs. Tucker convinced that she is indeed senile, but then she meets the nasty creature and in a satisfying surprise ending has the last laugh, both on gnome and daughter. *Australia's Children's Book of the Year for Older Readers Award.* *cmt*

**8.75** Wrightson, Patricia. **The Nargun and the Stars.** Macmillan, 1974. Originally published by Hutchinson in 1973. ISBN 0-689-50403-9. 184 p. (10-12). Novel. **Australia.**
Following his parents' death, Simon, eleven, goes to live with his middle-aged cousins on their isolated farm in northeast New South Wales. Loggers are cutting down a nearby forest, disturbing many ancient earth creatures and causing them to make contact with Simon. Another ancient creature, the rocklike monster, Nargun, is also in the area. This creature has been fleeing civilization and its noise for the last century, and now the loggers are making it angry. In protecting the farm from the Nargun, Simon becomes friends with his cousins and learns the

importance of responsible stewardship of the land. *Australia's Children's Book of the Year for Older Readers Award. cmt*

# INFORMATIONAL BOOKS

**9.1** Ayoub, Abderrahman, Binous, Jamila, Gragueb, Abderrazak, Mtimet, Ali , and Slim, Hedi. **Umm El Madayan: An Islamic City Through the Ages**. Translated by Kathleen Leverich. Illustrated by Francesco Corni. Houghton Mifflin, 1994. Originally published as *Umm El Madayan* by Editoriale Jaca Book SpA in 1993. ISBN 0-395-65967-1. 62 p. (10-14). Informational book. **Italy**.

Although a fictional city, Umm El Madayan represents the development of Islamic cities along the North African Mediterranean coast. From hunter-gatherer societies, through the influence of Phoenician, Carthaginian, Roman, and Christian cultures, to the growth and establishment of Islam, the city evolved over the millennia. Illustrations and text provide intricate detail about each time period. *CCBC Choices. jl*

**9.2** Brown, Fern C. **Teen Guide to Childbirth**. Franklin Watts, 1988. Originally published by Aladdin Books in 1988. ISBN 0- 531-10573-3. 62p. (12-14). Informational book. **Great Britain**.

The choices for place and method of delivery, the stages of labor, the birth itself, and the recovery period are clearly described. Photographs and diagrams enhance the text, and both give accurate biological facts and let a teen know exactly what to expect. *jg*

**9.3** Franklin, Kristine L. and McGirr, Nancy (Eds.). **Out of the Dumps**. Translated by Kristine L. Franklin. Photographs by Children from Guatemala City's Garbage Dump. Lothrop, 1996. ISBN 0-688-13923-X. 56 p. (10-14). Photo-documentary. **Guatemala**.

Guatemalan children document their lives in the dump in the center of Guatemala City that they call home. Using poetry and photography, they reveal tragic and gritty aspects of their everyday lives, such as death and starvation, as well as lighter and happier moments of mischief, sibling rivalry, and family love. The writing is notable for its lack of self-pity and its realism. *Booklist Editor's Choice. mew. Editor's note: Although first published in the United States, this book is included because its text and illustrations were created by Guatemalans in Guatemala.*

**9.4** Hollyer, Belinda. **Stories from the Classical Ballet**. Illustrated by Sophy Williams. Viking, 1995. Originally published by Macmillan Limited in 1995. ISBN 0-670-86605-9. 127p. (10-12). Informational book. **Great Britain**.

The stories of eight classical, world-famous ballets—*La Bayadere, Coppelia, The Firebird, Giselle, The Nutcracker, Petroushka, The Sleeping Beauty*, and *Swan Lake*—are narrated in compelling story form. Each ballet is introduced with notes about its origins and history. Former prima ballerina Irina Baronova opens the book with a description of her career in ballet and gives her own performance notes at the conclusion of each story. *jg*

**9.5** Lewis, Brenda R. **Stamps! A Young Collector's Guide**. Lodestar, 1991. Originally published by Simon and Schuster, London, 1990. ISBN 0-525-67341-5. 95 p. (10-14). Informational book. **Great Britain**.

This fascinating and informative book covers, briefly, every aspect of stamp collecting to start a beginner on the hobby or to intrigue the non-collector to pay closer attention to the history and details of stamp art. The art work is a combination of reproductions of stamps and illustrations in the form of stamps. Besides giving historical background, the author helps the beginner notice details and become acquainted with collecting techniques and strategies. One helpful highlight includes a map of the world which shows each country and gives both its English and its native name in its local alphabet. *jvl*

**9.6** Love, Ann and Drake, Jane. **Take Action: World Wildlife Fund.** Illustrated by Pat Cupples. Kids Can, 1992. ISBN 0-921103-43-3. 96 p. (8–12). Informational book. **Canada.**

Sections are entitled "Wildlife Matters," "Endangered Species," "Endangered Spaces," and "How to Take Action." Concise information is presented in reader-friendly style on subjects ranging from prairie ecosystems or oil spills to whooping crane eggs and rainforest bromeliad plants. Interspersed are suggested projects and word and picture puzzles, with answers at book's end. Instances of successful group environmental projects are appended, as are a glossary and index. Black and white illustrations on every page include detailed plant and animal drawings and humorous sketches of children in conservation activities like measuring acid rain, composting, and recycling. *jsn*

**9.7** Magubane, Peter. **Soweto: The Fruit of Fear.** Eerdmans/Africa World Press, 1986. Originally published as *June 16: The Fruit of Fear* by Skotaville Publishers in 1986. ISBN 0-86543-041-1. (paperback: 0-86543-040-3). 99 p. (12-YA). Photoessay. **Republic of South Africa.**

On June 16, 1976, thousands of middle and high school students in Soweto Township staged a peaceful protest against compulsory use of the Afrikaans language as a medium of instruction. A stone was thrown and a shot was fired, killing a student. This incident sparked the violent black African uprising that resulted, over a decade later, in the African National Congress governmental takeover. In this photoessay the uprising is dramatically documented in pictures of violent confrontation and sorrow. Excellent background reading for many RSA novels. *hr, cmt*

**9.8** Sanders, Pet and Farquhar, Clare. **The Problem of AIDS.** Gloucester, 1989. Originally published by Aladdin Books in 1989. ISBN 0-531-17191-4. 32p. (10-12). Informational Book. **Great Britain.**

Using a question and answer format, the authors describe AIDS, how it is transmitted, possible means of protection, and research on treatment. The text is simple but accurate, with the exception of treatment. Because of advances in this area made after this book's publication, the information presented here is dated. *jg*

**9.9** Sibley, Brian. **The Land of Narnia.** Illustrated by Pauline Baynes. Harper & Row, 1990. Originally published by Collins Lions in 1989. ISBN 0-06-025625-7. 96 p. (10-12). Informational book. **Great Britain.**

To anyone, adult or child, who is a Narnia series fan, this book offers much background information, including biographical information on C.S. Lewis and book-by-book plot lines and analyses. The lively writing style is geared to the child reader, and the many illustrations are well-placed and attractive. Though most of the art is by Baynes, the book also includes photos of Lewis and sketches by him and other artists. *bb*

**9.10** van der Rol, Ruud and Verhoeven, Rian. **Anne Frank, Beyond the Diary: A Photographic Remembrance.** Translated by Tony Langham and Plym Peters. Viking, 1993. Originally published by La Riviere & Voorhoeve in 1992. ISBN 670-84932-4. 113 p. (8-14). Photobiography. **Netherlands.**

A compendium of facts presented in readable narrative and original photographs, this book also contains maps, a time-line of the war years and significant events in the Frank family, letters, diary entries, and concentration camp photographs. An excellent supplement to *Anne Frank: The Diary of a Young Girl* (Doubleday, 1952). *Christopher Award; ALA Notable Book; Publishers Weekly Nonfiction Book of the Year; Booklist Editor's Choice; Best Books for Young Adults; Honor Book: Mildred Batchelder Award. mew, cmt*

# BIOGRAPHY

**10.1** Besson, Jean-Louis. **October 45**. Translated by Carol Volk. Harcourt, 1995. Originally published as *Paris Rutabaga*. ISBN 0-15-200955-8. 94 p. (9-12). Picture book for older readers. **France.**
These sequential diary entries describe the daily life of the author as a child (aged 7-12) in Paris during the Nazi occupation of France from 1939-45. Food rationing and bombing raids were common hardships, and many people used old tires as shoe soles, but the author realized that things could be worse for him. He saw his Jewish neighbors disappear and, at war's end, met an emaciated former classmate, the product of a German concentration camp. Frequent cartoon-like illustrations add to the child's perspective of this account and show the humor that provided relief during this sombre time. *sl*

**10.2** Buchignani, Walter. **Tell No One Who You Are: The Hidden Childhood of Régine Miller.** Tundra Books of Northern New York, 1994. Originally published in Canada by Tundra Books in 1992. ISBN 0-88776-286-7 (paperback 0-88776-303-0). 185 p. (10-14). Biography. **Canada**.
Living in Brussels, Belgium, in 1942, the Miller family—Jewish refugees from Poland—began to feel the threat of the Nazi Holocaust.

Régine's father arranged for her to be placed in a Gentile home, where she was to keep a very low profile, posing as a Gentile. Régine, then ten, spent the next three years in hiding, never knowing the fate of her family. Régine's memories of the four Belgian families who hid her are a testament to the warmth and love, as well as the cruelty, that humans are capable of. Includes photographs and a summary of related events. *cmt*

**10.3** Foreman, Michael. **War Boy: A Country Childhood**. Arcade, 1990. Originally published by Arcade in 1989. ISBN 1-55970-049-1. 94p. (8-12) Picture book biography. **Great Britain**.
Watercolors, comic-style drawings, and reprinted historical documents recount one boy's experience in Pakefield, England, during World War II. Daily events are interspersed with historical fact in this engaging autobiography for all ages. Sequel: *After the War Was Over*. *Kate Greenaway Medal. al*

**10.4** Kodama, Tatsuharu. **Shin's Tricycle**. Translated by Kazuko Hokumen-Jones. Illustrated by Noriyuki Ando. Walker, 1995. Originally published as *Shin-chan no Sanrinsha* by Doshin-sha in 1992. ISBN 0-8027-8375-9. 32 p. (9 and up). Picture book. **Japan**.
Shin, nearly four, wanted a tricycle more than anything. Although such toys were nearly impossible to get in wartime Hiroshima, Shin's uncle found a tricycle and made the boy's dream come true. On the morning of August 6, 1945, Shin was riding his tricycle with his best friend when the atomic blast destroyed Hiroshima. Forty years later, Shin's father donated the scarred remains of the tricycle to the Hiroshima Peace Museum in an effort to keep the dream of peace alive for children around the world. The depth of tragedy in words and illustrations make this a book for older readers. *jy, cmt*

**10.5** Little, Jean. **Little by Little: A Writer's Education**. Viking Kestrel, 1987. ISBN 0-670-81649-3. 233 p. (10-14). Informational book. **Canada**.
Jean Little, born in 1932 in Taiwan to Canadian parents who were both doctors, tells of her childhood in Taiwan and her life in Guelph, Ontario, where the family moved before World War II broke out. Jean had "bad eyes" yet she learned to read and went on to complete her university education and become a teacher. She took time off to write a novel about

a young girl with cerebral palsy which was accepted for publication. She was finally on her way to becoming a writer. *dd*

**10.6** Little, Jean. **Stars Come Out Within.** Viking, 1990. ISBN 0-670-82965-X. 260 p. (12-YA). Informational Book. **Canada**
Beginning each chapter of this autobiography with a quote from Emily Dickinson, Little describes her own development as a writer and her struggle to learn to live with her encroaching blindness. This moving account would interest not only her fans but also people who have never read her books before. *Parenting Award; Vicky Metcalf Award. jvl*

**10.7** Skira-Venturi, Rosabianca and Maquet, Yves-Marie. **A Weekend with Leonardo da Vinci.** Translated by Ann Beneduce. Rizzoli International, 1993. Originally published as *Dimanche avec Leonardo da Vinci* by Editions d'Art Albert Skira S.A. in 1992. ISBN 0-847-82440-8. 63 p. (7-12). Picture book. **Switzerland**.
As if entertaining the reader for the weekend, the fifteenth-century Italian artist, Leonardo da Vinci, talks about his life, world, work, and selected paintings. Includes reproductions of the artist's work and lists of museums where his works are on display. Also in the series: *A Weekend with Degas*; *A Weekend with Renoir*; *A Weekend with Van Gogh. cmt*

**10.8** Ward, Glenyse. **Wandering Girl.** Holt, 1991. Originally published by Magabala Books in 1988. ISBN 0-8050-1634-1. 183 p. (12-14). Biography. **Australia**.
At the age of one, Ward, an Aboriginal, was taken from her parents and placed in an orphanage to be raised according to European traditions. A straightforward, nonliterary style marks this memoir, set primarily in the 1960s, in which Ward recounts her childhood at the mission, her experiences when she is sent to be the only servant in the home of an upper-class white family, and her eventual escape from that servitude to a life of her own. *ss*

**10.9** Zhensun, Zheng and Low, Alice. **A Young Painter: The Life and Paintings of Wang-Yani—China's Extraordinary Young Artist.** Translated by Huang Long, Ding Lingqing, Ouyang Caiwei, and Song Xiaogang. Photographs by Zheng Zhensun. Scholastic, 1991. Originally published by New China Pictures Company in 1991. ISBN 0-590-44906-0. 80 p. (10-14). Biography. **China.**

This photobiography describes the life and works of Wang Yani, a child prodigy whose paintings from age three on, reveal both her astonishing skill and her delightful child's vision of the world. Photographs of fourteen-year-old Yani show her engaging in everyday activities, such as picnicking with friends and playing ball with her brother, but it is the photographs of her paintings of monkeys and other animals and scenery that bring her alive for the reader. The text explains how she learned to paint and the role her parents, especially her artist father, played in helping her to develop her art. *jvl*

# ANTHOLOGIES & SHORT STORIES

**11.1** Berry, James. **A Thief in the Village and Other Stories.** Orchard Books, 1988. Originally published as *A Thief in the Village* by Hamish Hamilton in 1986. (paperback: Puffin, 1990). ISBN 0-5305-745-3. (paperback: ISBN 0-14-032679-0). 148 p. (10-14). Short stories. **Great Britain**.

This collection of nine short stories presents a view of adolescent life in contemporary Jamaica. One story concerns a young girl's unusual desire for a bicycle; another is about a boy who endures the wrath of a hurricane in his quest to buy shoes so that he can play on the cricket team; another deals with a girl's adventures on a coconut plantation. *Smarties Book Prize; American Library Association Notable Books for Children. mja*

**11.2** Brooks, Martha. **Paradise Café and Other Stories.** Little, Brown, 1988. Originally published by Thistledown in 1988. (paperback: Point, 1993). ISBN 0-920633-57-9. (paperback: 0-590455-62-1). 108 p. (12-14). Short stories. **Canada.**

In fourteen short stories Brooks presents many faces and facets of love, whether of a teen-age boy carrying the memory of his uncle's long-dead fiancée, a youngster telling his dying dog every detail of his future life which he knows they will not be able to share, or a girl persuaded by her father's latest lady friend to take a chance on the boy who hitchhiked a hundred miles just to be with her. These teenagers struggle to make sense of love and of who they are. *Vicky Metcalf Short Story Award for "A Boy and His Dog"* (Canada). *jvl*

**11.3** Brooks, Martha. **Traveling On into the Light.** Orchard, 1994. Originally published by Groundwood in 1993. (Paperback, Puffin, 1996). ISBN 0-531-06863-3. (paperback: 0-140-37867-7). 146 p. (12–YA). Short stories. **Canada.**
Eleven short stories, most written in the first person, show teens on the edge of maturity interacting with each other and their parents. In the title story, sixteen-year-old Samantha struggles to resolve her hurt when her father goes to his male lover. Other stories tell of Laker, kicked out by his ex-hippie mother and coarse stepfather; Alvina, a slow learner trying to help her sister amid poverty; Jamie, haunted by his father's suicide; and Sidonie and Kieran, seeking love during family deaths, school exams, and a sibling wedding. *jsn*

**11.4** Carrier, Roch. **The Hockey Sweater and Other Stories.** Translated by Sheila Fischman. House of Anansi Press, 1979. Originally published as *Les Enfants du Bonhomme dans la Lune* by Éditions internationales Alain Stanké in 1979. ISBN 0-88784-078-7. 159 p. (12-14). Short stories. **Canada.**
The twenty short stories in this collection reflect contemporary French Canadian life. They are told by a young boy and are about school, church, his friend Lapin, the skating rink, and America. *dd*

**11.5** Crossley-Holland, Kevin. **British Folk Tales: New Versions.** Orchard Books, 1987. Originally published by Orchard Books, London in 1987. ISBN 0-531-05733-X. 383p. (10-14). Anthology. **Great Britain.**
Fifty-five tales are included in this comprehensive retelling which includes examples of many types of traditional literature. Folktale favorites include "Tom Tit Tot," "King of the Cats," "Goldilocks and the Three Bears" and "Jack and the Beanstalk." Fools tales, ghost stories, and legends, including some lesser-known tales, are complemented by scholarly notes, a glossary and a pronunciation guide. The author has sought in these retellings "to find the real meaning of these tales." *djg*

**11.6** De France, Marie. **Proud Knight, Fair Lady: The Twelve Laïs of Marie de France**. Translated by Naomi Lewis. Illustrated by Angela Barrett. Viking Kestrel, 1989. Originally published as *Proud Knight, Fair Lady* by Century Hutchinson Ltd in 1989. ISBN 0-670-82656-1. 100 p. (12-14). Anthology. **Great Britain**.

Marie de France, a twelfth-century Frenchwoman about whom little is known, collected these twelve laïs, or tales, heard from minstrels of Brittany and Celtic England. The tales speak of chivalry and courtly love, of brave knights and fair maidens. Swans carry messages of love; hawks turn into handsome men. *CCBC Choices. jl*

**11.7** Dickinson, Peter. **City of Gold and Other Stories from the Old Testament**. Illustrated by Michael Foreman. Pantheon, 1980. Originally published as **City of Gold** by Gollancz in 1980. ISBN 0-394-51385-1. 188p. (12-14). Anthology. **Great Britain**.

This brilliantly illustrated volume retells thirty-two Old Testament stories as they might have been told by Hebrew people prior to the time the Bible was written. *Carnegie Medal. al*

**11.8** Dickinson, Peter. **Merlin Dreams**. Illustrated by Alan Lee. Delacorte, 1988. Originally published by Victor Gollancz in 1988. ISBN 0-440-50067-2. 168 p. (12-14). Anthology. **Great Britain**.

Trapped beneath a rock on the moor for all eternity, Merlin dreams a world of Arthurian fantasy. The tales that he dreams are full of wit and magic: A girl uses her inherited gift to change with a greyhound to avenge her father's death; a slick mountebank underestimates the intelligence of "country bumpkins"; a young prince learns his own skills and abilities as a knight. The illustrations bring this dream world to life. *ALA Notable Books for Children. jl*

**11.9** Fienberg, Anna. **The Magnificent Nose and Other Marvels**. Illustrated by Kim Gamble. Little, Brown, 1992. Originally published by Little Ark Books in 1991. ISBN 0-316-28195-6. 48p. (7-9). Transitional/short stories. **Australia**.

Helped along by their special gifts and the magic of Aristan, a golden spider, five children decide to live their dreams and make the world a better place. Lindalou's skill as a woodworker, Andy Umm's ability to talk to animals, Ferdinand's great curiosity and knowledge of the human body, Ignatius Binz's unparalleled sense of smell, and Valentina Look-well's ability to paint the inner soul of her subjects add quirky humor to these five short stories. *Australian Children's Book of the Year for Younger Readers Award. cmt*

**11.10** Gavin, Jamila. **Our Favorite Stories.** Photography by Barnabas Kindersley. Illustrated by Amanda Hall. DK Publishing, 1997. Originally published by Dorling Kindersley Ltd. ISBN 0-7894-1486-4. 48 p. (6-12). Illustrated folktale anthology. **Great Britain.**

Ten folktales from around the world indicative of their country of origin are retold. Each tale is accompanied by a brief bio of a child from the featured country and informative marginal notes. Large, colorful illustrations help distinguish fact from fantasy. *cmt*

**11.11** He, Liyi and Philip, Neil (Eds.). **The Spring of Butterflies and Other Folktales of China's Minority Peoples.** Illustrated by Aiqing Pan and Zhao Li. Lothrop, 1986. Translated from the Chinese. Originally published by Collins in 1985. ISBN 0-688-06192-3. 144 p. (7-12). Anthology. **China, Great Britain.**

This anthology contains fourteen works of traditional fantasy, mostly folktales, from the Tibetan, Thai, Uighur, Bai, and other non-Chinese people living in China. (FirstSearch) *cmt*

**11.12** Howker, Janni. **Badger on the Barge and Other Stories.** Puffin, 1984. Originally published by Julia MacRae in 1984. ISBN 0-140-32253-1. 201 p. Short stories. **Great Britain.**

These five stories are set in small towns in northern England. Each explores relationships and understandings among the young and old. *(FirstSearch) International Reading Association Children's Book A-ward. cmt*

**11.13** Hughes, Shirley. **The Big Alfie and Annie Rose Story Book.** Lo-throp, 1989. Originally published by The Bodley Head in 1988. ISBN 0-688-07672. 58 p. (4-8). Illustrated anthology. **Great Britain.**

Delightful vignettes about toddler Annie Rose and her big brother Alfie alternate with poems about their family and events of their day. Implicit are the warm affection and bonding between brother and sister and their understanding mum and dad. The collection concludes with Alfie's participation in a wedding. Not to be left out of the excitement, Annie

Rose becomes the last little bridesmaid. Adult readers will cringe with embarrassment, while preschoolers will revel in triumph! Watercolor illustrations perfectly capture the humor of each episode. *djg*

**11.14** Hughes, Shirley. **The Big Alfie Out of Doors Story Book**. Lothrop, 1992. Originally published by The Bodley Head in 1992. ISBN 0-688-11428. 64 p. (4-9). Illustrated anthology. **Great Britain**.
Preschooler Alfie and toddler Annie Rose are the stars of this charming collection of short stories and poems. These episodes, as the title suggests, relate the children's outdoor escapades. In one story Alfie uses a cardboard box to set up a store for Grandma and Mum. In another, Alfie camps out in Grandma's back yard. Once again, Hughes masterfully portrays the universality of ordinary daily experiences of early childhood. *djg*

**11.15** Hughes, Shirley. **The Nursery Collection**. Illustrated by Shirley Hughes. Lothrop, 1994. Originally published individually as *Noisy*; *When We Went to the Park*; and *Bathwater's Hot* by Walker in 1985 and *Colours* and *All Shapes and Sizes* by Walker in 1986. ISBN 0-688-13583-8. 64 p. (3-5). Anthology. **Great Britain**.
Five stories center around concepts important in the lives of toddlers. Some stories, such as "Bathwater's Hot," use rhymed verse to present the concept of opposites, while others, such as "When We Went to the Park," "Colors," and "All Shapes and Sizes," are told in descriptive prose. "Noisy" depicts the chaos of a typical household, with telephone, dog, vacuum cleaner, and baby all raising the decibel level, and, befitting its place as concluding story, ends with the silence of sleep. Hughes's illustrations encompass a wide variety of childhood experiences and avoid stereotypical adult roles. *ss*

**11.16** Hughes, Shirley. **Tales of Trotter Street**. Candlewick, 1997. Originally published individually (see separate annotations) by Lothrop and Walker Books, 1989-1992. ISBN 0-763-60090-3. 64 p. (4-10). Illustrated anthology. **Great Britain**.
The author brings us four stories about the friends and neighbors who live on Trotter Street, a community somewhere, or anywhere, in England. The British text is preserved, and a brief glossary is included for American children. Tales included in this edition are: *Angel Mae* (1989); *The Big Concrete Lorry* (1989); *The Snow Lady* (1990); and *Wheels*

(1991). *djg*

**11.17** Jennings, Paul. **Unreal: Eight Surprising Stories.** Viking, 1991. Originally published by Penguin Books Australia in 1985. ISBN 0-670-84175-7. 107 p. (12-14). Short stories. **Australia.**
About his work the author says, "I try to put at least three of the following things in every short story: a surprise ending, something yucky, weird happenings, a lot of laughs, spooky events." Excellent for read-aloud or independent reading, these tall tale adventures of a fourteen-year-old boy are naughty enough to appeal to middle-graders and funny enough to appeal to everyone. A sprinkling of Australian terms adds interest. See other books in series: *Uncanny; Unbelievable; Unmentionable; Uncovered. cmt*

**11.18** Lively, Penelope. **A House Inside Out.** Illustrated by David Parkins. Dutton, 1988. Originally published by Andre Deutsch Limited in 1987. ISBN 0-525-44332-0. 128p. (10-12). Short stories. **Great Britain.**
These eleven short stories have as their protagonists various animals living within the contemporary English household of the Dixon family. Willie, the dog, gets caught in the Dixon's bed when he falls asleep there and does not hear them return; Sam and his extended family of mice have an adventure when Sam drops into the teapot and cannot get out; and a young pill bug helps a spider retrieve a pearl from the kitchen floor. The author claims that such adventures go on in most houses. *jg*

**11.19** Mahy, Margaret. **Nonstop Nonsense.** Illustrated by Quentin Blake. McElderry, 1989. Originally published by Dent in 1977. ISBN 0-689-50483-7. 120 p. (10-12). Short stories and poetry. **New Zealand.**
Hilarious vignettes and anecdotes about the ridiculous Delmonico family are interspersed throughout this collection of humorous poetry. Mahy's word wizardry creates fertile ground for Quentin Blake's imaginative pen and ink drawings. *djg*

**11.20** Oodgeroo [Kath Walker]. **Dreamtime: Aboriginal Stories.** Illustrated by Bronwyn Bancroft. Lothrop, 1994. Originally published as *Stradbroke Dreamtime* by Angus & Robertson in 1993. ISBN 0-688-13296-0. 96 p. (10-14). Anthology. **Australia.**
This authentic look at the culture of the Aboriginal people and their beliefs combines a section of reminiscences of the author's own child-

hood with a section of traditional dreamtime stories. Oodgeroo, who grew up on Stradbroke Island, off the Queensland coast, before it was despoiled by mineral seekers and tourists, recounts episodes that describe her Aboriginal family's way of life. These stories demonstrate the fundamental beliefs that shaped her family's behavior. They provide a link to the dreamtime stories—primarily creation tales—told in the second half of the book. *ss*

**11.21** Park, Ruth. **Things in Corners**. Viking Kestrel, 1989. (paperback: Puffin, 1993). ISBN 0140-32-7134. (Paperback ISBN 0140327134). 197 p. (12-14). Short stories. **Australia**.

These six stories, each told from the point of view of a young person going through an emotional or family crisis, are tinged with mystery, suspense, and a hint of the supernatural. In "What Kind of Lady Was Auntie Bev?", Aunt Bev, a strong-minded woman, mysteriously disappears just before Willamet's family, to whom she had deeded her house, moves in. The house seems alive with Aunt Bev's spirit and acts in spiteful ways whenever someone violates what would have been her sense of order and decorum. The tension drives a wedge between members of the family and accentuates their different needs and sensibilities. *jvl*

**11.22** Pearce, Phillipa. **Lion at School and Other Stories**. Illustrated by Caroline Sharpe. Greenwillow, 1985. *See Transitional Books*.

**11.23** Pearce, Philippa. **Who's Afraid? And Other Strange Stories**. Greenwillow, 1987. Originally published by Kestrel Penguin Books Limited, 1981. ISBN 0-688-06895-2. 152p. (11-14). Short stories. **Great Britain**.

These eleven short stories each contain a touch of the supernatural and explore the disturbing dark side of life. Some stories, such as "The Yellow Ball," exhibit Pearce's masterful literary talents. *cw*

**11.24** Rosen, Michael (Ed.). **South and North, East and West**. Candlewick, 1994. Originally published by Walker in 1992. ISBN 1-56402-396-6. 96 p. (4-6). Anthology. **Great Britain**.

In this well-designed collection, traditional tales from countries around the world are paired with distinctive artwork by mostly Canadian and British illustrators. *be*

**11.25** Singer, Isaac Bashevis. **When Shlemiel Went to Warsaw & Other Stories**. Translated by the author and Elizabeth Shub. Illustrated by Margot Zemach. Farrar, 1968. ISBN 0-440-49306-4. 115 p. (12-14). Short stories. **Israel**.

Eight stories are included in this collection. Some of the stories were told to the author by his mother and grandmother; others are from his imagination. They all ring true to the Jewish folktale tradition and are rich in fantasy and make-believe. *dd*

**11.26** Singer, Isaac Bashevis. **Zlateh the Goat and Other Stories**. Translated by the author and Elizabeth Shub. Illustrated by Maurice Sendak. Harper & Row, 1966. ISBN 0-06-025698-2. 90 p. (12-14). Short stories. **Israel**.

There are seven stories in this collection. The author bases these stories on his memories of people and the long ago which is still present to him. In this way he keeps family and friends alive in all their wisdom, strange beliefs, and their foolishness. *dd*

**11.27** Taylor, C. J. **How We Saw the World**. Tundra Books of Northern New York, 1993. Originally published by Tundra Books in 1993. ISBN 0-88776-302-2. 30 p. (7-9). Illustrated anthology. **Canada**.

The author, a Mohawk, retells and illustrates nine Native American creation stories from nine tribes living in various parts of Canada and the United States. Included are the Algonquin legend "The Birth of Niagara Falls," the Blackfoot legend "How Horses Came Into the World," and the Oneida legend, "Why the Dog Is Our Best Friend." Illustrations emphasize the Native Americans' reverence for nature. See also: *The Ghost and Lone Warrior*; *How Two-Feather Was Saved from Loneliness*; *The Messenger of Spring*. *cmt*

**11.28** Wilson, Budge. **The Leaving and Other Stories**. Philomel, 1992. Originally published by House of Anansi, 1990. (paperback: Scholastic, 1993). ISBN 0-399-21878-5. 208 p. (12-14). Short stories. **Canada**.

The nine short stories in this collection each has a teenaged female protagonist whose understanding of herself and others develops within family and community structures. The twentieth-century Nova Scotia settings are evoked clearly and lovingly. In "The Leaving," for example, the twelve-year-old narrator tells of the day her mother leaves the family farm in the early morning hours, takes her daughter with her to Halifax, explores ideas she has read about, and returns home to demand a new respect from her husband and sons. *Canadian Library Association Young Adult Book Award. jg, dd*

**11.29** Wynne-Jones, Tim. **Some of the Kinder Planets.** Orchard, 1995. Originally published by Douglas & McIntyre in 1993. (paperback: Puffin, 1996). ISBN 0-531-09451-0. (paperback: ISBN 0-140-38069-8). 130 p. (11–13). Short stories. **Canada.**
Nine stories feature pre- or early-teen heroes in whimsical, imaginative, or fantastic situations. In the title story, Quin must learn to show fear—or wonder—in her stage role and succeeds with a gift from her Nanny Vi. Ben's tale is a ghost story; Fletcher's, a humorous account of a school bully and travel dreams. "Tweedledum and Tweedledead" mixes friendship, a "summer vacation" writing assignment, and Alice in Wonderland. Postmodern lifestyle and tabloid sci-fi are spoofed in "Save the Mood for Kerdy Dickus," while "Star-Taker" is historical fiction about explorer Champlain's astrolabe. *Governor General's Award for Children's Literature; Canadian Library Association Book of the Year Award for Children; Vicky Metcalf Short Story Award* (Canada). *jsn*

**11.30** Yee, Paul. **Tales from Gold Mountain.** Illustrated by Simon Ng. Macmillan, 1989. Originally published by Groundwood Books in 1989. ISBN 0-02-793621-X. 64 p. (12-14). Short stories. **Canada.**
The author's purpose in telling these eight stories of Chinese people in Canada is to help today's Chinese-Americans appreciate the contributions of their ancestors as pioneers of North America. All the stories are bittersweet, and some border on folktales, such as "The Friends of Kwan Ming," where the hero's former traveling companions help him complete the three impossible tasks that he has been given by his employer. Other stories, like "Rider Chan and the Night River," feature the spirits of the dead. *bkn*

**11.31** Zhitkov, Boris. **How I Hunted the Little Fellows.** *See Realistic Picture Books.*

# Appendix

# *Children's Book Awards*

## International

### Hans Christian Andersen Award

This international award, sponsored by the International Board on Books for Young People, is given every two years to a living author and, since 1966, to a living illustrator whose complete works have made important international contributions to children's literature.

**1956** Eleanor Farjeon (Great Britain)
**1958** Astrid Lindgren (Sweden)
**1960** Erich Kästner (Germany)
**1962** Meindert DeJong (U.S.A.)
**1964** René Guillot (France)
**1966** Author: Tove Jansson (Finland)
Illustrator: Alois Carigiet (Switzerland)
**1968** Authors: James Krüss (Germany) and José Maria Sanchez-Silva (Spain)
Illustrator: Jirí Trnka (Czechoslovakia)
**1970** Author: Gianni Rodari (Italy)
Illustrator: Maurice Sendak

(U.S.A.)
**1972** Author: Scott O'Dell (U.S.A.)
Illustrator: Ib Spang Olsen (Denmark)
**1974** Author: Maria Gripe (Sweden)
Illustrator: Farshid Mesghali (Iran)
**1976** Author: Cecil Bödker (Denmark)
Illustrator: Tatjana Mawrina (U.S.S.R.)
**1978** Author: Paula Fox (U.S.A.)
Illustrator: Otto S. Svend (Denmark)
**1980** Author: Bohumil Riha (Czechoslovakia)
Illustrator: Suekichi Akaba (Japan)
**1982** Author: Lygia Bojunga Nunes (Brazil)
Illustrator: Zbigniew Rychlicki (Poland)
**1984** Author: Christine Nöstlinger (Austria)
Illustrator: Mitsumasa Anno (Japan)
**1986** Author: Patricia Wrightson (Australia)
Illustrator: Robert Ingpen (Australia)

**1988** Author: Annie M.G. Schmidt (Netherlands)
Illustrator: Dušan Kalláy (Czechoslovakia)
**1990** Author: Tormod Haugen (Norway)
Illustrator: Lisbeth Zwerger (Austria)
**1992** Author: Virginia Hamilton (U.S.A.)
Illustrator: Květa Pacovská (Czechoslovakia)
**1994** Author: Michio Mado (Japan)
Illustrator: Jörg Müller (Switzerland)
**1996** Author: Uri Orlev (Israel)
Illustrator: Klaus Ensikat (Germany)

# United States

## Mildred Batchelder Award

This award, sponsored by the ALA's Association for Library Service to Children, is given to the American publisher of a children's book considered to be the most outstanding of those books originally published in a country other than the U.S. in a language other than English, and subsequently translated and published in the U.S. during the previous year.

**1968** THE LITTLE MAN by Erich Kästner, translated from German by James Kirkup. Illustrated by Rick Schreiter, Knopf.
**1969** DON'T TAKE TEDDY by Babbis Friis-Baastad, translated from Norwegian by Lise Sömme McKinnon, Scribner's.
**1970** WILDCAT UNDER GLASS by Alki Zei, translated from Greek by Edward Fenton, Holt.
**1971** IN THE LAND OF UR: THE DISCOVERY OF ANCIENT MESOPOTAMIA by Hans Baumann, translated from German by Stella Humphries. Illustrated by Hans Peter Renner, Pantheon.
**1972** FRIEDRICH by Hans Peter Richter, translated from German by Edite Kroll, Holt.
**1973** PULGA by Siny Rose Van Iterson, translated from Dutch by Alexander and Alison Gode, Morrow.
**1974** PETROS' WAR by Alki Zei, translated from Greek by Edward Fenton, Dutton.
**1975** AN OLD TALE CARVED OUT OF STONE by Aleksandr M. Linevski, translated from Russian by Maria Polushkin, Crown.
**1976** THE CAT AND MOUSE WHO SHARED A HOUSE written and illustrated by Ruth Hürlimann, translated from German by Anthea Bell, Walck.
**1977** THE LEOPARD by Cecil Bödker. Translated from Danish by Gunnar Poulsen, Atheneum.
**1978** No Award
**1979** KONRAD by Christine Nöstlinger, translated from German (Austrian) by Anthea Bell. Illustrated by Carol Nicklaus, Watts.
RABBIT ISLAND by Jörg Steiner, translated from German (Swiss) by Ann Conrad Lammers. Illustrated by Jörg Müller, Harcourt.
**1980** THE SOUND OF DRAGON'S FEET by Alki Zei, translated from Greek by Edward Fenton, Dutton.
**1981** THE WINTER WHEN TIME

WAS FROZEN by Els Pelgrom, translated from Dutch by Raphael and Maryka Rudnik, Morrow.

**1982** THE BATTLE HORSE by Harry Kullman, translated from Swedish by George Blecher and Lone Thygesen-Blecher, Bradbury.

**1983** HIROSHIMA NO PIKA written and illustrated by Toshi Maruki. Translated from Japanese through Kurita-Bando Literary Agency, Lothrop.

**1984** RONIA, THE ROBBER'S DAUGHTER by Astrid Lindgren, translated from Swedish by Patricia Crampton, Viking.

**1985** THE ISLAND ON BIRD STREET by Uri Orlev, translated from Hebrew by Hillel Halkin, Houghton.

**1986** ROSE BLANCHE by Christophe Gallaz and Roberto Innocenti, translated from French by Martha Coventry and Richard Graglia. Illustrated by Roberto Innocenti, Creative Education.

**1987** NO HERO FOR THE KAISER by Rudolf Frank, translated from German by Patricia Crampton. Illustrated by Klaus Steffans, Lothrop.

**1988** IF YOU DIDN'T HAVE ME by Ulf Nilsson, translated from Swedish by Lone Thygesen-Blecher and George Blecher. Illustrated by Eva Eriksson, McElderry.

**1989** CRUTCHES by Peter Härtling, translated from German by Elizabeth D. Crawford, Lothrop.

**1990** BUSTER'S WORLD by Bjarne Reuter, translated from Danish by Anthea Bell, Dutton.

**1991** A HAND FULL OF STARS by Rafik Schami, translated from German by Rika Lesser, Dutton. Honor Book: TWO SHORT AND ONE LONG by Nina Ring Aamundsen, translated from Norwegian by the author, Houghton.

**1992** THE MAN FROM THE OTHER SIDE by Uri Orlev, translated from Hebrew by Hillel Halkin, Houghton.

**1993** No Award.

**1994** THE APPRENTICE by Pilar Molina Llorente, translated from Spanish by Robin Longshaw. Illustrated by Juan Ramón Alonso, Farrar. Honor Books: ANNE FRANK, BEYOND THE DIARY: A PHOTOGRAPHIC REMEMBRANCE by Ruud van der Rol and Rian Verhoeven, translated from Dutch by Tony Langham and Plym Peters, Viking. THE PRINCESS IN THE KITCHEN GARDEN by Annemie and Margriet Heymans, translated from Dutch by Johanna H. Prins and Johanna W. Prins, Farrar.

**1995** THE BOYS FROM ST. PETRIE by Bjarne Reuter, translated from Danish by Anthea Bell, Dutton.

**1996** THE LADY WITH THE HAT by Uri Orlev, translated from Hebrew by Hillel Halkin, Houghton.

**1997** THE FRIENDS by Kazumi Yumoto, translated from Japanese by Cathy Hirano, Farrar.

# Author-Title Index

# Country of Origin Index

# SUBJECT INDEX

# About the Author

Carl Tomlinson is professor of language arts and children's literature in the Department of Curriculum and Instruction at Northern Illinois University in DeKalb, Illinois. He is the coauthor of *Essentials of Children's Literature* (Allyn & Bacon, 1996), and has written about international children's literature in articles published in *The New Advocate*, *The Reading Teacher*, *International Education*, *The Social Studies*, *Early Child Development and Care*, and *The Middle School Journal*, as well as in chapters in various publications.